CHASING BIRDS ACROSS TEXAS

Number Thirty-five
Louise Lindsey Merrick Natural Environment Series

D0875141

Chasing Birds

across Texas

A BIRDING BIG YEAR

Mark T. Adams

Foreword by Brush Freeman

Drawings by Kelly B. Bryan

TEXAS A&M UNIVERSITY PRESS   COLLEGE STATION

Copyright © 2003
by Mark T. Adams
Manufactured in the
United States of America
All rights reserved
First edition

The paper used in this book
meets the minimum requirements
of the American National Standard for Permanence
of Paper for Printed Library Materials, z39.48-1984.
Binding materials have been chosen for durability.

Library of Congress Cataloging-in-Publication Data

Adams, Mark Thomas.
    Chasing birds across Texas : a birding big year /
Mark T. Adams ; foreword by Brush Freeman ;
drawings by Kelly B. Bryan.—1st ed.
        p.   cm.—(Louise Lindsey Merrick natural
environment series ; no. 35)
    ISBN 1-58544-295-x (cloth : alk. paper)
    ISBN 1-58544-296-8 (pbk. : alk. paper)
    1. Birds—Counting—Texas.   2. Birds—Texas.
I. Title.   II. Series.
QL684.T4A32   2003
598'.07'23209764—dc21   2003005681

Frontispiece: Black-capped Vireo. Drawing by Kelly B. Bryan.

TO MY DAUGHTER
Jennifer Michelle Adams

Contents

Foreword

Brush Freeman

Some may consider Texas more of a country than a state, which indeed at one time it was. It is huge; allow me to illustrate by example how huge. The total dry land masses in square miles of a number of nations would comfortably fit within the borders of Texas: France, Portugal, Malta, Belize, the Bahamas, Hong Kong, the island of Reunion, and four Singapores! That would still leave about a hundred square miles for a potential national park or a Texas-sized sandbox. Add to the state's 262,105 square miles of dry land another 6,687 square miles of Texas-owned waters, and one can only marvel at the birding potential the state possesses—or shudder at the effort required to take full advantage of it.

Among birders or birdwatchers, there is often a heartfelt need to see a high number of species within a certain geographical area. It may be a goal set on the basis of a specified time, on a regional basis, or on a time and regional basis. It can include yard lists, county lists, Big Days, Big Sits, Christmas Bird Counts, or any other parameter the participant wishes to set and follows. Many people consider birding a sport and approach it by competing either with their own previous tallies or with other folks of similar interests.

In terms of effort, time, and expense required to set a record, the biggest challenge of all in Texas is without doubt the statewide Big Year. A successful Big Year in Texas is not a matter to be taken lightly, should you choose to embark on one. It requires flexibility; at least moderately good physical condition; lots of time, money, understanding, and support from your family, boss, and birding peers; a good car; sacrifice; and most of all, a lot of determination and enthusiasm, especially as one approaches the end of the year when new additions to the list are few and often hundreds of miles apart.

In 1995, my friend Petra Hockey and I, following in the footsteps of Greg Lasley's 1994 Big Year, decided to give it a shot, well after January 1 had passed. It was a most memorable experience. Not only did we visit places in Texas we had never visited before, but we also met wonderful people during the course of our effort. This was before the days of instant information via e-mail news lists (that is, TEXBIRDS). Our on-the-road updates depended on nightly calls to several well-managed Rare Bird Alerts (RBAs), which consisted of telephone recordings at various numbers across the state. In addition, we seldom went a day without a call to a friend or two who kept us in tune with what was happening regarding rare birds or chaseable birds in the state. Long-distance phone calls alone during the year cost us well into four figures.

I put more than thirty-six thousand miles on my truck that year, and we used Petra's car at least half of the time. We never flew to any location. We visited every corner of the state, in many cases multiple times. At the end of the year we grew travel weary, frustrated, and, I must admit, a bit irritable. But on January 1, 1996, we both felt saddened that it was over. By pursuing the challenge, we were rewarded in many ways, and I don't think either of us has ever regretted the experience. We reveled in seeing twenty-seven bird species that are classified by the Texas Bird Records Committee (TBRC) as Review Species—birds considered rarities—and were able to see many species new to us within the state's borders.

Following our 1995 effort, Eric Carpenter made a run at the record and did wonderfully, though he was hampered by job responsibilities. When in late 1999 Mark Adams began talking about doing a state Big Year in 2000, I was somewhat dubious about his abilities and his resolve to endure the next 366 days and achieve even his initial goal (which was 450 species). I learned early on that I was greatly underestimating him, and by the end of the year I was astonished at his success.

As one reads the following account of Mark's experiences, it becomes apparent just how much determination is needed to reach the finish line and be successful. Mark describes in detail many of his joys, frustrations, and conflicting choices; and those hard or even danger-

ous times one is apt to face in the effort to get one more species despite weather, lack of knowledge of a given area, or downright absence of straight thinking.

If you are a birder who enjoys the allure of setting personal listing
goals in Texas, or even if you aren't, you will enjoy this book. Carefully written from notes taken daily as well as from his field notes for
documentation purposes, it is exacting and entertaining, incorporat-
ing loads of accumulated knowledge on various species found in Texas.
Alas, I am delaying you. With the account in hand, you and Mark
should hit the road. Good birding!

Acknowledgments

Throughout the year 2000, I was impressed by the generosity of Texas birders. I am especially indebted to Brush Freeman, Petra Hockey, and Eric Carpenter, whose Texas Big Year experiences and deep knowledge of birds, habitats, and our state helped me many times. As always, my Davis Mountains friends were immensely helpful, fun, and supporting: Rex Barrick, Kelly Bryan, Marc and Maryann Eastman, Linda and David Hedges, Tom and Carol Hobby, John Karges, and Dale Ohl.

I enjoyed the company of many birders in the field during the year and want to thank them for giving so freely of their time and knowledge: Noreen Baker, Keith Bartels, Nick Block, Tim Brush, Larry Carpenter, Mike Creese, Mel Cooksey, Mark Elwonger, Tim Fennell, John Gee, Brian Gibbons, Russell Graham, P. D. Hulce, David Knutson, Ed Kutac, Guy Luneau, Jay Packer, James Paton, Dwight Peake, Barrett Pierce, Randy Pinkston, Barbara Railey, Forrest Roweland, David Sarkozi, Rick Schaefer, Marcy Scott, Rosemary Scott, Jim and Phoebe Lou Sealy, Cliff Shackelford, Rose Marie Stortz, Tom Taylor, Ro Wauer, Jim and Lynne Weber, Ron Weeks, Matt Whitbeck, Matt White, John Whittle, Greer Willis, Jan Wobbenhorst, David and Mimi Wolf, and Jimmy Zabriskie.

I am grateful to many others who gave me valuable advice about places to bird or particular species: Ray Bieber, Ann Bishop, Lorie Black, David Bradford, Charles Brower, John Brunjes IV, Brian Cassell, Sheridan Coffey, Bob Doe, Andy Donnelly, Charles Easley, Ted Eubanks, Jesse Fagan, Mark Flippo, Connie Fordham, Bill Graber, Jeffrey Hanson, Derek Hill, Jimmy Jackson, Bob Johnson, Jane Kittelman, Rich Kostecke, Greg Lasley, Madge Lindsay, Mark Lockwood, Jeff Mundy, John Odgers, Brent Ortego, Laura Packer, Dick Peake, Jim Peterson, Ross Rasmussen, Martin Reid, Cecilia Riley,

Ellen Roots, Willie Sekula, Chuck Sexton, John Sproul, Sue Wiedenfeld, Alan Wormington, and Barry Zimmer.

I am especially grateful to Laura Long, whose careful readings, constructive advice, and thoughtful suggestions markedly improved this book.

CHASING BIRDS ACROSS TEXAS

Introduction

This is the story of a year-long quest, a venture that grew from my desire to spend a year's free time birding intensively across Texas. To this end, in the year 2000, I undertook what is known in birding as a "Texas Big Year."

The primary goal of any Big Year can be simply stated: to see as many bird species as possible in some well-defined geographic region in one year. Vast and varied Texas is a suitable canvas upon which to paint a Big Year. The sheer scale of the Lone Star State inevitably provides new experiences and adventures for those who seek them among the state's broad range of places, people, and birds.

My interest in a Big Year went beyond a desire to tally a long list of birds seen in Texas. I wanted to learn more about the birds themselves. Which birds were in what parts of Texas and when? Being relatively new to the state, I also wanted to learn more about Texas and its people. I looked forward to making new friends. Finally, the idea of a Big Year appealed to me because it gave structure and a sense of competition to my year's birding. Though I did not initially set my expectations too high, I was curious as to what I could achieve.

The final numerical result of my Texas Big Year is the most straightforward of my achievements: I saw and heard 489 bird species within the borders of Texas between dawn on January 1, 2000, and sunset on

December 31, 2000. This result far exceeded my expectations. A record was never my motivation, but my end result tied with the impressive Texas Big Year record established by Brush Freeman of Utley, Texas, and Petra Hockey of Port O'Connor, Texas, in 1995 and is the highest Big Year total recorded for any state or province.

Reaching such a large species total in one year in one state required much travel. The entire Texas coastline of the Gulf of Mexico became familiar to me, from the popular upper coast birding haunts such as High Island and the Bolivar Peninsula southward to the productive sites of the central Texas coast, such as Packery Channel, to the lower coast, where I sometimes roamed within a rock's throw of Mexico. Long weekends were spent in the rolling Hill Country. Airplanes, rental cars, and my own Jeep took me in and out of the larger Texas cities many times: Dallas, Houston, Beaumont, Austin, San Antonio, El Paso, Midland-Odessa, Lubbock, Amarillo, Nacogdoches. While in transit between these far-flung places, I was sometimes forced to sub-sist on airport food (Austin's Bergstrom Airport was the only place where this was pleasurable). I occasionally birded among the sights, smells, and sounds of the modern urban landscape. Necessity some-times required that I visit wastewater treatment plants. And chasing several species meant enduring roadside parks where I was enveloped in the stench of automobile exhaust and deafened by the roar of high-speed traffic.

But more often than not, I was surrounded by natural beauty and a gratifying lack of urban and suburban conveniences. In the Texas Pan-handle, I tarried at blessedly quiet parks and refuges. I traveled tens of miles without traffic lights and spent days in the company of just those persons who had departed the hotel or campground with me that morning. There were agreeable mornings in the stark beauty, heat, and solitude of the Chihuahuan Desert along the lonesome United States–Mexico border. I hiked and birded among the damp natural smells and towering forests of the East Texas Pineywoods. And I trekked many miles around my own "backyard," the Davis and Chisos mountains of Trans-Pecos Texas. Here, in one of the few frontiers re-maining in the continental United States, I have been privileged to explore the heart of these fascinating "sky islands."

This book chronicles my exploration and enjoyment of the land-scapes, habitats, flora, and fauna of Texas. It describes what I planned and what I could not possibly have planned: my often surprising field experiences and even a few misadventures. It includes fascinating, generous people. Though I was sometimes alone, I was frequently in the company of others who were uniformly helpful and intrigued by my quest. I turned numerous e-mail addresses and names into faces, voices, and personalities. I made new friends. The people of Texas and the people who visit Texas, birders and nonbirders, are featured players here.

Fortunately, I had been working hard since my arrival in April, 1994, at the University of Texas at Austin–McDonald Observatory. By the end of 1999, the university owed me more than three hundred hours of compensatory time and nearly as much vacation time. The nature of my job also assisted my Big Year ambitions. Few of my responsibilities were tied to the clock, giving me flexibility. Though I spent much time birding in 2000, I could always catch up at work by putting in long hours at the office before or after my time in the field. It was stressful but possible. Owing to this fortuitous combination of circumstances, I was able to do a Big Year without skimping on my job responsibilities.

A good fraction of the literature on the outdoors has been given over to authors who deliberately tempt fate and court danger, but a successful birding Big Year is unlikely to break any of your bones, require a hospital stay, or otherwise threaten your health. Though a Big Year is not extreme, it is nonetheless unpredictable and exhilarating.

Numerous Texas birding locations are discussed in these pages. Almost all are described in two widely available site guides: *Birding Texas* by Roland H. Wauer and Mark A. Elwonger (Helena: Falcon Publishing, 1998) and *A Birder's Guide to Texas* by Edward A. Kutac, 2nd edition (Houston: Gulf Publishing, 1998). When a public birding location is not described in either of these books, I provide directions.

I refer throughout to information that came to me via TEXBIRDS, an electronic list-server operated by the University of Houston. Such list-servers have revolutionized birding across the United States and

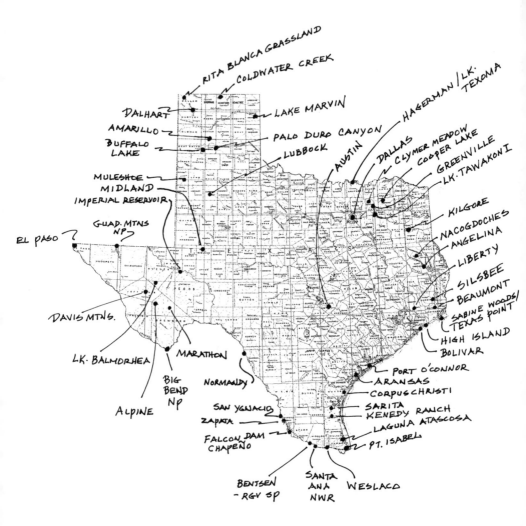

other parts of the world by providing near real-time information flow among birders. TEXBIRDS currently has more than a thousand subscribers. It is a data channel that few serious Texas birders can afford to do without.

At key milestones during the year, I list a number in parentheses beside a bird's common name, such as "Olive-sided Flycatcher (#400)." These numbers indicate at what point that species entered my Texas Big Year species list. Thus, Olive-sided Flycatcher was the 400th species I observed in Texas during the year 2000.

The common bird names used in this book follow those of the American Ornithologists' Union (AOU) in its *Check-list of North American Birds,* 7th edition (Washington, D.C.: American Ornithologists' Union, 1998). Common butterfly names have been adopted in accordance with those used by the North American Butterfly Association (NABA) in its *Checklist and English Names of North American Butterflies,* 2nd edition (Morristown, N.J.: 2001). Times given in the text are either Central Standard Time or Central Daylight Time, unless otherwise noted. All temperatures are in degrees Fahrenheit. Any date listed without a year should be assumed to be the year 2000.

Please join me now in reliving my Texas Big Year. I trust you will enjoy the experience and be impressed by where it takes us. And I hope you may be inspired to create and live your own adventures in the natural world.

## chapter 1

Birth of a Birder
and a Texas Big Year

W hile enduring that tortuous American rite of passage known as high school, I was a student in John Sharp's biology class. In the spring of 1970, Mr. Sharp took my sophomore class into the field to inventory a few remnant acres of woods at Warminster, Pennsylvania. Going outside the classroom was a novel concept to the children of suburban Philadelphia. We knew biology only as the stuff of textbooks and formaldehyde-fumed laboratories. Most wanted to get past the subject as quickly as possible. Confronting each of us with frog innards and similar unpleasantries, biology had already exposed most of the young men in my class as unfashionably squeamish.

As the school year drew to a close, our minds turned to thoughts of summer, but Mr. Sharp had one more biology hurdle for us: locate, identify, and study everything we could find in those woods. How interesting could that be? We were not enthusiastic.

Mr. Sharp was in charge, though. There was never any doubt of that simple fact. So every day for three weeks, we obediently marched outside and into the damp, tangled woods that bordered our school's parking lot. To our genuine surprise, we made many "discoveries."

Biological diversity thrived on our doorstep among the trees, grasses, ferns, wildflowers, shrubs, insects, mushrooms, birds, lizards, and mammals that inhabited our humble suburban tract. We learned the common and scientific names for many of these biological entities. Mr. Sharp knew what he was doing. We enjoyed this diversion from our increasingly warm classroom.

One sunny May morning, a classmate found a gaudy black, white, and red apparition perched in a tall tree. It was a bird, the likes of which none of us, Mr. Sharp excepted, had ever seen. Frantic paging through books and a noisy group consultation finally named the beast: an adult male Rose-breasted Grosbeak. Even among sophomore males, it created some excitement: a bird could be visually spectacular. Our books told us that some birds, like this one, migrated long distances every spring and fall. Wherever this bird's destination lay that spring, we had been privileged to see it.

My technicolor memory of this grosbeak remains vivid and pleasant, even after thirty-one years. I cannot say the same about many other high school memories.

Though I enjoyed this first field experience, there was a long pause before my interest in the natural world rekindled. I completed high school, college, and graduate school, abandoned my plans to be an academic astronomer, and sought a career in industry. I moved from Pennsylvania to Arizona to Florida.

In 1986, my family and I moved into a planned community where each middle-class residence was allocated a neat one-third-acre slice of the Sunshine State. Except for my lawn, I enjoyed this house. Like my neighbors, I was constantly at war with our lush, green lawn—suburbia's vilest lifestyle requirement—and the numerous critters that inhabited it. None of the occupants of our lawn was desirable by the standards of our homeowners' association. Maintaining this green carpet to the association's standards cost an exorbitant amount of money and weekend time.

There was good news, however, for my lawn brought birds into my life again. Each week, as I sweated and pushed my lawnmower through the dense Floretam grass, numerous insects fled skyward. In June, 1993, I first noticed a recurring spectator, a bird that always arrived shortly after I began my odious lawn-mowing chores. It perched atop the six-foot-high cedar fence that enclosed our backyard. This bird was distinctive: gray-bodied, dark masked, with a mostly black tail and wings that were accented by bold white highlights.

And it was entertaining. When a suitable living morsel fled before the roar and disturbance created by my mower, this avian Zorro saw a meal and dove perilously near the whirring blades to fetch its next bit of nourishment. My friend's antics alleviated some of the drudgery of mowing. Its daring impressed me.

Purchasing Roger Tory Peterson's *Eastern Birds* allowed me to name my companion. Since the order for listing species in most field guides, "taxonomic order," was a mystery to me, I paged through a good fraction of Mr. Peterson's book before I found my guest's picture and name: Loggerhead Shrike. The National Audubon Society's *Field Guide to North American Birds* further fed my newfound fascination by supplying me the Loggerhead Shrike's grisly nickname: "Butcher Bird." Since they lack talons, Loggerhead Shrikes often impale prey— an insect, a rodent, or even a small bird—on a thorn or a barbed-wire fence. Once immobilized, prey can be torn apart and consumed or stored for future consumption.

Having identified the Loggerhead Shrike, I found myself noticing other birds. My Florida home bordered a large working ranch, the legacy of a hardworking 1920s Czechoslovakian immigrant. The ranch would soon be sacrificed by the grandchildren to Florida's burgeoning real-estate market, but for many years, the vista behind our home was endless southern pine and palmetto occasionally visited by a few cattle.

Over this ranchland, unusual birds appeared just before or after sunset, careening among the pines. Their nasal voices called, loud and insistent, "peent, peent, peent," with a second or two between notes. They flew erratically and only in the weakening evening light. But I saw enough—dark brown bodies with long, pointed wings and a bright white bar near the wingtips—to find them in my field guides. Another small victory came my way: Common Nighthawk.

Those amusing long-legged, mostly white birds that graced our lawns, probing the sod with their curved bills, became known to me as White Ibis. On spring and summer mornings, when I retrieved the newspaper from the end of our driveway, I heard a bird singing brightly and soon identified it: Eastern Towhee. And the statuesque, mostly gray, red-capped, bugling birds that were the bane of the golf course groundskeepers: Sandhill Cranes.

Most birders keep a "life list," noting where and when they first see each species they encounter. I had unconsciously started building mine. But becoming a birder was not at all a part of my life plan. My personal address book contained no birders. I had no idea what being a "birder" meant. My suburban life continued, with my nonfamily playtime consumed by endless hours of golf.

Then, in mid-1993, I decided to turn my career back toward astronomy. The right opportunity eventually presented itself and in April, 1994, my family and I moved west. I went to work for the University of Texas at Austin as superintendent of the McDonald Observatory in the Davis Mountains of Trans-Pecos Texas.

Overseeing the operations for this world-class astronomical research, education, and public outreach facility was exciting. As I arrived, the observatory broke ground for the Hobby-Eberly Telescope, an innovative instrument that is the world's third largest astronomical telescope. Since public outreach was an important component of the observatory's mission, fund-raising was under way for a new, much larger visitors' center. There was a future here.

And West Texas was such a fascinating place. McDonald Observatory is one hundred miles north of the United States–Mexico border; the Davis Mountains are a "sky island" rising high above the surrounding Chihuahuan Desert. Here, at the best remaining continental astronomical site in the United States, the lack of city lights preserves the dark nighttime sky, enabling professional astronomical research. The Universities of Texas and Chicago established this observatory in the 1930s, using monies from the estate of the visionary banker William Johnson McDonald of Paris, Texas. Since that time the observatory has prospered, aided by the cooperation and pride of the communities that surround it and by the generosity of the University of Texas, the Texas Legislature, and private donors.

Though I had always wanted to live in the quiet of rural America, I was nervous about whether I could fit in and thrive in this community.

Other than a fifteen-month stint in rural northeast Pennsylvania when I was ten years old, my life had been spent in urban and suburban settings. The Davis Mountains are remote and thinly populated, one to two persons per square mile. This makes for special challenges, such as a forty-mile trek to the nearest large grocery store and a journey of 175 miles to the nearest commercial airport. Fortunately, the observatory is an integral part of the Davis Mountains communities. The local people are generous and friendly. I had no trouble making an interesting life, becoming part of the community. And my work was engaging.

Having moved to West Texas, I wanted to explore the region. When my mother, sister, and brother-in-law traveled across the country in May, 1994, to see West Texas, we made our first trip to Big Bend National Park. We marveled at the tree-clad Chisos Mountains; the forbidding lowland desert landscape; the life-giving riparian ribbon of the Rio Grande; hundred-mile-long views to distant, enigmatic mountains in Mexico and the United States; and the solitude. Although I recognized that exploring Big Bend needed to be a priority in my life, somehow it was a year before I returned.

In the spring of 1995, observatory colleague Marc Wetzel and I decided to go camping. Marc was a member of the Big Bend Natural History Association, a group that sponsors seminars on a range of topics. Marc suggested combining our camping trip with participation in a three-day birding seminar in the national park. This radical idea would never have occurred to me. Marc knew something of birds, especially raptors, and he wanted to know more. But other than the handful of elementary identifications I had pursued in Florida, I knew nothing of birds. Nonetheless, I agreed to Marc's intriguing seminar idea.

We arrived in Big Bend on a hot early May Thursday afternoon under a sky that threatened thunderstorms. Before setting up our tent, we parked among the cottonwoods and mesquite of the Rio Grande Village campground near the nature trail entrance. As soon as we stepped out of our car, we saw two showy birds, both red, one brilliant and small, the other larger and darker. I recall wondering—for just a few seconds!—whether a good number of Big Bend's birds were red. Such novice "insights" are embarrassing in hindsight but not uncommon. A mind is a dangerous thing. After a few minutes with a field guide, Marc and I determined that we had seen a male Vermilion Flycatcher and an adult Summer Tanager.

This was easy! Big Bend birds were straightforward to see and identify. But our walk along the nature trail soon proved how little we knew. Many birds escaped before we could decide what they were; others seemed to have few notable features, and we could not identify them with certainty.

The violent weather that sometimes awakens in the Big Bend visited our campsite that evening once the thunderstorms matured. Pea-sized hail pelted us, forty to fifty-mile-per-hour wind gusts thrashed our tent, and a wild downpour soaked belongings we had failed to protect.

Our seminar began the next morning, a typically warm and still Big Bend spring dawn. The night's fury had dissipated. Our leader, Anne Bellamy, introduced herself. Anne is a naturalist and artist, soft-spoken and given to listening carefully. She and her family lived in Big Bend National Park for several years. She knows the park well, is an expert birder, and is practiced at guiding a group with a range of birding talent. I was the rank novice, the person who knew the least about birds in this group on seminar day one.

Like all Big Bend birding seminars, this one included persons whose sole motivation was the addition to their life lists of the region's specialties: Colima Warbler, Lucifer's Hummingbird, and Gray Vireo. Two of our group would undertake the "Death March"—a ten-mile round-trip into the Boot Canyon high country with an elevation change of more than two thousand feet—only because that was where they could see the Colima Warbler. They would persevere through the heat of Blue Creek Canyon solely to add Gray Vireo and Lucifer's Hummingbird to their life lists. For them, the remainder of the seminar was a prelude to the real business.

After everyone had arrived and introductions were completed, we set off to bird the Rio Grande Village campground. I distinguished myself by dropping my binoculars onto the asphalt before we had walked ten paces. When I sheepishly picked up my binoculars and tried to focus on nearby cottonwoods, double images greeted me. Something in the optical train had been jarred out of alignment. This was a poor start.

Anne had seen me drop the binoculars. Without commenting on my fumble-fingeredness, she kindly offered me spare binoculars from her van. Apparently seminar attendees occasionally show up without optics or perform stunts such as mine. I was grateful for the rescue.

After lunch, I opened my binoculars and spent forty-five minutes repairing the problem, realigning the optics and undoing minor mechanical damage with my Swiss Army knife and a bit of know-how. This was not difficult for an astronomer. And to my relief, this recovery brought me back up a notch or two in Anne's eyes.

During those three days in Big Bend, Anne took us to many of the park's finest birding sites, all new to me: Rio Grande Village, Cottonwood Campground, Sam Nail Ranch, the Pinnacles Trail, Boot Canyon, Blue Creek Canyon. She showed us many birds. Anne made it all terribly interesting, peppering her discussion of bird identification with tidbits of natural history, geology, park history, and the high points of previous seminars she had led.

I learned so much, however, that information overload periodically clouded my brain. On the last day of the seminar, a well-intentioned but misguided expert birder quizzed me about every bird that popped into view. Before long, he was likely disheartened by my lack of skill. Until he corrected me, I claimed Ash-throated Flycatchers as Olive-sided Flycatchers; mistook several Brewer's Sparrows for Clay-colored Sparrows; and made one particularly egregious call, suggesting that a female Wilson's Warbler might be another species of warbler that is extraordinarily rare in Big Bend. Oops.

By Sunday afternoon, we had seen ninety-five species of birds, pleasing even the expert birders. The Boot Canyon Death March had yielded several Colima Warblers, and though Lucifer's Hummingbird had eluded us, we had sighted a singing Gray Vireo in Blue Creek Canyon.

From this seminar through the following spring, I did some birding, but not much. In May, 1996, Marc and I repeated Anne's spring Big Bend seminar. At home in the Davis Mountains, I met others whose passion for birds and birding was communicated to me, people like Kelly Bryan and Linda and David Hedges. More of my free time was spent birding and hiking. New worlds again opened up to me. I studied and soon understood my field guides. Part of the attraction of ornithology was that as in astronomy, it is an endeavor where the scientifically minded citizen can still play a role.

Three more Big Bend birding seminars guided by Roland (Ro) Wauer—August, 1996, and May and September, 1997—sealed my ambition to be a serious birder. Ro is a retired National Park Service employee who spent five seminal years of his career (1966–71) in Big Bend National Park as Chief Naturalist. He has crisscrossed the park numerous times and knows it as well as any person. During these three seminars, Ro transferred his infectious enthusiasm and respect for the Big Bend and its birds to each attendee. By the end of 1997, I had become an avid birder.

PERSONS WHO ENJOY BIRDING usually maintain several lists of which bird species they have seen and where. A yard list, for example, tabulates all species seen in or from one's backyard. County and state lists are also popular. On a larger geographic scale, North American birders might keep an "American Birding Association (ABA) Area" list for all species seen in the ABA Area, which has been defined as Canada and the United States excluding Hawaii. Adding up every species one has seen on the planet yields a birder's world list.

Founded in 1968 and devoted to the hobby of birding, the ABA now boasts more than twenty-two thousand members and fosters many aspects of the hobby, including its competitive side. The ABA has taken on the role of record keeper and rules setter for activities such as birding Big Days and Big Years.

During a Big Day, birders work to see and hear as many bird species as possible between one midnight and the next. Serious Big Day birders begin well before dawn, seeking the sounds of nocturnal birds, such as owls and rails. In the United States, a spectacular 258-species Big Day record was set in Texas by Bob Kemp, Dwight Peake, Giff Beaton, Adam Byrne, and Ron Weeks on April 24, 2001.

Big Years can be performed over any geographic scale. Some particularly ambitious souls have undertaken a Big Year over the entire ABA Area, an all-consuming and expensive task. New Jersey's Sandy

Komito holds the current ABA Area Big Year record: 745 species. Others have pursued Big Years on an even larger geographic scale. The world Big Year record, for example, is 3,631 species, achieved by globe-trotting Jim Clements in 1989. This record amounts to seeing 37 percent of the world's approximately 9,800 bird species in one year! The most popular type of Big Year in the United States, however, is one undertaken within the bounds of a single state.

As the popularity of birding has increased, with more sophisticated and timely communication between birders, Big Year possibilities have improved. Word-of-mouth and telephone Rare Birds Alerts have been superseded by the near real-time reporting of the Internet. Site guides have improved, too, and there are now volumes that can direct birders to the best locations for nearly every species.

With some effort, it is possible to see a good portion of a state's bird list in a single year. Through 1999, sixty-two Texas year lists of four hundred species or more had been reported to the ABA. All but nine of these were recorded in the 1990s. Table 1 lists the ten highest Texas Big Year totals through 1999. Each total is given as it was reported by the observer in the listing year. None has been updated to reflect changes in species status, such as the recent split of Solitary Vireo into Blue-headed, Cassin's, and Plumbeous Vireo, or the acceptance of previously uncountable species such as Green Parakeet. If such species status changes are taken into account, the 1995 tally of 485 species Brush Freeman and Petra Hockey chalked up becomes 489 species, the Texas Big Year record.

Freeman and Hockey started 1995 at their usual active birding pace, spending numerous days in the field. Brush was determined to observe several species that had eluded him in Texas in previous years. Multiday trips with Petra and others to key locations around the state were productive and yielded several rarities. At the end of March, Brush reviewed his year list and realized it was substantial. He started working on a Texas Big Year.

Petra did not commit to a Big Year in Texas until mid-April, but she soon caught up with Brush, even though she was out of the country for a month in the summer and another three weeks in the fall. By year's end, Brush and Petra had jointly established a new record, eclips-

Top Ten Texas Big Years as of January 1, 2000

Rank	Species	Observer	Year
I	485	Brush Freeman	1995
I	485	Petra Hockey	1995
3	468	Greg Lasley	1994
4	465	Don Alexander	1986
5	463	Petra Hockey	1999
6	458	Red Gambill	1995
6	458	Louise Gambill	1995
6	458	Red Gambill	1991
6	458	Louise Gambill	1991
10	453	Eric Carpenter	1999
10	453	Brush Freeman	1996

ing Lasley's 1994 mark. Though they did all their long-distance trips together, Brush and Petra's year lists differ by many first sightings and locations and by two species. Petra observed a Thayer's Gull in 1995; Brush did not. But Brush found a Shiny Cowbird.

In 1999, Brush Freeman, Petra Hockey, and Eric Carpenter introduced me to the idea of a Big Year concentrated in a single state. By October, the idea of attempting a Texas Big Year (hereafter simply TBY) seemed plausible and caught my fancy. I liked to travel. A TBY effort in 2000 would be an interesting way to learn a great deal about the birds of our state. It would motivate me to travel around Texas. I would discover new birding sites, hike and bird a wide range of new habitats. Bird species I had rarely or never seen, in or out of Texas, would become well-known to me.

Most of my field time up to that point had been in the Trans-Pecos. I had birded a little along the Texas coast and in the Austin area. But there were many parts of Texas that I had visited only once and others I had never visited. I had yet to see or hear numerous birds on the Texas checklist, including some relatively common residents and visitors, such as American Bittern, Rough-legged Hawk, and Acadian Flycatcher. Since the observatory owed me a large number of compensatory and vacation days and it was workable for me take quite a few of these in 2000, the requisite time off from work would be available. In December of 1999, my commitment to a TBY gelled.

Prior to 2000, I had seen no more than 375 bird species in Texas in one year. This led me to set the bar initially on my TBY at a target of seeing or hearing 400 bird species. I felt there was no chance of my TBY approaching Brush and Petra's record.

Through the influence and mentorship of Ro Wauer, 1999 was also the year in which I began to study butterflies. My original plan was to combine a bird and butterfly TBY. It held certain attractions. But I rejected this plan before the start of 2000, reasoning that the need to visit optimum bird and butterfly locations would create too many conflicts. The net result might be failure on both counts, bird and butterfly. After further consultation with Brush, Petra, and Eric, I decided that my initial target of 400 bird species was too low for the effort I was willing to invest. I beefed up my TBY target to 450 species.

As with any project that lasts for months, I knew that a good part of the challenge would be maintaining interest and motivation over an entire year. I did not want my TBY to sputter and come to an inglorious end in June. But now my targets were set. I had prepared as much as I could. The beginning of the year 2000 arrived. It was time to have fun with a Texas Big Year.

The birds that began my Texas Big Year on January 1, 2000: Pine Siskins feasting on niger thistle in my backyard, atop Mount Locke in the Davis Mountains (see chapter 2). Photo by Mark T. Adams.

A Big Year effort requires an observer to locate and see numerous birds, including relatively common species, such as this Yellow-headed Blackbird at Lake Balmorhea (Reeves County). Photo by Mark T. Adams.

Traveling long distances to see the rarest birds is a necessary component of a Big Year. This Rufous-backed Robin visited the town of Sarita (Kenedy County) for several weeks in January and February, 2000 (see chapter 5).
Photo by Mark T. Adams.

Specialties of Texas' montane habitats include Steller's Jay (year-round resident, Davis and Guadalupe mountains), Williamson's Sapsucker (winter resident, Davis and Guadalupe mountains), Colima Warbler (Chisos Mountains breeder), and Mountain Chickadee (year-round resident, Davis and Guadalupe mountains). This view is from the summit of 7,700-foot Pine Peak, looking southwest toward Mount Livermore, the highest peak in the Davis Mountains (Jeff Davis County). Photo by Mark T. Adams.

Multiple visits to the upper, central, and lower Texas coasts are required during a Big Year. This photo shows the author standing on the central coast near Freeport on May 5, 2000, not long after observing a vagrant Black-whiskered Vireo at the Quintana Neotropical Bird Sanctuary, a birding site that has produced a long list of rarities (see chapter 12). Photo by Ron Weeks.

Occasionally a very rare bird appears close to home. This adult male Berylline Hummingbird was seen and photographed at a private feeder in the Davis Mountains on May 25, 2000 (see chapter 13). Photo by Mark T. Adams.

The view from the Falcon Dam spillway (Starr County) in the Rio Grande Valley of Texas, looking east along the river. This part of the Rio Grande harbors Muscovy Duck, Brown Jay, Hook-billed Kite, and Red-billed Pigeon (see chapters 3 and 14). Photo by Mark T. Adams.

This singing male Slate-throated Redstart was at Pewee Springs in the Davis Mountains, June 21–25, 2000. This bird was the third Texas record for its species (see chapter 15). Photo by Mark T. Adams.

One benefit of a Big Year is spending many days in the field with friends. The author, on the left, is with Rex Barrick and Marc Eastman on a July 22, 2000, hike into Pine Canyon in Big Bend National Park (see chapter 18). Note that the book being consulted is a butterfly field guide! Photo by Maryann Eastman.

Discovering a Red-faced Warbler on August 6, 2000, near Bridge Gap on the Nature Conservancy's Davis Mountains Preserve was cause for excitement. This individual represented the first Davis Mountains record for the species (see chapter 19). Photo by Kelly B. Bryan.

One of two Long-tailed Jaegers observed by several people on September 1, 2000, at the Fort Bliss sewage ponds in El Paso. Note the limited white in the bird's primaries (see chapter 20). Photo by Mark T. Adams.

The author's Big Year was given a boost by the fall "invasion" of several species rare in Texas, including Lewis's Woodpecker (left) and Pinyon Jay (right), shown here at Frijole Ranch in the Guadalupe Mountains National Park on October 17, 2000 (see chapter 21). Photo by Mark T. Adams.

Alan Wormington discovered this gorgeous Olive Warbler on November 11, 2000, at Hueco Tanks State Historical Park. The author observed and photographed it the following afternoon (see chapter 23). Photo by Mark T. Adams.

A long New Year's Eve day in Lubbock, fighting snow and freezing drizzle, failed to yield a Long-eared Owl such as this individual, photographed at Mitchell Lake (San Antonio, Bexar County) on March 18, 1995 (see chapter 26). Photo by Greg W. Lasley.

chapter 2

Starting Close to Home

Though millions around the world celebrated the arrival of a new millennium (one year too soon), I attended no parties on New Year's Eve in 1999. My job required that I spend that Friday night awake as midnight came and went. Many feared that the Y2K bug would make an appearance, but no demons emerged from any observatory software or hardware. Everyone was pleased, especially the professional astronomers, who were working under a clear sky.

Since my Y2K vigil kept me up until well after midnight, it delayed the start of my Texas Big Year. Saturday, January 1, 2000, was unseasonably warm at my observatory home, which sits among alligator junipers, pinyon pines, and gray oaks at 6,800 feet elevation. The thermometer nudged sixty degrees. At 11:00 A.M. I refilled my feeders with thistle, black oil sunflower seeds, and white millet and spread seed on the ground.

I stayed home on day one, partly to be certain that my Big Year did not begin with an urban "trash bird," such as a House Sparrow, Rock Dove, or European Starling. At my house, well away from any town, the probability of seeing one of these species was zero.

At 11:35 A.M. on January 1, several birds with streaked breasts, sharp bills, and yellow wing patches settled on the thistle feeder hanging in a juniper outside my back door. I was nearly certain what they were, using only my naked eye. But absolute certainty was essential. I trained my binoculars on these ten birds and confirmed that they were Pine Siskins, fairly common in the Davis Mountains from fall through midspring. A few can even be found in the highest elevations of the Davis Mountains in summer.

I recorded Pine Siskin in my journal as species #1 for my Texas Big Year. It was an auspicious moment, this embarkation point for a year-long journey of uncertain dimensions.

I KEPT AN EYE ON MY FEEDERS between episodes of various moronic television programs and some light reading. By midafternoon, I had recorded several species that are year-round residents at the observatory, including fifteen Dark-eyed Juncos that gorged on my sunflower seed for more than an hour. Three of the Dark-eyed Junco subspecies were present in this group: "Pink-sided," "Oregon," and "Gray-headed" Dark-eyed Junco.

The junco subspecies are among the more straightforward to discern. Subspecies of the White-crowned Sparrow, however, are more subtle and require attention to detail for reliable identification with binoculars. Separating the "Gambel's" White-crowned Sparrow from the "Mountain" White-crowned Sparrow requires noting the bill color and the extent of black coloration between the eyes and the bill.

Many subspecies are impossible to separate using binoculars. This is work for ornithologists scrutinizing in-hand specimens. There are, for example, at least two species of Mourning Dove in Texas. Determining whether a given Mourning Dove belongs to one subspecies or the other rests on such esoteric measurements as the size of the bird's middle toe, a subtlety no credible binocular-bearing birder would claim to be able to distinguish.

What constitutes a species and a subspecies are fundamental questions in biological science. For decades, most ornithologists adhered to the biological species concept (BSC) definition, which holds that a species must be reproductively isolated from others. Distinctive geographical forms of the same type of bird are lumped as one species because these forms often interbreed if they inhabit common territory. To BSC proponents, if bird forms are only slightly different, they would probably interbreed if given the chance and so would be considered the same species.

The phylogenetic species concept (PSC) holds that geographic forms of the same type of bird should be treated as distinct species. PSC proponents argue that these forms have evolved separately and have unique histories. The PSC is currently gaining favor over the BSC. Since the PSC is a less restrictive definition, there would be more species of birds under the PSC.

In a less scientific vernacular, ornithologists who study species and subspecies definition fall into two broad categories: "lumpers" and "splitters." Lumpers advocate the BSC definition of a species. They are more likely to recommend combining two or more individual species into a single species than the reverse. Splitters favor the PSC and are usually the proponents for elevating individual subspecies to full species status.

Though lumpers held sway in the past, splitters currently outnumber lumpers among professional ornithologists. Several subspecies have been redefined as species in the recent past: Northern Oriole has been split into Baltimore Oriole and Bullock's Oriole; Rufous-sided Towhee has been split into Eastern Towhee and Spotted Towhee; Plain Titmouse has been split into Juniper Titmouse and Oak Titmouse. Since Big Year observers count the number of species they see and hear, the action of the splitters is a boon since it increases the species pool.

The Dark-eyed Junco subspecies seem unlikely to be elevated to individual species. But good bets for future splits include the several Fox Sparrow subspecies, at least two of which might be seen in Texas; and Warbling Vireo, which has distinct eastern and western forms that can be encountered on opposite sides of the state.

In addition to the siskins and the juncos, several Tufted (black-crested) Titmice roamed my yard's trees and climbed on my feeders on New Year's Day. In the late afternoon, the weather turned cloudy and much colder. A light rain fell and turned birds' minds to tasks other than feeding. Dusk fell with a modest three species in my TBY bank.

SUNDAY, JANUARY 2, was my first extensive field trip. Almost everything I would see would be new to my list, and my Big Year species counter would tick rapidly upward. I was eager to get outside and looked forward to a long day in the field with my friends David Hedges and Kelly Bryan.

David was born and raised in the Kansas City area in a birding family. After a twenty-six-year career with AT&T, he and his spouse sold their house, put most of their worldly goods in storage, and spent the next three years traveling and birding. This grand adventure eventually brought David and Linda to the Davis Mountains in November, 1993, as volunteer bird-banders. They have never left. David is now one of the busiest retirees on the face of the planet, volunteering for the Nature Conservancy of Texas and other organizations.

Whenever he is in the field, David strides along the trail with purpose and urgency. His sense of humor is legendary in and around Fort Davis, and our field trips are spiced by periodic outbursts of David's hilarious phraseology ("colder than a banker's heart" is a printable favorite).

Kelly Bryan started birding at thirteen, his interest sparked by a Waco schoolteacher's tutelage. In college, an unexpected observation of several Evening Grosbeaks led to a meeting with biologist Ralph Moldenhauer and a switching of Kelly's major from photography to biology. Moldenhauer introduced Kelly to bird-banding, which would become a lifelong passion. In 1974, he began a career with the Texas Parks and Wildlife Department, and he arrived in 1991 at the Davis Mountains State Park.

In the field, Kelly is an energetic presence, constantly disappearing over the next rise, anxious to know what lies ahead. Kelly endears himself to his field companions by always having an extra burrito to share. On many field trips, I run out of the house with minimal lunch and regularly face nothing more enticing to eat than a mushed banana or some preservative-soaked concoction. I would be much hungrier on the trail without Kelly.

The morning of January 2 dawned sunny and cool. There was little wind, a blessing one should rarely ignore in the Trans-Pecos. I met David at his home near Fort Davis at 7:30 A.M. We drove into town, added Kelly to our contingent, then headed to Balmorhea State Park and Lake Balmorhea.

Opened in 1968, Balmorhea State Park is a small facility of forty-six acres. Within its boundaries, however, lie the prodigious San Solomon Springs, gushing millions of gallons of water to the surface every day. When their flow was unconstrained, the springs created a cienega, a desert wetland. But as settlers moved into the Trans-Pecos in the late nineteenth century, farming took hold. Since that time, the springs have been modified to accommodate agriculture and pleasure. A pool was created where the springs breach the surface. Since this pool is as much as twenty-five feet deep, it is the centerpiece of the Balmorhea State Park and one of the few places in the Trans-Pecos where one can learn SCUBA. More recently, several agencies collaborated with Texas Parks and Wildlife to recreate a piece of the original cienega.

Excess water is channeled out of the park via a series of concrete sluices that extend many miles from the springs. This irrigation system has supported as much as twelve thousand acres of cantaloupe, cotton, and grain production.

When Kelly, David, and I arrived at the state park, there was little bird activity. We added just three common species to my year list: a single American Coot paddling on the pool; a Belted Kingfisher perched on a wire, occasionally emitting its signature "rattle"; and two Common Ravens that called as they flew past. We did not see the rare Pacific Loon that had been contentedly swimming in the pool through at least mid-December.

On Saturday, December 4, 1999, this adult Pacific Loon had "crash landed" on U.S. Highway 90 between Marfa and Alpine, in the open desert of Presidio County. Pacific Loons breed on lakes in the far North. During the winter they range southward, sometimes to inland lakes and reservoirs but more typically along the Atlantic and Pacific coasts. Few stray inland or as far south as Texas.

Fortunately for this Pacific Loon, a compassionate motorist stopped, retrieved the injured bird from the U.S. 90 roadside, and took it to Big Bend National Park. To nurse it back to health, the park's chief naturalist, Raymond Skiles, placed the bird in his bathtub, feeding it mosquito fish he had netted. I was in the park that December weekend, assisting Kelly with a Big Bend Natural History Association seminar. Raymond contacted Kelly and asked if he could arrange to release the loon at Balmorhea, a suitable environment.

Kelly and I went to Raymond's house in the park to retrieve the bird. Kelly held the loon while I snapped a few photographs to document this unusual Trans-Pecos record. The loon was not pleased. It struggled and pecked Kelly several times with its sharp beak, drawing blood.

With the permission of park personnel, the bird was released into the Balmorhea State Park pool later that day. The loon swam out a few feet and drank for several minutes. It then dove and fed, catching fish and crawfish. It was doing well.

This loon likely fell victim to exhaustion while flying over the Chihuahuan Desert. When it came down on the highway, it was in serious trouble. Since their legs are set far back on their bodies, loons cannot land on or take off from hard surfaces. Roadways glinting in the sunlight sometimes fool them: loons mistake these for water. Unfortunately for my Big Year effort, we saw no sign of the rescued loon at the Balmorhea State Park on January 2. The bird had evidently completed its recovery and departed.

Kelly and I drove four miles farther north along Texas Highway 17, stopping at the Balmorhea Grocery to invest in brisket, potato and cheese, and asado burritos.

Cottonwoods nurtured by the springs tower above the desert at Balmorhea, providing the only relief and shelter for miles in any direction. Travel-weary migrating birds often land here and rest when storms preclude going farther north in the spring or south in the fall. However, since this was January, we conjured up just the usual suspects, such as White-winged Dove and Rock Dove. Seeing little prospect for anything else, we moved on to Lake Balmorhea, two miles from town via Reeves County Road 319.

To the delight of birds and birders, several large reservoirs break the monotony of the Trans-Pecos desert: Imperial Reservoir in Pecos County; Lake Balmorhea in Reeves County; McNary and Fort Hancock reservoirs in Hudspeth County; and Tornillo Reservoir in El Paso County. Though their sizes vary with the growing season—

high in winter, low in summer—each of these reservoirs is several hundred acres in extent. Especially in winter, when ducks and other waterfowl head south, these bodies of water are bird magnets. Sorting through the hordes wintering at any of these lakes can take hours. But patient searches can yield West Texas treasure, such as a jaeger or a Long-tailed Duck. Fisherman often line the Lake Balmorhea shoreline, hopeful of snagging a catfish or a bass. But you will rarely find anyone at the other reservoirs.

With burritos in our bellies, Kelly, David, and I surveyed Lake Balmorhea and its environs for three hours. The lake was full. At 575 acres, it required a good scope if we were to identify birds at lake center. Our efforts yielded more than fifty species of birds, including a handful we had not anticipated. Common Ground Dove, for example, would be straightforward to find later in the year, but we were surprised to see one at Lake Balmorhea on January 2. We ranged around the entire shoreline, including the south side, where high clearance is always a good idea and four-wheel-drive is sometimes a necessity. We birded among the mesquite and salt cedar, too.

Attempting to relocate another unusual species that had been recorded in December, Le Conte's Sparrow, we formed a line and trudged across the sacaton grassland adjacent to the south-side inlet canal. Our target soon fluttered before us, barely above the tops of the grass, landing after a short flight. A bit more work yielded outstanding binocular views of two gorgeous orange and gray-faced Le Conte's Sparrows, a Trans-Pecos treat.

Overall, the winter of 1999–2000 was poor for sparrows owing to insufficient rains the previous summer and thus a poor seed crop. Nonetheless, in addition to the Le Conte's, we found small numbers of the more common sparrows, including Swamp, Vesper, Savannah, and Black-throated.

Ducks were present in good numbers, as were Western and Clark's grebes, specialties of Lake Balmorhea and McNary Reservoir. The lake shore was busy with foraging and resting winter residents such as Greater Yellowlegs, Snow Geese, Say's Phoebe, and Ring-billed Gull. A rare wintering Black-bellied Plover still patrolled near the water. The newly arrived adult Bald Eagle preened on his stump, several feet out from the south shore. Two immature Reddish Egrets, normally a coastal species, had recently taken up residence at the lake. There are few Reddish Egret records between the Gulf Coast and the Trans-Pecos. Yet, for several months, individuals of this species had been at Lake Balmorhea and Imperial Reservoir.

IT WAS A FRUITFUL TRIP around the lake, though we saw no sign of two other rarities that might have remained from late 1999: Surf Scoter and Black-legged Kittiwake. In late November, Pecos birder and minister Greer Willis had discovered an adult male Surf Scoter at Lake Balmorhea. Only a few of these oceangoing birds wander inland each year. Many people observed this bird through December, including me on December 11 and 18. But sometime before the New Year it departed, leaving me without an easy Surf Scoter for my Big Year.

I had also been at Lake Balmorhea on Saturday, December 4, 1999, with Cliff Shackelford and Linda and David Hedges. Among other things, we hoped to find a Crissal Thrasher for Cliff. This thrasher had become a personal nemesis to Cliff, constantly eluding him. An ornithologist who resides in Austin, Cliff works on several projects for Texas Parks and Wildlife, including the Partners in Flight (PIF) program, which was launched in 1990 in response to concerns about the population declines of many land bird species.

Before Cliff returned to Austin, we were squeezing in some birding. A more adventurous trip to Imperial Reservoir had been considered but rejected since the weather had turned abominable. Average wind speeds of more than fifty miles per hour had been recorded at Mount Locke the previous night, with gusts as high as seventy-one miles per hour, and it was cold. So rather than start in the predawn, we met at the Hedges' home for breakfast. While we ate pancakes and drank coffee, the sun warmed the air and the winds calmed. At 8:30 A.M., we hit the road.

Through the morning, we worked our way around the lake to the mesquite adjacent to the inlet canal, where I had often found Crissal Thrasher over the past couple of seasons. A medium-sized gull flew lazily and low, up and down the canal. At first glance, I thought this

Black-throated Sparrow. Drawing by Kelly B. Bryan.

was one of the fairly common wintering Bonaparte's Gulls. Its behavior was different, though, and little alarms were going off in my head. I had never seen a Bonaparte's Gull at the canal; they were always over or on the lake. As I was puzzling over this bird's behavior, Cliff shouted that the gull had a yellow bill. This was no Bonaparte's Gull. Cliff had made the correct call: it was a very rare adult Black-legged Kittiwake.

A quarter mile before reaching the lake, the inflow empties from the concrete canal into a dirt channel, creating a frothy three-foot-deep pool. The kittiwake liked this pool. When not flying, it settled here, allowing Cliff and me to approach to close range with cameras. To see an adult of this species in Texas was exceptional. Ninety percent of the kittiwakes discovered in the Lone Star State are immatures.

After this success, we confronted a setback. The Crissal Thrashers were hiding. We never found one for Cliff on Saturday. On Sunday, however, Cliff relocated the Black-legged Kittiwake and found a Crissal Thrasher where I had suggested he might. For a few moments, Cliff had a Crissal Thrasher in the same binocular field of view as a Black-legged Kittiwake, a stunning juxtaposition of an oceangoing species with a bird of the desert. The kittiwake remained at Lake Balmorhea for at least a week but did not stay into the New Year. It was a shame that this bird was not more cooperative, since I never saw a Black-legged Kittiwake during my Big Year.

## chapter 3

The Rio Grande Valley in Winter

The "Rio Grande Valley of Texas" is a magical phrase to anyone interested in birds. To Texans, this place is simply the Valley, a treasure trove of year-round outdoor opportunities along the Rio Grande as it completes its run to the Gulf of Mexico. Though only 5 percent of the Valley's original habitat has escaped conversion to agriculture, housing, and commerce, several organizations—notably the Texas Parks and Wildlife Department, the Texas Nature Conservancy, and the U.S. Fish and Wildlife Service—have preserved key portions of this species-rich corridor for resident and migratory birds.

Since October of 1999, Linda and David Hedges and I had been anticipating our trip to the winter meeting of the Texas Ornithological Society (TOS) in the Valley. My only prior experience with this region had been a single day's birding with fellow West Texan John Karges in December, 1996, a brief diversion before we headed into Mexico.

TOS was founded in 1953 to promote and encourage the observation, study, and conservation of birds in Texas. Field trips are the centerpieces of the semiannual TOS meetings. In addition to providing guided tours of public birding sites, local organizers always gain access to choice private and government properties that are usually off-limits. This TOS meeting was based in McAllen, a thriving border city and an excellent base of operations for visiting and birding the Valley's numerous refuges and parks.

Traveling to McAllen from the Trans-Pecos requires a full day's drive across most of southern Texas. Our travel day started early and cold. In the predawn, as the Hedges and I drove through Musquiz Canyon between Alpine and Fort Davis, their car's exterior thermometer registered just twenty-two degrees. The Valley's warmth beckoned. Since we had so many miles to cover, David insisted we minimize stops. By midmorning we were within hailing distance of the Rio Grande, near Eagle Pass. Ready for a break, we spent a half hour at a birdy resaca and cemetery just a quick right turn off U.S. 277, near Normandy.

On an earlier trip to this resaca, John Karges, Francie Jeffery, and I had stumbled upon a local homeowner and Border Patrol captain. He had greeted us with a friendly wave but warned us to be gone by dusk and to be wary all along this stretch of the U.S.-Mexico border. The area was apparently rife with drug smuggling and illegal immigrant traffic.

My memories of that unsettling conversation returned as I revisited the Normandy resaca. But in the light of day we felt safe, especially since we were only one hundred yards from a major highway. Golden-fronted Woodpeckers, Osprey, and Belted Kingfishers flew and called from the trees that line this cutoff waterway. We had no contact with the seamier, desperate side of border existence and soon continued toward McAllen.

East of Laredo and traveling on U.S. 83, the "Texas Tropical Trail," we passed Falcon Dam. In most people's minds, the Valley begins here. Dedicated in October, 1953, this immense dam halts the Rio Grande's flow near its confluence with the meandering Pecos River and creates a sixty-mile-long lake. The riparian area below the dam can be excellent for birding, though this is another area where caution is advisable. An old hobo camp is a feature of the U.S. side, and transients can still be encountered anywhere along the river. It should not be birded alone.

Given my Big Year mission, I convinced David that another brief stop was in order. At San Ygnacio, I could search the cane along the Rio Grande for a rare Texas bird and Valley specialty: White-collared Seedeater. This small finch with a stubby, conical bill is common throughout Mexico and Central America. It was fairly common in the Valley as recently as the 1940s. Now, it can be found only in small numbers at scattered sites along the Rio Grande from Zapata to San Ygnacio to Falcon Dam. At sleepy San Ygnacio, healthy stands of river cane are accessible from the ends of several streets, including Washington and Grant streets, where searching for the seedeaters has become a local industry.

At Washington Street, a whiteboard carried the glad news that others had seen the seedeaters that morning. A smaller, crudely lettered sign advised us that a fee of three dollars per person was required to bird the area. This request was new, and its validity was the subject of much discussion at the McAllen TOS meeting. Our fees would theoretically be used to purchase food for the seedeaters and to maintain the area. Giving those who had erected this sign the benefit of the doubt, we paid, stuffing one-dollar bills through a slot in a metal canister.

Sunny, humid warmth and a modest breeze made our walk among the cane pleasant. We studied an accommodating perched Gray Hawk, an immature. Squawking Great Kiskadees patrolled the area, dashing from tree to tree. A calling Chihuahuan Raven passed overhead. Picking our way among the reeds and riverside shrubs and trees, we found a small foraging flock, but it contained only gnatcatchers, Orange-crowned Warblers, and "Myrtle" Yellow-rumped Warblers. An hour's intensive search yielded no seedeaters. We posted our strikeout on the whiteboard and left.

Farther east along U.S. 83, we struck out again at another well-known seedeater stop, the cane encircling the Zapata Library pond. Though we were disappointed by failure in our first attempts to see a Valley specialty, it was likely just a matter of the midday doldrums.

DAVID HAD LONG AGO LOST the battle to push on to our day's destination with no more stops. He was a sport and a birder; he didn't mind. A small green and white sign on U.S. 83 pointed zealots to the right, to Salineño, one of the most productive birding spots in the Falcon Dam area. We turned.

The road to Salineño terminates at the Rio Grande with broad views up and down the water. Near the river is a fenced-in lot under a canopy of trees. From November to March, retirees from other states—"Winter Texans"—live here, tending feeders that provide hours of Valley birdwatching pleasure for visitors. We parked, then opened the long entry gate and walked through onto the property of Pat and Gale deWind, the gracious hosts at Salineño. David and Linda, well-traveled and sociable, already knew the deWinds. Our arrival was a reunion for them. But, as always in the birding community, the deWinds' welcome extended to anyone with binoculars and a smile, such as myself.

From outdoor chairs alongside the deWinds' RV, we monitored the feeder activity with other TOS-bound birders. Brilliant, noisy, and gregarious Green Jays swooped in for a snack, creating a clamor. Bulky White-tipped Doves strolled the grounds. A Long-billed Thrasher briefly mixed with the more common residents, such as House Sparrows and Inca Doves.

We enjoyed this avian cornucopia while softly chatting with the group, recovering from the ill effects of our long car confinement. The conversation stoked our anticipation for the weekend. There was talk of Clay-colored Robins at Bentsen–Rio Grande Valley State Park, wintering warblers and a Northern Beardless-Tyrannulet at Anzalduas County Park, multiple Aplomado Falcons at Laguna Atascosa National Wildlife Refuge, and other juicy tidbits. We relished and contributed to the birding and travel "war stories" being traded. Several people wanted to hear the latest from the Davis Mountains and the Big Bend.

Knowing that the available time was limited, I pulled myself away from the feeders and strolled down the partially paved hill to the Rio Grande's muddy bank. The murky flow washed slowly past my feet, looking much as it does in the Big Bend. Everything else was different, of course. The flora and fauna were of the Valley, not the cane-lined river edges and Chihuahuan Desert of the Trans-Pecos.

Anglos and Hispanics fished from the bank and from a few small boats scattered across the river. A handful of birders intently scanned the river and skies, exchanging comments about what was in view and what they wished would come into view. Wintering waterfowl floated nearby on the river, some of which were new to my Big Year, such as Gadwall and Common Moorhen. At this well-known haunt of the rarest Texas birds, a place where every birder's eyes are alert for Mexican strays, I added one of the state's most abundant birds to my year list: Northern Cardinal!

My next scan of the river brought me a colorful Valley gift: a male Ringed Kingfisher with bold rufous belly, rusty breast, and white undertail. He attracted my attention with his harsh rattle and his size, twice that of a Belted Kingfisher. He flew across the river, oblivious to my interest, then perched along the bank a few feet above the waterline. I had expected this bird to be a challenge, yet it had required just a five-minute investment. The birding gods had smiled on my efforts, and I thanked them.

The time to depart Salineño came too soon. We said our good-byes to those assembled at the deWinds' place, returned to the car, and made a beeline for Weslaco. As we pulled alongside the curb at Madge Lindsay's house, it was seventy-five degrees on a magnificent early January evening.

Blessed be the South.

THOUGH SHE WAS BUSY WITH WORK and could not join us in the field, Madge kindly invited us into her Weslaco home for the weekend of the TOS meeting. She had known David and Linda for years, both as friends and, in Linda's case, as a fellow Texas Parks and Wildlife staff member. Madge is a tireless worker for conservation efforts in Texas, especially in the Valley. She has had a major hand, for example, in the planning and development of the soon-to-be-realized World Birding Center. When we visited, she was getting serious about a home in the Davis Mountains. She would soon be a neighbor.

Madge had alerted us to the habits of her local Red-crowned Parrot troop. These Valley birds are descendants of escaped caged birds and strays from northeast Mexico. Now well established at many locations, they were formally added in 1995 to the *Checklist of the Birds of Texas* published by TOS (3rd edition, Austin: Capital Printing, 1995).

The next morning, at exactly the time predicted by Madge (7:10 A.M.), the parrots left their nighttime roost, shrieking in a manner that would wake any birder who had mis-set the alarm clock. I ran out of Madge's front door, casting around in the sky for their unmistakable shapes. Against a cloudy sky that leaked a light warm rain, seventy parrot silhouettes wheeled across my line of sight. Their calls were unrelenting and carried for blocks. If I lived with them, this shrill morning chorus might be unwelcome. As a visitor, though, seeing and hearing these Red-crowned Parrots was an exciting start to our day.

After enjoying the parrots and breakfast, we drove literally around the corner to meet well-known Valley birder Richard Lehman and a group he was leading on a TOS field trip into the fifteen-acre Frontera Audubon Center. A Blue Mockingbird had wandered these acres, and occasionally into Madge Lindsay's yard, since early May, 1999. It had last been seen in October. This tropical bird would dart in and out of sight here throughout 2000, satisfying some but frustrating me and many others.

Outside the sanctuary, I met Richard. Everyone tried to guess what the weather would do next. As though in answer, the rain intensified. Larger drops forced a retreat to the car where David, Linda, and I voted to bird elsewhere, hoping to outrun the weather.

UNTIL SHE AND DAVE GOT TOGETHER in 1988, Linda Hedges was not much more than a backyard birdwatcher. Dave hooked her on birding the first time they visited Cheyenne Bottoms, a huge inland marsh in central Kansas. Birding suddenly became an important pastime in their shared lives. After she and Dave settled near Fort Davis, Linda returned to school, earned a master's degree in biology from Sul Ross State University, then went to work for Texas Parks and Wildlife.

The three of us drove to the Santa Ana National Wildlife Refuge, leaving the rain showers behind us to the east. Santa Ana's 2,088 acres of undisturbed riparian forest is the largest remaining block of such habitat between Falcon Dam and the Gulf of Mexico. We were eager to see what birds were present.

A dozen Plain Chachalacas called and foraged at the entrance, within a few steps of the parking lot. As with the Ringed Kingfisher, I had anticipated that seeing this species would be at least a minor challenge. Not so!

After a short walk down the trail to Willow Lake, we spied a roosting Common Pauraque just inches off the trail. While we observed this resting bird from a respectful distance, a German couple caught up to us. They were burdened by a huge load of photographic equipment: a weighty tripod, two expensive camera bodies, and several long focal length lenses wrapped in camouflage. The gentleman seemed happy; the lady did not. Having studied German for five years, I knew enough of the language to tell that she was repeatedly asking when this humid jaunt would end. His reassurances were not having the desired effect. She sat down on a bench in a huff.

We exchanged information with the man about the birds we had seen, and we showed him the pauraque. This may not have been one of our better ideas. He took tens of photographs of this bird, some from very close range. We worried that he was disturbing the bird's rest, but it never flushed.

A short distance west of Santa Ana NWR, Anzalduas County Park is visually unimpressive. The lower limbs of every tree are neatly trimmed, the grass is mowed and the understory has been swept clear for human convenience. Nonetheless, several rare birds, such as Rose-throated Becard, have been recorded at this small park on the Rio Grande. It can be a good location for Valley specialties in any season.

Our noon arrival at Anzalduas meant that we shared the park with picnicking families. Nonetheless, the birds were unfazed. A flock of notable winter residents had been reported, and it was these that we sought and found near the park's center. A splendid Black-throated Gray Warbler joined a Black and White Warbler, Orange-crowned and Yellow-rumped Warblers along with the real prize, a Northern

Beardless-Tyrannulet, which proclaimed its location by uttering its call note multiple times.

As we finished our last round of the park, we consulted with a recently arrived TOS tour, passing on our sightings of the warblers and the tyrannulet, which we knew would be high on everyone's wish list.

BENTSEN–RIO GRANDE VALLEY STATE PARK, generally acknowledged to have the best winter birding in the Valley, was our next stop. The day had grown warm and the birds were becoming sluggish when we reached this park, where the premium we sought was Clay-colored Robin. This Mexican thrush is a rare winter visitor to the Valley, though breeding has been documented on several occasions at scattered locations along the Rio Grande.

Our first hour-long attempt to find the robin was a bust. Earlier in the day, the bird had been seen feeding in an anacua tree in the tent campground just south of the newest restroom. We drove straight to this spot. But the eyes of a dozen birders could not relocate the robin. It was somewhere else; we hoped it was still in the park. David and I returned Linda to the TOS headquarters hotel for her 5:00 P.M. Board of Directors meeting, then zoomed back to Bentsen to renew our pursuit of the Clay-colored Robin.

The lack of success through the afternoon had thinned out the group holding watch in and around the anacua tree. Only a handful of hard-core hopefuls remained. After thirty minutes of searching an ever-increasing area, we saw a bird of the appropriate size and color dart past us and into the anacua tree. We all craned our necks for a look: a thrush that was brownish olive above, with a lightly streaked throat. The Clay-colored Robin foraged for three or four minutes, feeding on the anacua's yellow berries. Then a territorial Northern Mockingbird chased our prize around and out of the tree. We followed the robin's flight, hoping to see where it would land, but it disappeared over the tops of nearby trees.

A vanload of hopeful birders arrived minutes after the Clay-colored Robin's departure. As David and I prepared to head off in search of dinner, it was our sorrowful duty to give those just arriving the news that every birder dreads: "You should have been here five minutes ago!"

ON THE THIRD DAY OF THE TOS MEETING, we decided that a trip to the coast would yield the greatest bounty. For the morning, we joined an official TOS field trip to Laguna Atascosa National Wildlife Refuge, a forty-five-thousand-acre miracle of subtropical, coastal, and desert habitats located north-northeast of Brownsville, nestled against the Texas coast. This property was set aside in 1946 as a wintering site for ducks and geese. But a far wider range of species can be seen there, and the refuge is managed for much more than waterfowl alone.

On this cloudy morning with a light wind and pleasant sixty-degree temperatures, we arrived early and birded around the refuge headquarters while waiting for our tour to begin. We were entertained by the birds coming in to seed and water at a nearby photographer's blind: Olive Sparrows, Green Jays, House Wrens, Plain Chachalacas, Long-billed Thrashers, and Northern Cardinals. Though jays are often bold, Olive Sparrows are notorious skulkers, yet here they were in good light at less than twenty paces. The ready availability of breakfast apparently made them bold.

To the delight of the assembled group, an Ovenbird strutted in plain view. I had not imagined seeing this bird before spring migration, and in past years it has been something of a nemesis to me, making me work hard for a few brief looks.

At the appointed tour start time, we loaded a minimal number of vehicles. Our guide led us west toward Osprey Overlook, then through a locked gate and onto a good dirt road. The first raptor of the day was a White-tailed Hawk carrying a limp duck it had plucked from some other part of the refuge.

Our next sighting trumped the White-tailed Hawk. Not far along this normally off-limits dirt road, our caravan halted. Our leader gestured urgently to the southwest, where a falcon was perched on an old fence post. Its brilliant white breast stood out even to the naked eye: an Aplomado Falcon.

Though it was once a fairly common resident of grasslands and deserts from southern Texas to southern Arizona, the Aplomado Falcon had been extirpated from all of its range in the United States by the early twentieth century. Owing to this sad plight, a reintroduction program for these falcons has been under way for some time. Between

1986 and 1989, twenty falcons were released at Laguna Atascosa NWR and at the adjacent Buena Vista Ranch. As of the end of 1999, 466 falcons had been released in South Texas.

This project, like several others, has used a release technique called "hacking." Captive-raised young are placed into an artificial nest, known as a hack box. Refuge personnel monitor the young, and captive-bred parents care for the young for several weeks until they learn to fly and hunt, at which point the hope is that they are savvy enough to be wild birds, capable of fending for themselves. The long-term goal is for the Aplomado Falcon once again to reproduce in the wild in numbers that will maintain the species in Texas.

These South Texas Aplomado Falcons cannot be counted on a birder's year tally or life list until they are reestablished in the wild. A formal decision by the state bird record committee (see following chapter) is required to sanction this milestone. So the lure of seeing these falcons was not an additional Big Year tick but the thrill of seeing a success story, a return from near extinction in the United States.

Individual wild Aplomado Falcons have occasionally been documented in West Texas, most recently in October, 1997, and summer, 2002. Such birds originate from the small remnant population of northern Chihuahua, Mexico. They are not the hacked birds of the lower Texas coast. In 2002, the Peregrine Fund initiated an effort to reintroduce the Aplomado Falcon in West Texas by releasing thirty-six birds on private ranches in two counties.

ONLY RECENTLY HAD THE GREEN PARAKEET, a Mexican species, become countable in Texas, since all of the observable individuals were considered to be recent kin of escaped cage birds. But they were now officially on the state's checklist and fair game for a Big Year. There were several Green Parakeet roosts in the Valley. One of the most reliable had been at the corner of 10th Street and Violet Road, a busy intersection in McAllen. Since this was directly north of the TOS host hotel, we put off dinner to chase the parakeets.

At 5:00 P.M. we found ourselves enmeshed in horrendous traffic, an unfamiliar situation for residents of the Trans-Pecos. We passed traffic light after traffic light on 10th Street, each somehow managing to turn red as we approached. These minor delays actually helped our cause. As the Violet Avenue sign came into view, numerous parakeets were just coming to roost. We estimated that there were three hundred of the foot-long green missiles in the southeast corner lot, with more still arriving. What made this location special to the parakeets was not clear. But they loved the place, lining up like swallows on the utility wires. Some of the parakeets were atop a commercial building; and yet others clung to the sides of the building. They were all squawking. It was anything but a subtle experience.

By Sunday morning, our clock had run out. We reluctantly headed west. Outside McAllen a thick fog slowed our progress and dimmed our hopes of having a last productive hour at Salineño. But the fog relented just east of Salineño. We spent a few more minutes at the deWinds' feeders, admiring two of the Valley's most dazzling species: Altamira Oriole and Audubon's Oriole. These sizable birds feasted on orange slices, a perennial oriole favorite. We had already seen Altamira Orioles at Bentsen, but Audubon's was new for our trip and my year.

Though our watches urged us to leave, since we wanted to be home before midnight, David and I could not resist a final check at the Rio Grande. We scanned up and down the river, hoping for a Hook-billed Kite or a Muscovy Duck. Though neither of these showed, the Valley did have a going-away present for us, another Mexican species that reaches the northern limits of its range along the Rio Grande. David saw it in his scope first: a plump, dark bird perched in the top of the tallest trees on the broad island that splits the Rio Grande just upstream of Salineño. As soon as David called it to my attention, this Red-billed Pigeon took wing, flying downstream toward us. We had no trouble picking it up in binoculars, getting definitive views of its plumage and bill. It passed just a few tens of feet above our heads.

When golf was my principal weekend leisure pursuit, I always tried to end each round or practice session on a positive note: an especially fine drive, a beautifully arched iron shot, a solidly stroked putt. David and I agreed that similar notions seemed apropos for a Big Year. Red-billed Pigeon can be difficult to find, and we had just been treated to an orchestra-seat view. This seemed a good note on which to call an official end to our Valley trip.

We had birded many fine sites, spent time in the field with interesting people, and seen many Valley specialties. Given our limited time, we had missed—"dipped on," in birding parlance—only a few species, such as White-collared Seedeater, Brown Jay, Hook-billed Kite, and Muscovy Duck. I would need to address these misses later in my Big Year.

But we had done very well. Upon our return to the observatory on January 9, my Big Year stood at 158 species.

## chapter 4

Pursuing Varied Thrush

The Texas Bird Records Committee (TBRC), a nine-person standing committee of the Texas Ornithological Society, tracks the occurrence of rare birds reported from within the state and the adjacent portions of the Gulf of Mexico. The committee actively solicits reports, photographs, and audio records of the rarest birds, particularly those on its "Review Species List" and any species that are not on the official Texas State List (621 species as of July, 2002). Committees of this sort exist in most states, staffed by skilled and committed volunteers.

The Texas Review Species List includes, as its best known and most referenced component, "Review List A: Rarities." More than 140 species are currently on Review List A. Each has occurred less than four times per year in Texas over a ten-year time span. Review List B includes species for which distribution and status in Texas are under special study by a TBRC subcommittee. This list currently contains two species for which midwinter (December and January) records are solicited: Swainson's Hawk and Semipalmated Sandpiper.

The TBRC also seeks documentation for subspecies that have been recorded only rarely in Texas and that may eventually be elevated to species status: "Eurasian" Green-winged Teal, "Mangrove" Yellow

Warbler, "White-winged" Dark-eyed Junco, and "Fuerte's" Orchard Oriole. This group of species constitutes Review List C.

A "presumptive" species has had at least one sight record accepted by the TBRC, but the species has not yet met the requirements for full acceptance on the Texas State List. Full acceptance requires a specimen, photograph, video, or audio recording for at least one record. White-crowned Pigeon, Black Swift, Social Flycatcher, Crescent-chested Warbler and murre species, all extraordinary records for Texas, are currently on the state's Presumptive Species List.

Under the leadership of Greg Lasley and Mark Lockwood, the TBRC has gathered and scientifically evaluated many new bird records for the state, including species as varied as Stygian Owl, Orange-billed Nightingale Thrush, Stejneger's Petrel, and Buff-breasted Flycatcher.

PURSUING REVIEW SPECIES is a fundamental part of any serious Big Year effort. Given their rarity, one cannot predict which Review Species will be seen in Texas in any given year, but there will always be some. With a willingness to travel, especially on short notice, it is possible to record more than twenty Review Species in a year.

On Christmas Day in 1999, Anthony Floyd and Melissa Abbott discovered two Varied Thrushes in Lubbock's Clapp Park, near the center of this city of two hundred thousand people. Varied Thrush is seldom seen in Texas, so it appears on the TBRC's Review Species List. A bird of the northwest United States and Canada, the Varied Thrush resides in dense wet coniferous forests. Every winter, some move south into California. A handful undertake long-distance winter treks, straying as far east as the Atlantic Coast. And in some winters, a few Varied Thrushes make their way into Texas.

From their discovery at Christmas through mid-January, Lubbock birders and visitors regularly reported the Clapp Park Varied Thrushes. Most who pursued these birds had little difficulty finding them. It finally dawned on me that if I was committed to a Big Year, chasing these birds should be a priority.

Prior to this chase, no rarity had pulled me more than 150 miles, the distance from my home to the center of the Big Bend National Park, a drive of two and a half hours. Though Lubbock is as much a part of West Texas as the Davis Mountains, three hundred miles and five hours of high-speed driving lay between my front door and Clapp Park. Fortunately, the observatory had recently hired Rex Barrick as its assistant physical plant manager. Rex's interest in exploring and the outdoors is at least as great as mine. We had done some adventuring over the previous months. But I had no idea if he would be interested in an arduous, long-distance, one-day rare bird chase.

When I approached him, Rex thought my proposed mission worthwhile. He even solicited use of his spouse's Ford Explorer. To my delight, Kathy permitted us to travel in the comfort of her SUV. Compared to my ragtop 1995 Jeep Wrangler, this would be upper-crust motoring. Rex and I departed from Mount Locke on Sunday, January 23, at 4:30 A.M. under a sky filled with the stellar glory of a cold, clear West Texas night. The trip passed partly in darkness, partly in the wan rays of an early morning winter sun. I worked on my laptop computer during the drive to Lubbock and kept up a conversation with Rex, to make sure he did not nod off.

We arrived at Clapp Park at 9:40 A.M., pleased by the partly cloudy sky, slight north wind, and temperature rising into the fifties. From a baseball field parking lot on the park's north side, we walked toward the trees where we had been told the thrushes were roosting and foraging. A Sharp-shinned Hawk struck a flock of grackles, scattering them and creating a ruckus, but came up empty. We hoped that the thrushes had not been recently eaten by this or any other sharpie!

Rex first sighted the Varied Thrushes in the highest bare branches of a cottonwood on a levee across the pond. We trained my scope on them and confirmed that they were indeed our targets for the day. The ubiquitous Great-tailed Grackles flew into the cottonwood as we celebrated. The grackles flapped their wings as they squawked at and harassed our thrushes, chasing them from branch to branch. The thrushes moved lower in the cottonwood, trying to avoid the grackles, eventually flying away to escape. But they had not gone far, and after some searching we found them again on the levee.

We stalked them so that I could obtain photographs for the TBRC. Throughout the morning, the thrushes flew back and forth across the pond, into and out of the junipers, to and from the levee. While they were in the junipers, they fed on berries. On the levee, the birds twice took turns venturing to the water's edge to drink. Whenever I tried to approach more closely, they froze. They were wary. I shot two rolls of film, but none of my photos was from as close a distance as I had hoped to achieve.

Our lengthy observations allowed us to discern fine details. As noted by Petra Hockey and others on TEXBIRDS, the plumage of these Varied Thrushes differed somewhat from their depiction in the National Geographic Society field guide. The eyestripe of one Clapp Park thrush was noticeably different in length and shape from the field guide illustration, where it is shown as straight and uniform in width. On one of the live birds that Rex and I studied, the eyestripe was narrow above the eye, then curved back and down behind the eye, flaring down the bird's nape to the edge of its mantle, in a manner reminiscent of a Louisiana Waterthrush. This same Varied Thrush's black face mask and breast band nearly connected, framing the orange throat. In the National Geographic guide, the face mask and breast band are well separated.

Birds are individuals, products of their place and time. Such minor plumage variation is normal. Studying and recording these differences is an excellent way to train one's eye and mind to produce good field observations.

Pleased with our success, Rex and I left Clapp Park at 11:45 A.M. With much of the day still ahead, we consulted our maps and guides over lunch at a Lubbock sandwich shop and decided to drive sixty-five miles northwest to the Muleshoe National Wildlife Refuge. The shortgrass prairies at this refuge illustrate the look of the southern high plains before agricultural development. The management program consists of grazing and controlled burning, with some use of mechanical methods of vegetation and shrub control. The goal is maintenance of a winter resting area for Sandhill Cranes and waterfowl and of diverse habitat for other wildlife.

En route to Muleshoe NWR, between the towns of Whiteface and

Morton, we encountered three thousand or more Sandhill Cranes settling into fields of winter stubble. Neither of us had ever seen as many cranes at one location, and we stopped to enjoy the sight and sound of them. Muleshoe NWR itself disappointed us with dry playas and no cranes. Other than calling Western Meadowlarks, which were new to my Big Year, there was little to see or hear. To add to our difficulties, the wind blew at fifteen to twenty miles per hour and grew gusty.

Rex and I started home on Texas Highway 214, a straight line south across the sparsely populated plains of Bailey, Cochran, Yoakum, and Gaines counties. The mostly sunny, warm weather was a boon, but it made me drift off into sleep. My nodding head bounced off the passenger side window more than once on this stretch. It had been a long day after a short night.

In Cochran County, an imposing raptor caught Rex's attention and helped wake me up. From atop a power pole, the hawk surveyed the area. We pulled over. My naked-eye impression, as we passed the bird, was of a Golden Eagle. After we stopped and I contemplated the bird through binoculars, I realized my mistake: this was a dark "morph" Red-tailed Hawk.

Raptors show astonishing, often confusing variety in their plumages. Many hawk species have dark and light morphs or plumage varieties, including Red-tailed, Swainson's, Short-tailed, and Broad-winged hawks. The relative numbers of dark and light morph birds varies from species to species and, within species, by location. In general, light morph hawks are more common.

This dark morph Red-tailed Hawk allowed me to study it and take several good photographs, perched and in flight. It seemed as curious about me as I was about it. While the dark in a Harlan's Red-tailed Hawk is black, this bird's dark was the rust-red coloration on its body and wings. Since they are visually distinguishable, hawk morphs are another means to expand the scope and fun of a Big Year list. However, regardless of how many morphs are observed, a species can be counted only once.

An hour farther down the highway, ten miles south of Seminole in Gaines County, we stopped again, this time to observe the antics of a

Prairie Falcon pair. They chased each other across the sky at high speed and grappled, talons locked for a few seconds as they tumbled, recovering their composure uncommonly close to terra firma.

As the falcons headed off to the north, our warm afternoon segued into a cooler evening with a mostly cloudy sky that squeezed the usual colors from the sunset, leaving metallic grays. A high-cholesterol meal at a fast-food restaurant and a convenience store caffeine boost fortified us, and we completed our trip home in one long drive.

AT DEPARTURE, when one cannot be certain that several hundred miles of travel will yield a coveted rare species sighting, hesitation is a common and understandable emotion. Will the bird already have departed by the time I get there? Will the weather cooperate? Do I have enough information to find the bird myself if I arrive and no one else is looking? How can I get the latest information? These and other questions plague you as you drive or fly, as you pursue the chase.

In retrospect, with my Big Year complete, it seems that the decisions regarding which rarities were worth long-distance chases and which were not should have been easier. This reflects what I have learned, of course, as opposed to what I knew at the time. The only sure thing is that you will not see a rarity if you fail to chase it.

Successful chase efforts are readily justified. After returning from Lubbock, Rex and I had good stories for our respective dinner tables. A failed chase requires longer explanations, more detail, all of which spawns quizzical looks and questions from nonbirding family members. You didn't see the bird? Why not? What went wrong? But success or failure in notching another species cannot be the sole gauge of a day's value. Whether I was seeking common or rare birds or simply the solace of a hike in the company of friends, every venture I made into the field during my Big Year yielded unanticipated insights and treasured moments.

This trip to Lubbock was no different. We had "bagged" the target by 10:00 A.M. That was a relief. But more important, we had enjoyed a day away from the cares of business and the minutiae of daily life. We had been blessed with a warm, sunny winter day on the southern high plains; we had savored the pleasure of seeing a huge Sandhill Crane flock waiting for winter to pass; we had stopped for a few minutes' visit with a dark morph Red-tailed Hawk as it sought a late afternoon meal; we had been entertained by the winter play of a pair of Prairie Falcons. As I walked in the front door of my home that January evening, I recall hoping that the majority of my future rarity-chasing trips would be this engaging. They were.

chapter 5

Home and Away Games

The last weekend of January was for birding in the Davis Mountains. My Saturday morning began at the Eppanauer Ranch pastures north of the McDonald Observatory, where a flock of twelve Mountain Bluebirds, including three powder-blue males, posed on the fence posts. Ten miles farther north on Texas 118, I turned left into the Madera Canyon (Lawrence E. Wood) picnic area. Most birders visiting the Davis Mountains stop here. It is one of the few publicly accessible locations where higher elevation species can be seen.

On this morning, I found two adult male Williamson's Sapsuckers at the picnic area, both clinging to ponderosa pine bark below their sap holes. Some winters, this species is fairly common from November through March. In other years, they have been rare and difficult to find. Not long after my discovery of these sapsuckers, two Michigan birders drove into the picnic area. With my help, they soon had Williamson's Sapsucker on their life lists and were happy.

On Tuesday, February 1, after four hours of effort over two days, I finally managed to see the eight Eastern Bluebirds that irregularly came to water at the home of my friends the Hobbys. Tom and Carol live in Limpia Crossing, five miles south of the observatory. The pleasure of spending time over coffee and muffins with them was reason enough to visit. And their birds completed my Davis Mountains winter blue-bird trifecta: Mountain, Eastern, and Western bluebirds.

The Davis Mountains are one of the few locations where all three bluebirds can be seen in the same season. As a game within the game of my Big Year, I tried to find these bluebirds from locations separated by a minimum number of miles. I had seen several Western Blue-birds near the observatory's visitor center on January 16. Thus, the maximum distance between my winter bluebird sightings was the mileage from the Mountain Bluebirds on the Eppanauer Ranch fence posts to the upturned trashcan lid that served as a water basin and attracted the Eastern Bluebirds to the Hobbys' home: just six miles.

BUSINESS TOOK ME TO AUSTIN on Wednesday, February 2. Prior to leaving West Texas, I had contacted Cliff Shackelford for advice about several species I might find around Austin. Cliff gave me the information I needed and offered to accompany me into the field, an overture I welcomed. Late on Thursday afternoon, my first opportunity, I drove to Cliff's Texas Parks and Wildlife Department office in south Austin. We left seeking our first target: Monk Parakeet.

Since their initial escape from captivity years ago, Monk Parakeets have thrived in the wild. These birds are hardy and are now a fixture in many cities across the South. They can survive cold weather, and colonies exist as far north as New England, Chicago, and Oregon.

Cliff and I headed east to Krieg Field, a baseball complex on the south side of the Colorado River and the Longhorn Dam. As at any major baseball complex, tall metal poles thrust into the sky, topped by banks of high-intensity lights. Near each pole's summit was a maintenance platform, and almost every one was home to a cylindrical Monk Parakeet nest several feet across, composed of interwoven sticks, all a particular size and thickness. As we stepped from our cars, we heard and saw two Monk Parakeets weaving sticks into a nest. Another fifteen parakeets waddled on the ground nearby, screeching.

Many equate "parakeet" with the popular small cage bird called the Budgerigar, a native of Australia. These Monk Parakeets were not small, however. Typically they are a foot in length, with whitish breast and throat, yellow-green belly, and green back. When they flew, bright blue highlights in their wings attracted one's eyes. If the Monk Parakeets decided to have a conversation, I imagine an umpire would have a hard time hearing and being heard while a Krieg Field baseball game was in progress.

Mary Moore Seawright Metropolitan Park was within walking distance of Cliff's home. After visiting the baseball-loving Monk Parakeets, we toured this second park, sharing the trails with Austin residents walking their dogs, jogging, or riding their bikes, unwinding after a day's work.

The target species here, Harris's Sparrow, came easily. Though birders sometimes use taped owl calls to excite winter birds and bring them into view, Cliff accomplished the same thing with his own voice, imitating an Eastern Screech Owl with remarkable fidelity. In the middle of the park, amidst some shrubs and trees, two Harris's Sparrows responded. With black crown, face, and bib, they were unmistakable. To our surprise, three Fox Sparrows also hopped into view, chipping—the first individuals of this species that Cliff had seen in the park.

JULIE, CLIFF'S SPOUSE, arrived home not long after Cliff and I. We had an excellent pizza dinner. Since I wanted to hear and see an Eastern Screech-Owl, we did not tarry after eating and were outside again by 8:00 P.M.

Everyone who had shared the sunlit Mary Moore Seawright Park with us was gone. Outside the white circles our flashlights inscribed on the pathways, little was visible other than the silhouettes of the trees against the light-polluted sky. Only traffic and the occasional scuffle of a feral cat or other nocturnal creature disrupted the peace. Despite a clear sky that allowed the day's heat to ascend, the nighttime temperature remained pleasant. We wore light jackets.

For twenty minutes, Cliff worked to call up an owl just inside the park boundary, a place where he had recently heard an Eastern Screech-Owl. But this owl was either not home or not interested. At our next

Eastern Screech-Owl. Drawing by Kelly B. Bryan.

stop, a short walk down the path, an Eastern Screech-Owl answered, its voice soft, mournful, seemingly distant. Cliff guessed that the owl was actually nearby, that it was using what ornithologists have dubbed a "whisper call." These calls are used, for example, when a bird wants to inform its mate quietly that it is present and vigilant.

Cliff panned a spotlight around the woods and found the owl nearby, as he had predicted. Just eight inches tall, our quarry sat twelve feet above the ground, twenty yards from us. Keeping the spotlight's bright center off the bird so that it would not flush, we examined it in binoculars for as long as we wished.

As a small return for their hospitality, I toured Julie and Cliff around the winter constellations and the available planets: Taurus, with the Seven Sisters, the Pleiades; Orion the Hunter with the brilliant red star, Betelgeux, at his shoulder; the twins of Gemini; Canis Major, sporting the night sky's brightest star, Sirius; the planets Mars and Jupiter shining orange and yellow-white, respectively, from within the clutches of Pisces the Fishes; and ringed Saturn, just a bit fainter, cavorting with Aries the Ram.

To close our day, we celebrated at an ice cream shop where we enjoyed a delectable caramel and cashew custard in a waffle cone. Losing weight was not a component of my Big Year.

OVER THE PREVIOUS WEEK, Austin birders William Reiner and Jeffrey Hanson had posted TEXBIRDS messages about Eurasian Collared-Doves in Austin. A century ago, these doves were found only on the Indian subcontinent and in Turkey. Early in the twentieth century, the species began expanding its range. Introduced into the Bahamas in the 1970s, these doves migrated to Florida sometime in the 1980s, for unknown reasons. From Florida they rapidly spread across the South, soon reaching Texas.

In south Austin, my Eurasian Collared-Dove trek began with a right turn from the Interstate Highway 35 frontage road into a jammed Wal-Mart parking lot. Harried Austin consumers rushed in and out of the store. In the parking lot, I dodged cars and drivers rushing for 'coveted parking places. In a long-sleeved white dress shirt, dress pants, and tie, I scanned the few remaining big oaks with binoculars. Four Eurasian Collared-Doves huddled in a majestic oak that had somehow avoided the bulldozer's blade. To be certain they were not the similar Ringed Turtle-Doves, a common cage escapee, I watched the birds fly. Ringed Turtle-Doves are characteristically pale, with diagnostic white undertail coverts; Eurasian Collared-Doves have gray undertail coverts. And while the dark primaries of Eurasian Collared-Doves contrast strongly with their other wing feathers, the Ringed Turtle-Dove's primaries contrast only slightly with the rest of the wing.

Throughout the year 2000, Eurasian Collared-Doves continued their march across Texas. By December, Balmorhea, Marfa, Fabens, and other Trans-Pecos towns counted them as regular inhabitants.

ON JANUARY 31, Paul and Val Kitchens found a Mexican stray in Sarita, a tiny town in rural Kenedy County south of Kingsville along the lower Texas coast, where cattle outnumber humans. The Kitchenses had been on their way from the Rio Grande Valley to an American Birding Association conference in Corpus Christi. They had stopped at Sarita for a few minutes, and the impulse had netted them a gem, a Rufous-backed Robin.

This robin inhabits the forests of western Mexico from Sonora south to Oaxaca, eleven hundred kilometers or more from Texas. It has a reputation as a wanderer and had previously been recorded in Arizona, California, and Texas. Its appearance is well described by its name. Through at least midweek, the Sarita robin had been seen every day since its discovery. From the moment that my Austin trip was set, I had plotted a path that would permit a try for this rare bird on Sunday, February 6.

Cold water splashed on my face at 3:40 A.M. in my aunt and uncle's Corpus Christi home suppressed my urge to go back to bed that Sunday morning. This excessively early start was necessary to assure a predawn arrival in Sarita. Sunrise was at 7:10 A.M. The Rufous-backed Robin had been fairly regular for an hour or two after sunrise but had been difficult to find later in the day and often was not found at all.

I drove south on Texas 77 as fast as the law allowed and arrived in Sarita at 6:30 A.M. I parked across the street from Our Lady of Guadalupe Catholic Church. One other car hugged the same curb, with a probable robin-seeking birder slumped against the driver's side window, asleep.

As the mostly cloudy sky lightened, a Common Snipe flew into the short grass of a small lot adjacent to my car. This was encouraging. Previous days' reports had mentioned the robin foraging with a snipe on this lawn of just a fraction of an acre. The arrival of a Killdeer ten minutes later momentarily raised my pulse, too, since the sun had yet to crest the horizon. The assembled birders soon numbered fifteen. As anxious persons congregated in the street, the tension was palpable. Would the robin show?

Relief swept the group when the Rufous-backed Robin arrived from the south at 7:02 A.M., dropping into the very lot we were watching. The robin perched on a branch at eye level, then hopped to the ground and fed with the Common Snipe and the Killdeer, eating small fruits, catching insects, probing the ground. Hushed snippets of conversation replaced the earlier, more boisterous tone of the crowd. All eyes were screwed tight to binoculars and scopes. Camera shutters clacked. There was more than enough time for all present to get their visual fill.

Walking away from a Rufous-backed Robin proved difficult. But an equally amazing visitor, a Cape May Warbler, had been reported for several days from across the street on the grounds of the Catholic church. A wintering Cape May Warbler in Texas is an extraordinary event. This species' normal winter haunts are the West Indies. A few off-course individuals are seen every year on the Texas coast in migration, but one could easily bird the coast through spring and not see a Cape May Warbler.

Walking across the street, I joined the half dozen birders congregating on the sidewalk in front of the church, each staring through binoculars into a tall, wispy mesquite. The focus of their attention was a small bird hopping from branch to branch. Centering this bird in my binoculars, I spent several minutes observing a streak-breasted, sharp-billed, faded yellow-green wood warbler, a definite Cape May Warbler in winter plumage.

Delighted by this easy success, I walked back to my original post for more study of the Rufous-backed Robin, which was still delighting the crowd. After a few minutes, though, without warning and as suddenly as it had arrived, the robin brought the curtain down on its show, flying off to the southwest at 8:20 A.M. It was not seen again that day, though hopeful birders continued to arrive from points near and far. The robin did return, however, every morning through Sunday, February 13.

MY PLAN FOR MONDAY, February 7, was to join Russell Graham for a boat trip to Aransas National Wildlife Refuge, primarily to see the endangered Whooping Cranes, one of the two crane species regularly found in North America. Russell is a skilled lifelong birder who lives in Carrollton in the Dallas–Fort Worth area but often roams the state. I was looking forward to having company in the field.

Several boats ply the waters of Aransas Bay, showcasing the refuge and the cranes. Between November and March, captains guarantee that their guests will see Whooping Cranes. In April, cranes depart Texas and, after a four-thousand-kilometer flight north, arrive at their breeding area in Canada's Wood Buffalo National Park in the Northwest Territories. By September's end, Whooping Cranes set out southward again for Texas and Aransas NWR.

Named for their loud, resonating call, Whooping Cranes can have a seven-foot wingspan and, at four to five feet in height, are the tallest North American birds. The 180 Whooping Cranes that winter at Aransas represent a substantial portion of the remaining wild population.

In the late nineteenth century, a thousand or more Whooping Cranes were living in the aspen parkland and prairie regions of western Canada and the United States. Their range extended from the far North to central Mexico, and from Utah east to New Jersey, into South Carolina, Georgia, and Florida. Whooping Cranes bred across the north-central United States and the Canadian provinces of Manitoba, Saskatchewan, and Alberta. A nonmigratory breeding population resided in southwestern Louisiana.

But by the 1940s, the world population had plummeted to a mere fourteen birds. The Whooping Crane teetered on the verge of extinction. A serious conservation effort began in 1938, when many feared it was too late to save the species. But the U.S. and Canadian resources put into this effort have resulted in an encouraging recovery.

My alarm clock roused me from a fitful sleep that Monday morning at 4:45 A.M. Russell and I had reservations for the suitably named *Whooping Crane,* a fair-sized craft operated out of Fulton by Captain Ted. I needed to be on the road by 5:30 A.M. for an on-time arrival at the dock. After a few minutes of wakefulness, however, I became nauseous. The source of my queasiness was unclear, though it was probably exhaustion. I had been sleeping too little, working and birding too much. I dressed and forced down a bowl of cereal, hoping my misery would fade. It did not. Ten minutes of additional rest made no difference, either.

I persevered, packing my rental car and sliding into the front seat. I still felt horrible but loathed the idea of wasting a day on the coast. As I prepared to turn the key in the ignition, my stomach somersaulted. I bolted from the car, bent at the waist, convinced I would vomit in my aunt and uncle's driveway. After several dry heaves, I shut off the car, went back into the house, and called Captain Ted's to cancel my reservation. The woman I spoke with promised to get a message to Russell Graham about my predicament.

I lay down without resetting my alarm clock.

Still weak but no longer nauseous, I awoke at 9:15 A.M. Disappointed that I had missed the Whooping Cranes, I constructed Plan B, settling on a trip to Corpus Christi's Elliot landfill. The scenery would be a far cry from the beauty of the inland waterway, and I worried that the smell might cause a recurrence of my stomach problems. But the Corpus Christi landfill probably held at least one rare bird. Lesser Black-backed Gull had recently been reported there. If I could find it, this species would be a fair substitute for having missed the Whooping Cranes.

The guard at the landfill gate was an effusive fellow who wanted to talk. Since it was winter, he had signed in several other birders over the past week and was curious to know what I hoped to find. It is a privilege (an odd one, admittedly) to bird at landfills such as Elliot, so I made time to talk birds with the gatekeeper.

Lacking guidance as to where the gulls might be concentrated, I followed a line of dump trucks as they rumbled along well-used tracks. Monstrous mounds of a modern city's refuse rose before me, several stories high. The trucks lumbered up the mounds to the summit, where they added their cargo to the landfill. Thousands of gulls perched atop Elliot's Everest, my nickname for the summit. Several hundred more gulls circled just above the refuse heap, calling. Innumerable urban generalists—European Starlings, Great-tailed Grackles, and similar species—rummaged through the trash with the gulls.

A side track passed near these birds. I took it and parked out of the way of the trucks. On this warm morning, the smell of trash stung my nostrils but did not threaten my stomach. The smell lingered in my nose and clothes for hours after I departed, though.

Gulls are the bane of many birders. Reliably identifying them can be difficult. Understanding their range of plumages can take even a keen observer years. Some gulls mature in two years. Other gull species require three or four years to mature. Until maturity, each year's plumage is different, and the variation among individuals of similar age can be daunting.

Within the hobby of birding, there is a subculture of birders who revel in studying and understanding gull plumages, striving for ever deeper knowledge of these birds and for reliable subspecies discrimination. Adding to the complexity of this task, gulls are prone to hybridization, interbreeding between species. Most birders can be sent into despair just by hearing the "H-word" together with the names of any two gull species.

But where there is variety, there is challenge and opportunity. After a couple of hours of studying the hordes of common gulls, I separated out two individuals of the relatively rare species I had hoped to find, one second-year Lesser Black-backed Gull and one third-year bird, salvaging something from an otherwise difficult day.

## chapter 6

Northeast Texas Rarities

uring the first few weeks of my Big Year, I had sampled the Trans-Pecos, the central Texas coast, and the Rio Grande Valley and had spent a single day in Lubbock. Numerous species awaited me elsewhere around the state.

Winter weather and work pressures prevented my getting another trip organized until the third weekend in February. I selected Northeast Texas as my destination because of the presence of two rare gulls: Little and Black-headed gulls, both Texas Review Species. My destination decision was also swayed by the generosity of two expert local birders, Matt White and Russell Graham, each of whom spends a good fraction of his free time outdoors. My morning of illness having forced me to abandon plans to meet Russell for the Whooping Cranes earlier in the month, I now looked forward to getting out into the field with him on his home turf. Though I had been exchanging e-mail with Matt, I had not seen him since the TOS meeting of November, 1997.

A teacher and a historian, Matt has deep family roots near Greenville, a small town north and east of Dallas–Fort Worth. His knowledge of the region's birds is superb, and in his recently published book, *Birds of Northeast Texas* (College Station: Texas A&M University Press, 2002), he imparts much of what he has learned. Matt is by nature generous.

His assistance would be crucial at several key times during my Big Year effort.

On Friday afternoon, February 18, I left the observatory for Northeast Texas. My itinerary began, as it often did, with the two-hour and forty-five-minute drive from my front door to the Midland Airport. After an hour's flight, I drove away from Dallas-Love Field with every local flag and pennant snapping at the behest of a stiff breeze.

Black-headed Gull is the familiar small gull in many parts of Europe, the Middle East, and North Africa. The first records of this species in North America date only from the 1920s, with the continent's first breeding record occurring in Newfoundland in 1977. Over the past few decades, increasing numbers of Black-headed Gulls have migrated across the Atlantic to winter in Newfoundland and Nova Scotia. A few winter farther south in New England, and the species has been recorded in Alaska after straying across the Bering Sea from Asia. Any Black-headed Gull in Texas is extraordinary.

Little Gull is downright dainty, the smallest gull in the world and another European invader of recent vintage, the first North American records dating from the early twentieth century. Since 1962, there have been several breeding records in the Great Lakes region, but any Texas Little Gull is big news.

SATURDAY, FEBRUARY 19, dawned frosty. Though I was up at 6:15 A.M., I lost time to a recalcitrant toilet. Fearing an unsanitary flood in my motel room, I undertook a jacketless run through the parking lot to garner a plunger, courtesy of a bleary-eyed front desk clerk. It solved the problem. A few minutes at the motel's minimalist continental breakfast—cold cereal, a glazed doughnut that could have bounced, and two cups of weak black coffee—gave me a sugar buzz but quieted my hunger.

Sunrise peeked through a partly cloudy sky as I pulled into Matt's driveway, my vehicle's heater running full blast to dispel winter's chill. We wasted no time. We agreed on our mission and put rubber to the road.

An adult Black-headed Gull had been discovered in late December, 1999, at the Village Creek Water Treatment Plant in Arlington, west of Dallas. This bird, which had been banded as a chick in Finland in June of 1996, was returning for its third successive winter at Village Creek, a remarkable site fidelity record. I had been looking forward to seeing this Finnish native, but it did not wait for me, disappearing in early February. Fortunately, Matt had located another adult Black-headed Gull at Big Creek Reservoir in November.

At the reservoir, we wanted to set up our tripods and scopes on a county road that passed near a lone rundown home sitting on a few fenced lakeside acres. But there were two problems with this plan. The homeowner had demonstrated blatantly antisocial behavior in the past, hassling Matt and even brandishing a weapon on one occasion. And the homeowner's hefty, growling, free-roaming brown mutt was not going to allow us to birdwatch from his territory, which apparently included the public county road. Every time we drove by, this mutt dashed after our vehicle, working himself into a loud-mouthed, slobber-spewing frenzy. I christened this monster "Thud the Wonder Pup," abbreviated simply to Thud when he appeared poised to do something unpleasant and fast action was in order, as in "Floor it, Matt! Thud's looking to chew on our left rear tire!" We belatedly thought of a strategy to distract Thud but could not execute it since we had no bones in our cooler.

The good news was that Thud's owner seemed to be away. His house was shut and quiet. It also became apparent that Thud understood his territory's boundaries. As we passed some magic invisible line in the dirt, Thud halted his teeth-baring snarls and trotted back to the center of his kingdom, content but glaring our way, daring us to be careless.

We flirted with disaster by setting up our scopes near Thud's domain. This gambit gained us nothing, unfortunately, and after nearly an hour seeking the Black-headed Gull, we moved on. Distressed by this miss, I consoled myself with the thought that though Review Species were a Big Year's trophies, each species counted only once.

Having left Thud to bark at squirrels, Ring-billed Gulls, and imaginary Delta County demons, we crunched slowly along remote dirt roads, looking and listening. At midmorning, we stopped alongside an enormous field brimming with geese feeding on the leftovers from last season's grain crop. Hundreds of Snow Geese, several tens of Canada and Greater White-fronted geese, and three Ross's Geese were in this field, conversing loudly and simultaneously, a cacophony that reminded me of a crowded high school cafeteria at lunchtime.

To obtain better light on the flock, we made two quick right turns, then walked out into the field's grain stubble. The geese shared their bounty with longspurs, several of which flitted across our line of sight. They were easy to hear clearly but tough to see well. We struggled to center a Lapland Longspur in my scope but finally won the battle. The field was alive with American Pipits, too.

Our archenemy the wind reappeared, increasing to fifteen miles per hour over no more than a quarter hour. My numb hands, cheeks, nose, and ears pained me. My eyes watered. But this was good fun.

Matt and I made a wide loop on multiple Delta County roads, eventually returning to Thud and Big Creek Reservoir. Checking many of the same locations we had visited earlier, we still could not find the Black-headed Gull. As 10:00 A.M. approached, we were ready to give up on this Review Species again.

As a last resort, we scoped the lake from a small park and boat launch on the reservoir's east end. My concentration had begun to lag when a fleeting glimpse of a possible Black-headed Gull resuscitated my interest. The gull flew with two Ring-billed Gulls at a moderate distance, disappearing in the direction of a small cove about halfway to Thud's place.

I yelled at Matt, who was not far away, relating what I had seen, and we took off. In the vicinity of the cove, our only access to an open water view required a bushwhack through woods cluttered with thorns and downed timber. As we cleared the trees and tangled undergrowth, Matt saw the bird briefly and agreed with my assertion that it was likely a Black-headed Gull. But the gull slipped from our grasp again, heading farther up the lake.

We jumped into the car and roared to the other end of the lake. Just beyond Thud's domain, we quickly set up our scopes and located the Black-headed Gull on the water near shore, its red bill steering us to the correct identification. We relished this treat for twenty minutes, studying it in flight, floating, and standing. Thud behaved well throughout this interval, content to chew on the remains of some hideously multicolored toy.

WHITE ROCK LAKE is several hundred acres, the centerpiece of an urban park surrounded by Dallas. Jogging trails hug the lakefront. On a busy Saturday afternoon, we pursued the Little Gull that had made the lake its home since being discovered by Peter Billingham on February 5.

Matt and I sorted through the gulls along the lake's northwest and west shores but found only the usual suspects. The Little Gull had been seen most often near Tee Pee Hill. Unfortunately, we had neglected to learn where Tee Pee Hill might be. We asked two resting, sweaty joggers and a couple of other passersby. They were all clueless.

As I quizzed yet another couple, Matt spied hundreds of gulls to our south. Since the TEXBIRDS descriptions of the Little Gull's favorite haunts had mentioned a multitude of gulls, we headed south. And found Tee Pee Hill!

As we set up, this looked to be Mission Impossible. Hours might be needed to sort through these gulls to find one individual of the world's smallest gull species. But after just ten minutes, Matt announced he probably had the bird. With his careful directions, I found the putative Little Gull. To the naked eye, it was a buoyant speck far out on the lake; in binoculars, it was clearly a gull; and in our scopes, it seemed Matt had made the right call. I was impressed. The Little Gull's white primaries were visible. Several Bonaparte's Gulls floated near the Little Gull, which was definitely smaller and sported a darker head and primary flight feathers.

Russell Graham arrived as the Little Gull was brought to the center of our scopes' fields of view. The three of us watched the bird bob aimlessly on the lake surface for a while. Then it took flight over the lake's north side and a Little Gull's most notable features—dark underwings, white trailing wing edges—were revealed.

Russell departed after this triumph. He had been up since 4:00 A.M. and had worked most of the day. Matt and I drove to the nearby

Old Fish Hatchery, a wooded center-city birding spot on the south side of White Rock Lake Park. We found numerous winter residents, including my year's first Blue Jay and Brown Creeper.

There remained one more important target: Rusty Blackbird, which we hoped would be our day's capstone. To find it, we drove to a Hunt County property owned by Matt and his family. We arrived in the day's last hour by design, with the weather turning mostly cloudy and colder. From the highway, we turned onto a rutted private dirt road, entering sixty-two wild acres. Matt led me through woods and across fields, through scratchy weeds and thick, thorny shrubs, over dead tree limbs. American Robins were everywhere. Two Winter Wrens met us along a small creek, but our only views of Rusty Blackbird were two dark flying forms that Matt's greater skill allowed him to identify as they passed high overhead. I needed better.

Daylight faded further without any Rusty Blackbirds. Ten minutes after sunset, I deemed our cause lost. But Matt was not ready to give up, and his persistence was rewarded as our quarry streamed onto the property to roost. The first Rusty Blackbird in our binoculars was a female. To assure us of its identity, it called thrice. Soon six Rusty Blackbirds, two males and four females, occupied a small tree. Then more came to roost, and yet more.

When the light faded to uselessness, I thanked Matt for his expertise and company. We had covered 210 miles since dawn and had capitalized on every second of daylight.

ON SUNDAY MORNING, Russell Graham and I met in the predawn at a gas station in McKinney, north of Dallas. Once we had been fortified with coffee and convenience store "health food," we drove north to Lake Texoma, a large, narrow body of water that straddles the Texas-Oklahoma border and is an excellent winter birding spot.

Pursuit of the lake's most recent rarity and Review Species, a Red-throated Loon, was our goal. At the Lighthouse Marina, where the loon had last been sighted, we scrutinized every square foot of the calm lake surface. We tallied twenty-five Common Loons, the most frequently encountered loon in Texas, before we hit upon a promising bird.

The suspect was distressingly distant. Even aided by quality optics and a high magnification eyepiece, discerning this bird's identity posed a challenge. The still early morning winter air provided some advantage: fine image quality. Distant details were crisp. On many days, the image degradation caused by solar heating can be horrendous. Even minor amounts of heat shimmer can relegate distant birds to the "unidentified" category.

This bird's lackadaisical nature permitted leisurely consideration of its identity. We strained our eyes and eventually agreed that our loon had a thin bill, which eliminated Common Loon and the very rare Yellow-billed Loon. The bird's apparent size was smaller than that of the nearby cormorants. Pacific and Red-throated loons are similarly sized, however. Only adult Pacific Loons have a dark "chin strap," but seeing this subtle plumage feature at a great distance was not feasible. Our bird held its head tilted up from the horizontal, a secondary behavior characteristic of Red-throated Loon, but not Pacific Loon, which holds its head level.

Aided by the excellent conditions, we studied the pattern of light and dark on the bird's neck and face. Russell and I agreed, after much discussion, that the multiple clues we had painstakingly assembled built a story with one confident conclusion: Red-throated Loon (#242).

THROUGHOUT MY TEXAS BIG YEAR, I was struck by the generosity and friendliness of the state's birding community, who gave me more than I had any reason to expect. People were invariably willing to share their experience and knowledge of the state's birds and habitats. Novices, persons of intermediate skill, and birders with the broadest knowledge of the Lone Star State's avifauna, such as Matt White and Russell Graham, all gave freely of their time and energy. People who had never met or talked with me prior to my Big Year went out of their way to assure that whatever time I devoted to their part of Texas would be maximally productive.

I made many new friends while spending mornings and afternoons in the company of others, chasing birds across Texas. And making new friends—attaching smiles, voices and personalities to names— was my year's most treasured result.

## chapter 7

A Long Weekend in the Pineywoods

N orth of Houston, Beaumont, and the upper Texas coast, the Pineywoods make up a humid region of low elevation and hilly forests bordering Arkansas and Louisiana. Some have dubbed this area the "wooded eastern quarter" because dense forests of hardwoods and conifers are common. Loblolly, short-leaf, long-leaf, and slash pines dominate where there is good drainage. All but the fast-growing slash pine are native species. It reigns wherever the original woodland was cut and replaced with introduced trees. Hardwoods prevail in the floodplains, and bald cypress swamps are scattered throughout the region. The Big Thicket National Preserve is the heart of the remaining Pineywoods, a forty-five- by fifty-mile area containing impressive wild timber in several discrete tracts of pine, mixed hardwood, and bottomland hardwood forest.

As I began my Big Year, the Pineywoods and its birds were unknown to me. But help was available. As a benefit to its membership, the Texas Ornithological Society scheduled field trips throughout 2000 to key locations around the state. These excursions, led by first-class guides, were inexpensive one- or two-day affairs. When TOS offered a Saturday–Sunday Pineywoods field trip, I signed on without hesitation. The trip targeted four East Texas specialties, each a lifer for me: Red-cockaded Woodpecker, Brown-headed Nuthatch, Henslow's Sparrow, and Bachman's Sparrow.

Were I to bird the Pineywoods on my own, Brown-headed Nuthatch would cause me little trouble. It is a common species in appropriate East Texas habitat. The inclusion of Red-cockaded Woodpecker on the trip's itinerary was a different matter and a major inducement to register. These woodpeckers are rare. A guide with knowledge of their current roosting sites would save me precious time.

Henslow's Sparrow is a skulker and uncommon, even in appropriate habitat. Finding this species in Texas is a formidable task. If we could find Henslow's Sparrow on this trip, a potential major time sink would be removed from my Big Year. Though Bachman's Sparrow is an uncommon pine forest resident, it can ordinarily be found without undue strain during the breeding season, when the males sing from low exposed pine branches. Outside the breeding season, when they are silent, these sparrows are far more elusive and can easily be missed. I feared that our trip's late February dates might be too early to find a singing Bachman's Sparrow.

BEFORE MY ALARM CLOCK RANG on Saturday morning, February 26, I awoke in the predawn to peals of thunder and rain thumping my motel room window. The news from the Weather Channel was grim. The sky still rumbled as rain showers came and went while our group gathered for introductions and an overview of the next two days. Our leaders, David and Mimi Wolf and Rick Schaefer, were optimistic that the precipitation would end by noon. The weather did little to dampen our spirits.

David and Mimi Wolf make their living from birds and the natural world. David has a wide-ranging interest in all aspects of natural history and is a senior member of the Victor Emmanuel Nature Tours staff. Mimi is a talented naturalist and artist whose work has been widely published in books and magazines. Their home is East Texas, and they know the area like few others.

Rick Schaefer is a biologist at the U.S. Forest Service research station in Nacogdoches. He works with threatened and endangered species, including the Red-cockaded Woodpecker. As our group assembled and Rick visited with each participant, his appreciation for and knowledge of the Pineywoods enlivened each conversation. The plan was to spend the morning with David and Mimi, then meet Rick at mid-afternoon to pursue Red-cockaded Woodpeckers.

Refusing to let the light sprinkles deter us, Mimi and David began our morning with a hunt for Henslow's Sparrow on private land along FM 1275 near Nacogdoches. As a favor to David and Mimi, the landowner had granted access.

Our group of twelve formed two lines, each person an arm's length from the neighboring ones, to march back and forth over several acres of a thick, wet, and weedy field. Henslow's Sparrows live and hide in such places. When flushed, they fly weakly for a short distance and land. Sometimes they disappear into the grass and scurry from view. If luck were with us, a Henslow's would perch high enough in the grass for us to admire it.

Tromping through the mat of damp brown weeds soaked my pant legs, shoes, and socks. Multiple passes across the field yielded nothing. David and Mimi had cautioned us that patience and a willingness to stomp around for awhile were prerequisites to seeing Henslow's Sparrow. Their confidence that these sparrows were in this field inspired us.

A bit more slogging earned our first success. A probable Henslow's Sparrow startled us and flew weakly. We surrounded the grassy mound into which it had disappeared, hoping to freeze the bird and prevent it from scurrying away between someone's legs. The bird cooperated, remaining seated low in the grass but not invisible. Almost all of us had our first views of a Henslow's Sparrow courtesy of this bird. The greenish cast to its head and nape were apparent, more so than I had expected, especially in the dim light of the cloudy morning. Further effort led to another Henslow's flying into a small copse, where it sat at knee height and in plain view.

Satisfied with our mastery of Henslow's, we birded the remainder of this property, hearing the musical trill of Pine Warblers in the lofty pines. After yet another Henslow's Sparrow popped up at midfield, we were satisfied with our take. We made our way back to the gate and encountered the most boldly marked Yellow-bellied Sapsucker I had ever seen, a bird destined for breeding success. An "Audubon's" Yellow-rumped Warbler was in a roadside tree. This is the rare Yellow-rumped Warbler subspecies in East Texas, where the "Myrtle" Yellow-rumped Warbler is fairly common. In years past, the "Myrtle" and "Audubon's" forms had been separate species, but ornithologists were now convinced that the scientific evidence merited lumping them.

At Saint's Rest Road, ten miles south of Nacogdoches along a levee above the surrounding swamp and bottomland hardwoods, Brown-headed Nuthatches twittered in the trees. A flock of Golden-crowned Kinglets passed quickly through the woods above our heads. An accommodating Winter Wren appeared and disappeared among fallen logs. Pileated Woodpeckers called loudly. One of these colossal woodpeckers flew so close that its flaming red Woody Woodpecker crest would have caught the attention of even the most nature-blind individual.

AT 4:00 P.M., WE MET RICK SCHAEFER at our motel and drove in a caravan to a Red-cockaded Woodpecker roost site in the Bannister National Wildlife Area of the Angelina National Forest. When we reached the designated place, we easily found the active Red-cockaded roost trees since each trunk was ringed with a broad stripe of blue paint at head height.

Though it was once fairly common across its range, the Red-cockaded Woodpecker is now a rare species. No more than ten thousand individuals survive in the southeastern United States. The Red-cockaded Woodpecker's decline has been caused by the decreasing availability of the habitat it requires: mature pine woods. Within such woods, these woodpeckers nest only in cavities they excavate in large live pines infected with the red heart fungus. This infection turns a tree's center soft while leaving its exterior hard.

Once a roost tree has been located, seeing these birds requires waiting until they return in the evening, often with great fanfare. At day's

Brown-headed Nuthatch. Drawing by Kelly B. Bryan.

end, three Red-cockaded Woodpeckers displayed and called for us from outside their roost holes, forty feet above the forest floor. Inspection of these roosts in our scopes showed their exteriors to be rimmed by small holes oozing resin, protecting the nest from the ravages of tree-climbing predators, such as snakes.

ON SUNDAY MORNING, February 27, our group visited the Angelina National Forest Boykin Springs Campground, thirty miles southeast of Lufkin and a few miles from the town of Zavalla. We hiked a muddy track through the dense pine woods. Brown-headed Nuthatches darted through the canopy. Pine Warblers vocalized. And a Bachman's Sparrow sang: a single introductory note followed by a melodious trill.

Our singer perched on a mid-elevation pine branch. Several scopes focused on the bird, which held remarkably still. Two other Bachman's Sparrows broke into song nearby, and two Red-cockaded Woodpeckers meandered through the same pines. These Bachman's Sparrows allowed our weekend to be declared a complete success. We had found every one of our target species. The group had seen each species well, a tribute to the scouting, skill, and determination of our leaders.

We ended our trip at Sam Rayburn Reservoir. At 115,000 acres, Sam Rayburn is the largest lake entirely within the state's boundaries. We stopped at pullouts along the Texas 147 bridge. The lake surface hosted the usual wintering species and one rarity, a Pacific Loon, a trip bonus discovered west of the bridge by David Wolf.

Our group dispersed at noon after a round of good-byes. Prior to departing, I asked our leaders' advice about Hairy Woodpecker and several other species I hoped to find. David, Mimi, and Rick suggested a visit to Jackson Hill Park, north of the reservoir, and a visit to Alazan Bayou, near Nacogdoches.

A two-hour investment in Jackson Hill Park paid handsome rewards. Bushwhacking through the woods, I found a Downy and a Hairy Woodpecker clinging to adjacent trees, affording an excellent comparison. As I combed through a foraging flock, a Red-breasted Nuthatch jumped into view, puttering down a tree trunk. At my last stop, near campsite 39, a familiar song greeted me with the news that spring was near. Having likely just reached Texas from the south, two adult male Northern Parulas in gray-blue, yellow, and white plumage took turns serenading me.

From Jackson Hill I traveled north to Nacogdoches and Alazan Bayou. Along County Road 628, a spot David had suggested, I struggled to find an Eastern Towhee. Since the winter day was expiring, I broke off from my failing towhee search and hiked into the Alazan Bayou meadows. Not a soul was in sight. After I had been there a quarter hour, three Sedge Wrens chattered from the field's dense, low grasses and showed themselves, earning a spot on my year list.

With only the fringes of daylight remaining, I again birded along CR 628 seeking a towhee. Two howling but harmless hound dogs trailed me for a quarter mile. With the last of the sun's rays disappearing from the treetops, I played an Eastern Screech-Owl tape. Several birds responded. As the tape neared the end of its brief run, a single bird of the right size, color, and shape emerged from the edge of the woods: Eastern Towhee! It hesitated, then flew across the road, landing where the light was as good as it could be at sunset. I had never seen this bird in Texas. To add species number 255 to my year list, my day's birding had gone down to the wire, to the very last bit of sunlight.

## chapter 8

Big Year Nemesis Number One

Painted Redstart

Т he American wood warblers, including the Painted Redstart, are the most pursued species of the northern hemisphere. Few can resist the bright colors of these birds and the excitement of their frantic spring migration.

An adult Painted Redstart, male or female, is sumptuous, certainly one of the most breathtaking warblers in North America. Though a good fraction of its plumage is jet black, much of this redstart's breast and its entire belly are "painted" brilliant red. Whether the bird is flying or perched, a conspicuous white wing patch cannot be missed, even on juvenile birds. And, like the more familiar American Redstart, this painted cousin fans its tail while foraging, advertising its identity even to the naked eye.

I had seen numerous Painted Redstarts on winter trips into Mexico. Painted Redstart is a common breeding species, for example, in the wooded canyons of Mexico's Maderas del Carmen mountain range, fifty miles southeast of Big Bend National Park. But I had yet to see one of these birds in Texas or anywhere else in the United States.

The TOS *Checklist of the Birds of Texas* (3rd edition) describes the Painted Redstart's status in Texas as "uncommon, irregular and very local resident in the high canyons" (127) of Brewster County in the Trans-Pecos. Roland Wauer, in his *Field Guide to the Birds of the Big Bend,* 2nd edition (Houston: Gulf Publishing, 1996), catalogues Painted Redstart as a "sporadic summer resident" of Big Bend National Park, with records extending from March 12 through September 4. All but two of the park's records come from the high elevation canyons, with Boot Canyon being the most likely place to find this species. In their *Birds of the Trans-Pecos* (Austin: University of Texas Press, 1998), Jim Peterson and Barry Zimmer note: "Populations apparently fluctuate. In some years [Painted Redstart] may be absent altogether."

With the continuation of the drought that had plagued the Trans-Pecos for more than half a decade, the year 2000 offered little to entice Painted Redstart to breed in the area. Luck seemed on my side, though, on Friday evening, March 10, when Dale Ohl called me at home with the news that an adult Painted Redstart was in a private yard in the tiny West Texas town of Marathon. Dale had heard about the redstart that afternoon. She had driven to Marathon to see it. Within seconds of her opening the yard gate, a Painted Redstart had presented itself for her enjoyment. I very much hoped for a reenactment of this scene the following day.

On Thursday, Alan Tennant had discovered this gem at his home in Marathon, a Chihuahuan Desert oasis forty miles north of Big Bend National Park. Established many years ago as a railroad waystation, Marathon sits out in the rugged Trans-Pecos ranch country. With human occupation and the passage of time have come trees that tower far above the surrounding desert, attracting migrating birds in need of rest and sustenance. It was not hard to imagine a Painted Redstart visualizing Alan's yard as an invitation to refuel.

Early on Saturday morning I attended a meeting at the Fort Davis National Historic Site, then leaped into my Jeep for a sixty-mile drive to the southeast along Texas 118 and U.S. 90, arriving in Marathon near noon.

Alan had given me permission to bird his property. My optimistic mindset envisioned success in an hour or less. But over the next sixty minutes, only the usual town species—House Sparrow, Rock Dove, European Starling, House Finch—were visible from the street outside his home. I opened his yard gate and entered. Ruby-crowned Kinglets and Yellow-rumped Warblers occupied the yard's greenery. A flock of adult and immature White-crowned Sparrows pecked at the ground. A Ladder-backed Woodpecker tapped on a tree trunk and occasionally uttered its diagnostic "whinny" call. A Yellow-bellied Sapsucker, rare in West Texas, clung to an adjacent tree.

After an hour's birding, I widened my search, reasoning that the redstart might choose to wander. I walked a circle of ever-increasing radius around Alan's home, scrutinizing every tree, fence, and shrub in yard after yard. My optimism began to ebb.

Five miles south of Marathon lies a spring-fed riparian area known as the Post. A park and a weekend hangout, it features old cottonwoods that stand guard over a few grassy acres. Worth a look in any season, the Post can be a hotspot during spring and fall migration. In October, 1982, for example, its reed-choked pond edges had hosted a Northern Jacana, a particularly rare Texas Review Species.

On this Saturday afternoon, several families were enjoying picnics in the park. A pair of young children laughed while working to force the park's swings to unrealistic heights. Undeterred by the human activity, Golden-fronted Woodpeckers, Dark-eyed Juncos, and Vermilion Flycatchers attended to their business in the cottonwoods. Cactus Wrens, Northern Mockingbirds, and a Loggerhead Shrike stayed to the park's desert edges, while a Black Phoebe and several American Coots were around and on the water, respectively. I hoped that the Painted Redstart deemed the Post a worthy stop. But there was no sign of the bird.

I repeated my search pattern: another hour in Alan's yard, a walk on the surrounding streets, another visit to the Post. I patrolled every street in Marathon that had trees or shrubs of any kind. I craned my neck out of the open window of my Jeep, hopeful for the sight of an active black, red, and white-splashed warbler. Hope waned, but as long as there was daylight, I refused to give up.

At 3:00 P.M., I returned to Alan's yard yet again. I had been there only a few minutes when Alan came home. I introduced myself. We chatted, maintaining a vigil for my elusive target. Impatience was getting the better of me, so I headed off to the Post for a third time.

When I came back, still empty-handed, Alan gave me the sad news that while I had been at the Post, he had seen the Painted Redstart for a few seconds at the rear of his yard, along his fence. On this note of good and bad news, Alan departed, wishing me luck and welcoming me to continue looking for as long as I liked.

His brief sighting rejuvenated me. I repeatedly scoured the yard, concentrating my energies on the trees, shrubs, and tall grass near the fence. The bird had to be nearby. But whatever the redstart had been doing when Alan saw it, it was apparently no longer in the mood and had moved on.

Out of light and time, I stuck a thank-you note on Alan's front door, reluctantly started my Jeep, and drove home without a Painted Redstart. This was only the first individual of this species to torture me in the year 2000. There would be others.

HAVING READ DALE'S ORIGINAL TEXBIRDS post, four Dallas birders contacted her, expressing their interest in the Painted Redstart, requesting that Dale notify them if anyone saw the bird on Saturday. That evening, Dale relayed my failure and Alan's momentary midafternoon sighting. Since Alan had seen the bird, the Dallas birders drove all night to reach Marathon. They spent their Sunday repeating my Saturday, never finding the redstart, despite the availability of four sets of eyes.

## chapter 9

Dawn at the Lek

E very other year, the International Society for Optical Engineering organizes a conference for astronomers and engineers who design, construct, and operate large telescopes. In March of 2000, more than a thousand persons from around the world converged on Munich, Germany, to attend the Astronomical Telescopes and Instrumentation meeting, myself among them.

German species would obviously not count toward my Big Year. And a ten-day absence from Texas just as spring migration accelerated would not help my Big Year. But I was not retired. This meeting was important business. And while I was in Germany, there was time for a half day in the field with Stefan Tewinkle, a local birder I had met two years before. Birding in Germany did assist my Big Year by providing opportunities to study multiple individuals of species that appear in Texas but only as great rarities: Garganey, Eurasian Wigeon, Tufted Duck, Black-headed Gull, Ruff, "Eurasian" Green-winged Teal, and others.

On Saturday, March 25, under a mostly cloudy sky that threatened rain, Stefan and I set off to bird at several reservoirs in and around Munich. In February, I had worked hard to see a single Black-headed Gull in northeast Texas. Stefan and I found more than 150 Black-headed Gulls congregated around one of the smaller reservoirs, displaying a variety of plumages.

As we walked along one shoreline, accompanied by a few exercising early risers from a nearby town, Stefan spotted a male Garganey near a line of reeds. In the shallow water behind the Garganey, four Ruff strutted, and we spied several Eurasian Wigeon, another Texas Review Species. I lingered over these, preparing for some future day when I might find one of their lost cousins in Texas.

THE LAST OF MY HOMEWARD flights from Europe touched down at eleven on the night of Sunday, April 2, leaving me exhausted from an itinerary of Munich to New York to Dallas to El Paso. Much as I wanted to see my family and sleep in my own bed, the Earth had passed the vernal equinox. The sun had moved north of the celestial equator. Spring was under way. I spent Sunday night in an El Paso motel, looking forward to a noon departure for Amarillo and a hurried Panhandle trip targeting Lesser Prairie-Chicken and other regional specialties.

Though travel had left me feeling frayed and weary, I spent an hour on Sunday night electronically reconnecting to the Texas birding community. As expected, vivid accounts of early spring migration were accumulating on TEXBIRDS, relaying word of the increasing volume and diversity of migrants landing at coastal hotspots such as High Island, Sabine Woods, Packery Channel, and South Padre Island. And since I had been away for more than a week, it was inevitable that something "juicy" would have been discovered in my neck of the woods, the Trans-Pecos, while I was in Europe.

Jim Paton, an expert birder and El Paso resident, had attempted to alert me that a Painted Redstart and a Ruddy Ground-Dove had been seen in a west El Paso yard on March 25 and 26. The owner had not told anyone about these birds until the evening of March 26. Paton saw and photographed the Painted Redstart the next day, but the Ruddy Ground-Dove had vanished. By the time I returned to Texas, both of these rare birds were gone. Ruddy Ground-Dove, a Review Species, would have been a lifer and an excellent Big Year bird. Painted Redstart had definitely become a nemesis.

MY MONDAY AFTERNOON FLIGHT from El Paso to Dallas to Amarillo, a city of 150,000 Texans, was nearly on time, an agreeable change of pace. There would still be a couple hours of daylight remaining after we landed. From the airport, I drove west on Interstate 40.

Flat and devoid of trees, the northwest corner of Texas is the Llano Estacado. Prior to the extensive settlement that occurred in the nineteenth century, this region was a horizon-to-horizon shortgrass prairie. Much of the land has since been converted to agriculture and ranching. With limited time, I headed for several large feedlots where Ring-necked Pheasant, a Panhandle specialty, was a possibility. Along the way, I spied my year's first Swainson's Hawk, perched on a fence pole, an imperturbable light morph adult being harassed by an agitated American Kestrel.

Farther west, a crude sign for the Amarillo landfill caught my eye. I had not known of this place but exited immediately, curious to compare its avian fare with what I had sampled in early February at Corpus Christi's Elliot landfill.

A short drive north on a two-lane road brought me to the landfill's open gates. Adjacent to the gate was a black-tailed prairie dog colony covering many acres. Several prairie dogs ran along the surface between their dirt surface mounds. Others disappeared into their underground tunnels when I stepped from my car. The bravest held their ground, chirping at me as I advanced toward their territory. As I had hoped, scanning the colony with my binoculars revealed Burrowing Owls standing guard at entrances to some of the prairie dog caverns.

The landfill itself disappointed, holding just a few Franklin's Gulls. But on the drive back to the interstate, in an agricultural field west of South Hill Road, my year's first Ring-necked Pheasant headed in the opposite direction when I stopped to look at it. The bird was not happy to see me, but I was pleased to see it.

THE "SPRING FORWARD ONE HOUR" rule that defines the annual switch from standard to daylight saving time had taken place in the wee hours of the past Sunday morning. As I often do, regardless of my motel's pedigree, I had brought a reliable battery-powered alarm clock with me. Unfortunately, I paid inadequate attention to the time on its illuminated digital face. On Monday night as I laid my head on my pillow, I neglected to notice that the clock was still on standard time. Thus, on Tuesday morning, April 4, when I stumbled from bed and sleep at 4:15 A.M. according to my clock, it was actually 5:15 A.M. already.

My error did not register until after I had dressed, packed, and checked out of my room and was seated in my car warming my hands over the heater's output. The dashboard clock read 5:39; I expected it to read 4:39. My foggy brain puzzled over this inconsistency. The clear, brightening morning sky promised a fine day—but it was too bright. Dawn should not be so near! Something was awry. I checked the clock and my watch and realized what had happened.

I had planned on a leisurely, cooked breakfast at a nearby diner: bacon and eggs, toast, coffee, orange juice. But losing an hour scrapped this plan and sent me on a mad dash into a convenience store where a tired graveyard shift clerk took an inordinate amount of time ringing up my stale doughnuts and burnt coffee. The day's first stop was for Lesser Prairie-Chicken in Lipscomb County, eighty miles northeast of Amarillo near the tiny town of Glazier. I had been advised to arrive before dawn. That was going to be a challenge.

Lesser Prairie-Chicken had once been common on the southern plains, such as those of the Texas Panhandle. But no longer. Hurt by fire ants and the continual loss of the shortgrass prairie, Lesser Prairie-Chicken populations have been in serious decline for decades. Still, beginning in late winter and continuing into spring, male Lesser Prairie-Chickens gather to attract females for nesting. They come together in groups, choosing locations on sparsely vegetated rises that afford good local visibility. These places are known as leks.

Male prairie-chickens establish territories at a lek, with the dominant birds taking the choice center sites. Each male divides his time between territorial defense and complex courtship displays. Seeking the favor of one or more hens, a male prairie-chicken fans his tail feathers, leans forward, drops his wings, raises the pinnae or "ears" on his neck, and inhales air to inflate his orange-red neck sacs. The males also call or "boom" for the hens, especially in the early morning. These calls can be heard as much as a mile from the lek.

With a full hour accidentally chopped from my day by a bit of carelessness, I feared being late to the lek. If the chickens were not booming, they would be easy to miss. To recover time, I drove faster than I should have, all the while scolding myself for my mistake. Fortunately, I tend to cushion my travel estimates for uncertainty about road conditions and traffic, and this assisted my recovery. At 7:25 A.M. as the sun crested the horizon, I turned onto the dirt county road along which I hoped to find Lesser Prairie-Chicken, relieved to be less than a mile from my destination.

The lek was on private land but viewable from this county road and so close by that I had been advised to drive slowly and not get out of my car until I passed the lek. Since I had arrived in time, my mood improved, allowing me to appreciate the early spring sunshine and cathedral-like quiet of this rural place. The temperature hovered just below freezing. A five- to ten-mile-per-hour wind added to the chill, but it was not hard to endure. I drove with the windows open, the car's heater set to the highest possible temperature and air flow.

Several Lesser Prairie-Chickens were on the lek, an ill-defined, slightly elevated open area encircled by a broad grassy field. The males' colorful neck sacs and dark, erect pinnae made separation of the sexes straightforward. Several males boomed as I passed within thirty yards, their calls reverberating over the quiet countryside. I drifted another fifty yards along the road and then exited my car, taking care not to slam the door. For the next eighty minutes, I studied these fascinating birds. They were totally involved in their spring ritual.

Typically eight to thirteen birds were in sight, strutting on the lek. A total of seventeen to twenty Lesser Prairie-Chickens were present, almost all males. Only three were females. The competition for hens was fierce.

When an adult female Northern Harrier flew over, barely above the grass, every prairie-chicken flushed into taller grass, seeking cover and safety. Every quarter hour or so, a chicken would fly across the road to another part of the prairie or return from some other location. West of the county road, at a distance of 100 to 150 yards, prairie chickens boomed from another lek.

It was difficult to leave this spectacle, but other places and species demanded my attention.

BLACK-BILLED MAGPIE is regular in winter in the Panhandle of Oklahoma and in northeastern New Mexico, but the species is very rare in Texas, and well-documented records are few. Hence Black-billed Magpie is on the TBRC Review Species List, and it was exciting news when on the afternoon of December 5, 1999, Eric and Larry Carpenter, son and father, discovered a Black-billed Magpie at Coldwater Creek. This creek crosses Texas 136 in Hansford County, north of Gruver, less than ten miles south of the Texas-Oklahoma state line. The Carpenters saw the magpie on the bridge and along the creek to the southwest.

Between this discovery and the New Year, several Texas birders relocated one magpie or more at Coldwater Creek. Chuck Sexton, a U.S. Fish and Wildlife Service biologist with a long track record of ornithological research in Texas, noted in his TEXBIRDS post that the magpies were following the cattle—they were attracted to the water troughs, cattle feed, and cow manure. At the time of my early April Panhandle trip, there had been no magpie reports since January 15, when Tom and Phyllis Frank had seen two birds at Coldwater Creek. I wondered whether they were still present. Few birders roam this part of Texas. It was conceivable that no one had even looked for the Black-billed Magpies since mid-January.

After leaving the Lesser Prairie-Chicken lek, I added a few arriving migrants to my year list, though none of these would be difficult to see elsewhere during spring. With the day coming to an end, I debated whether a long drive to Hansford County was worthwhile and decided it was.

My car coasted to a stop at Coldwater Creek at 4:40 P.M. From several places along Texas 136 and County Road F, I surveyed up and down the creek, over and over, but saw no magpies. As sunset gained on me, I recalled Chuck Sexton's advice about checking areas holding cattle. East of the highway and south of the creek, at a distance of a half mile, I noted a group of fifteen cattle that had previously escaped my attention. Moving to a vantage point on the east shoulder, atop a hill north of the Texas 136 bridge, I scoped the area that held these cattle.

After a minute or so, a large, dark, partially hidden bird perched in a tree caught my eye. There were no Great-tailed Grackles here. What could this be? As I pondered this question, the bird swooped from the tree to the ground: a Black-billed Magpie! Besides size and silhouette, the bright white in the wings and on the bird's belly were beacons in my scope, even at this great distance. One could never hope to identify a Chipping Sparrow at a half-mile range, but one could be sure of a magpie.

The magpie stayed on the ground a few seconds, then flew into a tree's midlevel branches. It was joined by a second magpie. Then a third magpie appeared, flying into an adjacent tree.

The area occupied by these birds had all the ingredients Chuck Sexton had listed: cattle, a water trough, cow manure. Over the next hour, whenever I returned to my scope from writing field notes, relocating one or more of these birds rarely required a wait of even two minutes. Sometimes, while the magpies were on the ground, they were hidden by foreground landscape obstructions, such as toppled trees or tall grass. But they would soon reappear. Given the time of year, I wondered if they might be breeding in Texas.

While I reveled in this spectacle, two ranch hands stopped their battered pickup truck alongside my rental car.

"Evenin'. What're ya lookin' at?" the older man asked as he sauntered over.

"Some interesting birds. Black-billed Magpies. Care to take a look?" I offered my scope.

"Ha! What did I tell ya?" the older man said to his young friend, smiling broadly. "Pay up!"

In January, the winner of the bet had met a group of birders who were pursuing the Coldwater Creek magpies. Prior to stopping to talk to me, he had bet his friend that I was looking for them, too. The loser of the bet was astonished by the turn of events but laughed off the obviously minor cash loss. Both men looked at the magpies in my scope and in my National Geographic field guide. I explained why birders would be interested to see them in Texas.

We had a fine conversation.

THE GREATER AND LESSER PRAIRIE-CHICKENS are
separate species, with the Greater being a bit larger and darker than
the Lesser. The Greater Prairie-Chicken is now struggling for survival,
though it also was once a common bird over its range. The Atlantic
Coast subspecies, the Heath Hen, became extinct in 1932.

The Texas subspecies, "Attwater's" Greater Prairie-Chicken, is endangered; other subspecies, such as those in Colorado, are faring better. Small managed populations of the Texas subspecies remain at only
two preserves: Attwater Prairie Chicken National Wildlife Refuge at
Eagle Lake and the Texas City Prairie Preserve on Galveston Bay.

Because biologists have mixed captive-raised birds with wild birds
at these preserves, it was questionable whether the species was still
"countable" in the Lone Star State. According to the ABA Big Year
rules, an observer must see a wild bird for the species to be countable.
I knew of no way to separate a wild bird from a captive-raised individual visually, and there was no public access to these leks; thus the
effort required to see a Greater Prairie-Chicken at either site would be
substantial and might be wasted. Since I could not afford to invest in
a species for which countability might be questioned, I passed.

## chapter 10

Into the Ooze

L ate on Thursday afternoon, April 6, I was working in my observatory office when the operator informed me that David Hedges was on the phone.

"Brush Freeman just called from Imperial Reservoir on his cell phone," David said. "He and Petra Hockey were looking at a drake Eurasian Wigeon while we talked. How's that for interesting?"

"Fantastic!" I said. There might not be another Eurasian Wigeon opportunity in Texas in 2000. "Want to take a shot at it this evening?" I said, hopeful that David would accompany me for the two-and-a-half-hour drive, 130 miles one way.

"Sure," he said. "We can take my truck. But we should go as soon as you can get away. Any chance of that happening?"

"Give me a half hour to wrap up," I said.

AS THE ONLY LARGE BODY OF WATER in an otherwise dry landscape, Pecos County's Imperial Reservoir is a bird magnet. This remote, seldom visited place is a hotspot for West Texas rarities, having hosted Pacific and Red-throated loons, Pomarine Jaeger, Red-necked Grebe, Red Phalarope, Surf Scoter, Black-legged Kittiwake, and other goodies. Much like a visit to the high country of the Davis

Mountains, a day's birding at Imperial Reservoir that fails to produce a rarity leaves one feeling that something must have gotten away.

In the early evening, David and I followed the bumpy dirt road along Imperial Reservoir's east side, turning right to parallel the south shore. Chihuahuan Desert surrounds the reservoir. Scattered creosotebush and mesquite extend to the horizon in every direction. Along the lake's shoreline, exotic salt cedar groves have taken root and thrive. A handful of unkempt, rarely occupied mobile homes sit on the sandy north shore. Much of the land to the west is leased for oil production. Pumpjacks lazily haul oil into pipelines, with no humans in sight.

As winter gives way to spring, the reservoir is drawn down to satisfy local agricultural and ranching water needs. When the water level drops, the southwest portion of the lakebed is exposed. Driving on this reclaimed lake bottom is tricky, demanding a watchful eye and occasional forays from the vehicle to check the ground's ability to support a vehicle.

Over the past winter, our mutual friends John Karges and Kelly Bryan had recovered from a near hopeless situation, having stuck their four-wheel-drive truck in wet sand and muck along the northwest shore. David and I knew this story well and had no interest in reliving it. If you cannot extract yourself from the sand and mud at Imperial, summoning help means a wrecker from Fort Stockton. The principle governing such rescues is "whatever the market will bear." If one is stuck at Imperial, one had better be prepared to bear a great deal.

Our car shuddered along the washboard road surface. We soon reached the limits of judgment-free driving and stopped. Brush and Petra had discovered the Eurasian Wigeon while scoping a raft of Lesser Scaup and American Wigeon from roughly our position. With growing excitement, we saw some Lesser Scaup and numbers of American Wigeon.

Enthusiastic that a Eurasian Wigeon sighting might be near, we set up our scopes. Conditions were less than optimal. As often occurs in a Trans-Pecos spring, a twenty-mile-per-hour wind howled and gusted, picking up sand particles. My mouth turned gritty, and I needed frequent breaks to rinse sand out of my eyes. The wind had also whipped the reservoir's surface into frothy whitecaps, causing every waterfowl to disappear and reappear annoyingly, over and over. To make matters more challenging, the afternoon's warmth created a thick layer of heat shimmer, turning each of the bobbing ducks in our scopes into blobs that only rarely steadied. The conditions demanded patience to squeeze information from the fleeting seconds when image quality improved. It was trying.

Confidently separating a female or immature Eurasian Wigeon from a female or immature American Wigeon is a task reserved for experts in conditions of good lighting and image quality. However, even in these difficult conditions, a Eurasian Wigeon drake would stand out. The drakes of this graceful, medium-sized duck species from the Old World have a creamy forehead and crown, reddish brown head and neck, pinkish breast, and grayish body, while an American Wigeon drake features a white forehead and crown, grayish face with a wide, curving green eyestripe, and chestnut breast and body.

We scrutinized the scaup and wigeon for forty-five minutes without finding a Eurasian Wigeon. The ducks slowly motored away, receding into the shimmer and whitecaps. To view them from a closer range and to examine other more distant ducks, we drove west. A smaller vehicle, a Suzuki Samurai, was ahead. A young man and woman strolled nearby.

David shifted into four-wheel-drive. We drove between the winter high water mark and the thinly vegetated desert. Along the reservoir's northwest shoreline, we encountered a field of uncomfortably large and jagged rocks. David turned right, intending to drive lower and closer to the water for several hundred feet on what appeared to be hard, smooth sand. This seemed a reasonable course of action. We feared a tire puncture if we continued to lurch over the rocks, and the sand's color and visual texture was consistent with other sand that had supported David's vehicle.

But as soon the truck's wheels left the rocks and hit the sand, we began to sink. David turned the wheel back left, trying to accelerate as he uttered expletives.

The wheels spun without traction. We were stuck. David turned the truck off. We looked at each other, shared a few more expletives, then got out. The situation was grim. All four wheels had sunk several inches. Just underneath the thin layer of relatively dry surface sand, the lakebed was thick, gelatinous and foul-smelling.

We scooped muck away from the wheels with our bare hands and jammed the largest, flattest rocks we could find against, behind, and in front of all four wheels, seeking to create an impromptu roadbed and escape route. We failed, accomplishing nothing more than sinking the truck a bit deeper.

David took out a lengthy, strong chain, but it dangled uselessly in our hands because there was no suitably strong attachment point in the desert. We needed a towering oak or a stop sign to be our anchor, not a withered creosotebush. We worked to jury-rig an anchor. The land surrounding the lake was littered with the detritus of oil production. We wandered among this material seeking a solution and eventually found a bent and rusting axle, perhaps from a vehicle that had gotten stuck and been abandoned. We connected the chain to the rear bumper of David's truck and then to the rusted axle, but we could not anchor the axle firmly enough in the ground.

As our situation deteriorated, I remembered the other vehicle, now well to our south. With binoculars, I saw that they were stuck, too. It seemed that they were unlikely to provide any assistance.

Over the next ninety minutes, David and I got steadily dirtier but were no closer to driving away. We were about ready to call a wrecker when another glance to our south revealed that the young man and woman had somehow freed their vehicle. They were driving away.

David and I waved, whistled, and shouted: "Hey! Don't leave! Help!" The car stopped. We waved, whistled, and shouted some more. The car turned in our direction. Our relief was palpable. It seemed more likely that we might get home that night.

Once the Samurai arrived at our location, a few minutes of discussion with the young man and woman resulted in our chain being connected from their front bumper to our truck's rear bumper. We were hoping that they could pull us out. For our next rescue attempt, we decided that I would sit in the driver's seat of David's truck, David would manage the operation from a point midway between the two vehicles, and the young man would be at the wheel of his Samurai. With the chain in place, we prepared to go at it one last time.

The woman was standing near David, who now insisted she get in the Samurai. "We need all your weight in the car, ma'am," David said. The woman was heavyset. Neither David's tone or his intent was mean-spirited, but it would have been easy for the young man or woman to have heard otherwise. After David's request, there was a pause, a few moments when I thought they might undo the chain and drive off, leaving us either to conjure a miracle or to provide a massive cash infusion to a Fort Stockton wrecker. But the woman squeezed into the Samurai's front passenger seat.

David's countdown reached zero. Furious seconds of mud spewing, pulling, and wheel spinning followed, with loud encouragement from David. I worked the gas pedal of David's truck, finally accelerating in reverse out of the grasp of the lake bottom back onto the relative safety of the rocks.

As we removed the chain, delighted, David and I thanked our saviors profusely. We were plastered with mud and smelled awful. The young couple refused to accept any money and drove off, waving. We half-heartedly resumed our search for the Eurasian Wigeon, but the daylight soon faded.

I returned to Imperial Reservoir two days later, investing another five hours on the Eurasian Wigeon. Under sunny morning skies with no wind and excellent image clarity, I surveyed every square centimeter of the reservoir's surface. Pecos birder Greer Willis did the same. If the Eurasian Wigeon had been present, we would have found it. But it had likely departed on Thursday afternoon and was now floating on some other reservoir.

## chapter 11

Spring Migration

S pring is the season that every birder anticipates. Millions of birds from hundreds of species cross the southern coastline of the United States in the span of a few short weeks. Each northbound male and female migrant is focused on its destination, intent on propagation of its species. Gaudiness abounds, with male migrants clothed in their finest colors.

Departing from southerly staging areas, such as the Yucatán Peninsula, many migrating birds take a daredevil's route across the Gulf of Mexico, their wings beating nonstop for several hundred miles, always at the mercy of the weather. Others choose land routes through Central America that avoid the Gulf crossing, but these are also fraught with peril. Mid-March brings the first migrants to Texas. By mid-April, the trickle turns to a flood that crests in late April and early May. Stragglers continue to reach Texas through late May. Then, as quickly as it began, migration is over and the breeding season is on.

At the end of the first week of April, migrants and newly arrived residents reinvigorated the West Texas landscape with color and song each spring morning. On April 7, a gorgeous black and yellow torpedo landed at my hummingbird feeders to extract nectar, my year's first Scott's Oriole, its melodious song unheard since the previous summer. It perched precariously on the feeder's narrow rail, spinning.

A lone Least Tern and a Cliff Swallow duo joined me at Imperial Reservoir during my second try for the Eurasian Wigeon on April 8. The same afternoon, a migrating Pectoral Sandpiper wandered the muddy south shoreline at Lake Balmorhea.

A Davis Mountains Preserve hike on April 9 yielded singing Grace's Warblers and Hutton's Vireos in the Madera Canyon ponderosa pines. A scolding Steller's Jay, black crest erect, met me at the trailhead into Tobe Canyon, at 6,700 feet. The tittering of forty White-throated Swifts caught my ear as they zoomed over a nearby high ridge. A bumpy slog in my Jeep to Bridge Gap, at 7,300 feet, brought me to the territory of three playful Zone-tailed Hawks chasing one another on the thermals. The steep trail above Bridge Gap led to a fleeting encounter with a flock of Pygmy Nuthatches, their high-pitched calls informing me of their presence. At day's end, returning through the lower elevations, I greeted my first Wilson's Warbler.

I HAD BEEN ANTICIPATING a mid-April trip to the upper coast since the previous fall, when the idea of a Big Year had first entered my mind. Finally, at midafternoon on Friday, April 14, I stood at the far southeast corner of Texas with just Sabine Pass separating me from Louisiana, the coast only a few miles ahead.

Evidence of spring surrounded me. At the junction of Texas 87 and FM 3322, in the town of Sabine Pass, I swerved my rental car into a tackle store parking lot to watch arriving Chimney Swifts. Their rapid wingbeats and pointed wings telegraphed their identity to me before I raised my binoculars.

As I continued west along Texas 87, migrating birds streamed by, making landfall. These individuals had survived the demanding Gulf crossing, but their fuel reserves were depleted. They fed continuously in the roadside trees and shrubs. Multiple dark red, adult male Summer Tanagers chased each other; more than two dozen Orchard Orioles, mostly rust and black males, worked for food in a loose pack. Dark blue iridescent Indigo Buntings dashed across and down the highway. Black and white Eastern Kingbirds veered about the mostly cloudy sky catching insects, only rarely resting on a wire.

White-throated Swift. Drawing by Kelly B. Bryan.

At Sabine Woods, cars and pickups filled the roadside parking area. This isolated thirty-two-acre coastal oak motte, owned by the Texas Ornithological Society, is one of the most productive "migrant traps" along the upper Texas coast. Having made the crossing, fatigued migrants often drop into the first available habitat. The conservation of coastal sanctuaries such as Sabine Woods, which function as migrant traps, especially in the spring, is vital to the future of avian migration.

My midafternoon arrival was intentional. The likelihood of seeing migrants along the coast is governed by the weather and the time of day. Given their starting points and the hours required to cross the Gulf, waves of migrating birds usually reach the upper Texas coast between 3:00 and 6:00 P.M. Migrants may suddenly be present in large numbers, with the transition from calm to substantial activity occurring in a remarkably short interval.

The impact of weather conditions on spring migrants is the subject of endless debate, though the major factors are clear. Migrants are headed north. When the wind is from the south or nearby points on the compass, many migrants choose to continue inland with the aid of a following wind, rather than stop at the coast. In the presence of a heavy north wind, however, birds will stop at the first land they see. Rain and opposing north winds can lead to spectacular "fallouts" of exhausted birds on the coast. Though fallout conditions are good news for birders, they are bad news for birds, killing thousands of migrants that have no energy left to fight the weather. Fallouts sometimes leave coastal beaches littered with the carcasses of warblers, thrushes, and vireos.

I WANDERED AMONG THE TREES of Sabine Woods, on and off the wooden boardwalk, sharing these acres with fifteen other birders, all pleased with the afternoon's offerings. Shortly after I entered the shelter of the intertwined oaks, a Red-eyed Vireo at eye level was centered in my binoculars, bird #300 for my year.

The action was unceasing. My preoccupation with the migrants meant that the swarming mosquitoes barely registered with me. My year list leaped forward with multiple Chestnut-sided Warblers; more than two dozen Hooded Warblers, male and female; numerous Wood Thrushes; and my year's only Yellow-throated Warbler, a male barely within the focus range of my binoculars. The following hours yielded two striking Prothonotary Warblers, a female and a male; several Kentucky Warblers; multiple American Redstarts of both sexes; many Tennessee Warblers; Swainson's and Gray-cheeked thrushes; and Worm-eating Warblers.

The activity continued into the next morning. An adult male Cerulean Warbler, white and turquoise, greeted me at the Sabine Woods entry gate. A male Painted Bunting, looking as though he had been dipped in seven Crayola colors, sang from a high perch. Gray Catbirds hid in every shrub; Kentucky Warblers waddled along the ground; and an Ovenbird sat quietly among the dead leaves that carpeted the earth. Rummaging on the ground, turning over leaves and twigs with its outsized bill, a Swainson's Warbler allowed itself to be seen. This drab, secretive bird, clothed in shades of brown, was an especially sweet find, only the second individual of this species I had ever seen.

A short drive west on Texas 87 brought me to the oceanside vistas of Sea Rim State Park. The Marshlands Unit, north of the highway, was unproductive. Across the highway, the Beach Unit included a boardwalk that extended far out into a healthy marsh. On my second circuit of the boardwalk, an American Bittern flew low over the marsh, an adult with dark wing uppersides, a streaked neck, and the classic malar stripe. Twenty minutes later, I accidentally flushed a Least Bittern.

As I walked and birded along the beach, a Common Tern flapped along and above the water's edge. Shorebirds congregated where frothy waves lapped the sand, and among them was my first Semipalmated Plover.

A midafternoon return to Sabine Woods continued my "Christmas in April." An Eastern Wood-Pewee called. Baltimore Orioles arrived in impressive numbers, along with a tail-less Yellow-breasted Chat, several Blackburnian Warblers, and a Yellow-billed Cuckoo, its long tail and russet wings an immediate giveaway.

Strolling the boardwalk, I was invited into a conversation with two women who were puzzling over a flycatcher's identification. We exchanged opinions about this bird, an *Empidonax* flycatcher, then went on to introductions and chat about homes and travel. I discovered that Sandra Hathaway, one of my new acquaintances, and I had mutual friends, two of whom were present that afternoon at Sabine Woods. I had passed them on the boardwalk. Being focused on the birds, I had failed to recognize them!

Sandra and I talked for a long time. At the conclusion of our conversation, she invited me to a dinner party that night at her home in Beaumont, an hour's drive north. Sandra's party was a welcome change of pace from my usual solo evening meal at a low-budget eatery. She was a gracious and entertaining hostess who counted among her friends many interesting people. One of this party's unexpected benefits for me was the wealth of local birding knowledge I accrued from several guests. I stayed too late at the party, of course, though only by a birder's definition.

ON SUNDAY MORNING, April 16, I traveled southeast along FM 3322, with Sabine Pass to my left and the extensive *Spartina* grass marsh of the 8,952-acre Texas Point National Wildlife Refuge on my right. Hard-hatted workers were arriving for their morning shift at plants and sites along my route. Shipping, oil exploration, and refining dominate the local economy. Towering offshore rigs and the huge industrial paraphernalia associated with their repair and construction imposed their jagged geometry on the skyline.

As the sun crested the horizon, I stopped along a quiet stretch of a potholed two-lane road. The salt smell of the Gulf mixed with the organic tang of the marsh. Two sparrows and a rail were among my goals for the day. Seaside Sparrow is an uncommon to common year-round resident in coastal marshes. I expected little trouble seeing it. Finding a Nelson's Sharp-tailed Sparrow, a far less common winter resident along the upper and central Texas coast, would be the greater challenge.

I also hoped to find a Clapper Rail, a common coastal marsh resident. Rails are among the more difficult bird species to see or hear. They inhabit dense marsh vegetation, where they are often active at night. Secretive and shy, they rarely stray into the open. Rails can sometimes be drawn into sight by persistent playing of taped calls, but I had no interest in that tactic. To decrease the likelihood that birders, especially hard-core "listers," would be tempted to harass birds such as rails, the ABA listing rules specify that "heard only" species can be counted for Big Year and life lists.

Six rail species are normally observable in Texas: Yellow, Black, Clapper, King, and Virginia rails and Sora. On February 7, at the DuPont Wetland near Victoria, Ro Wauer and I had spied three Soras. The Hedges and I had studied three King Rails from a South Texas roadside on January 8. Persistence and patience had yielded an unobstructed twenty-second binocular view of a Virginia Rail on January 30, as it walked slowly along the border between the dense reeds and the water's edge at San Solomon Cienega in Balmorhea State Park. Seeing a Yellow Rail, a rare winter resident of upper and central coast marshes, would require a major effort since these birds do not vocalize while in Texas. The tiny, extraordinarily secretive Black Rail would be problematic, too, though hearing it in the summer was a distinct possibility at one of several sites traded among avid Texas birders.

Despite much searching, I found no Clapper Rails. I fared better with Seaside Sparrow. This species breeds from Massachusetts to Florida and along the Gulf Coast to Texas. Its winter range extends to the southernmost portions of the Texas coast. An investment of fifteen minutes of walking yielded good looks at two separate birds flying above the marsh. The second perched long enough for me to study it in my scope.

The Seaside Sparrow's appearance varies significantly with geographic location. Most ornithologists recognize nine subspecies. The "Dusky" Seaside Sparrow (now extinct) and the "Cape Sable" Seaside Sparrow have been regarded as distinct species in the past. My Texas birds were the "Louisiana" Seaside Sparrow subspecies, rather dark birds that breed along the Gulf from extreme western Florida to San Antonio Bay in East Texas.

After a fast-food lunch, I explored the 27,500 acres of the Anahuac National Wildlife Refuge, one of the best coastal marsh birding sites in Texas. Located adjacent to the arm of Galveston Bay known as East Bay, Anahuac NWR is managed primarily as a wintering site for ducks and geese, though birding is good all year. The land throughout the refuge is low and often wet and covered by *Spartina* grasses.

On Shoveler Pond Road, I visited a small migrant trap called the Willows, where a few healthy willow trees poke up from an otherwise treeless landscape. An alligator floated in a shallow pond. A quick circuit of the pond and trees yielded my year's first Northern Waterthrush, tracked down after I heard its hard "chink" call note. But there was no sign of the Palm Warbler that others had reported.

At the start of the 2.5-mile Shoveler Pond Loop, three Purple Gallinule swam in a reed-filled ditch. Migrants and residents crammed Shoveler Pond. From its rear edge, five Fulvous Whistling-Ducks stared at me and my scope. As I drove along the loop, two Least Bitterns stood in open view.

With the day moving toward midafternoon, returning to a coastal migrant trap seemed wise.

Driving south across the Texas 124 bridge that rises high above the Intracoastal Waterway, a birder gains an inkling of the view High Island presents to migrants weary from a Gulf crossing: a slightly higher piece of ground right at the coast, capped with mottes of dark green oak, hackberry, and tallow trees. These mottes, alive with the foods that birds crave, revitalize a migrant's fat stores.

Like many others, I turned left at the High Island Post Office, at the corner of Texas 124 and 5th Street. Parked cars lined the roadside and filled the lot at the Houston Audubon Society's Louis Smith Woods Sanctuary (aka Boy Scout Woods). I grabbed a departing birder's spot in the lot and walked the short distance into some of birding's most hallowed ground, arriving at 3:30 P.M. Since the reputation of High Island as one of the best migrant traps anywhere in the United States is deserved, birding there on a mid-April weekend was not a solitary experience. After paying for an annual pass, I reviewed the sightings list posted at the information booth and chatted with the volunteers. A typically varied assortment of migrants had been recorded prior to my arrival, including several species I still sought.

Two dozen people packed the bleachers near the information booth, all theoretically watching the nearby woods and a small pond created by a water drip. A family reunion–like atmosphere prevailed, the antithesis of a serious, hushed birding session. Several conversations were under way at all times, a couple of them uncommonly loud. It was a measure of the migrants' need for food and water that the cacophony from the bleachers did not bother the birds. While I was perusing this scene, a Yellow Warbler jumped into sight and onto my year list. He shared the stage with several Tennessee Warblers, a Kentucky Warbler, and multiple Indigo Buntings and Summer Tanagers.

Unhappy with the human noise level at the bleachers, I strolled along a wooden boardwalk, ambling through a space framed by tall trees and known as the Cathedral. High in the canopy and almost directly overhead, my year's first Golden-winged Warbler greeted me. The striking black throat and facial mask of this male grabbed my attention. To avoid straining my neck muscles by looking straight up, I lay down on the boardwalk planks. A Golden-winged Warbler is one of nature's finest, well worth additional effort for a good view. From a comfortable prone position, I relocated the bird, noting its powdery, golden crown. A broad stroke of the same delicious hue decorated each wing.

The afternoon was sunny and warm, with a moderate southerly breeze. No threatening weather was in sight or forecast. A strong influx of birds seemed unlikely anytime soon.

But at 5:15 P.M. the birding segued from fair to excellent, as though someone had simply flipped a switch. The diversity of this sudden activity dazzled everyone. For just over an hour, almost every tree in the Boy Scout Woods harbored migrants. Every birder could see numerous thrush, warbler, and vireo species without walking far or searching hard. Not surprisingly, the natural noise level hardly increased despite the influx of substantial numbers of birds. Though a few migrants uttered an occasional understated call note, nearly all remained silent, saving their voices for the breeding grounds.

A half hour after the arrival of this migrant wave, a particularly delightful sight appeared in a catalpa tree just a dozen feet from my eyes: a sumptuous male Golden-winged Warbler foraging with a vivid male Cerulean Warbler.

I partook of this High Island visual feast until, at 6:20 P.M., the majority of the migrants suddenly departed for points farther north and inland.

FOG SHROUDED THE COAST at dawn on Monday, April 17. I ventured down the Bolivar Peninsula, following Texas 87 along this narrow, twenty-seven-mile-long spit of land. Seven miles from High Island, near Gilchrist, a canal was cut between the Gulf of Mexico and East Bay, creating Rollover Pass. Depending on the tide and wind, birds congregate on the bay or Gulf side.

Seeing large numbers of birds on a bayside sandbar, I stopped. A Clapper Rail was in the open in the parking area, working along the seawall. Scanning the birds on the sandbar added Sandwich Tern and Black Skimmer to my year.

An hour later, at the southern end of the peninsula, I entered the Bolivar Flats Shorebird Sanctuary, owned by the Houston Audubon Society. This popular beach and Gulf-view site held, among others, thirty calling Short-billed Dowitchers, three Wilson's Plovers, and a single individual of the increasingly rare Piping Plover.

David and Mimi Wolf, the husband and wife team who had made my February Pineywoods weekend such a fine experience, had recently reported Nelson's Sharp-tailed Sparrow on Frenchtown Road, a narrow two-lane road that winds through marshes at the peninsula's southwest end. At noon, with my stomach grumbling, I walked along Frenchtown Road with water lapping over my sneakers every time a car passed and forced me onto the flooded shoulder. A half hour's effort produced excellent looks at the gray napes and ochre crown stripes of two Nelson's Sharp-tailed Sparrows low in the marsh grasses. I was especially pleased by this find. These sparrows would travel north soon.

Farther west on Frenchtown Road, I scanned ships inbound from the Gulf to Galveston Bay and several platforms near shore. A huge, white-headed bird sat high on a platform: a juvenile Magnificent Frigatebird.

Returning north along the peninsula, I found hordes of birds still occupying the bayside sandbar at Rollover Pass. Several plovers had joined the gulls, terns, peeps, and pelicans that had been present earlier. I searched for an American Golden-Plover among these new arrivals since I had yet to find this species during my Big Year. Though they mainly inhabit fields of short grass in migration, American

Golden-Plover are occasionally seen on coastal mud tracts. Of the birds at the pass, one struck me as a promising candidate. While I studied it, a car pulled up alongside mine. An older man clambered out, accompanied by a younger woman. The way they interacted, it seemed likely that she was his daughter.

"What do you see out there?" the man asked me as he set up a tripod and scope.

"Lots of stuff," I said. "I'm trying to figure out whether this plover could be an American Golden-Plover."

"Out there?"

"Yes."

"You're wasting your time. There aren't any American Golden-Plover out there."

His dismissive tone irritated me, though I knew he was likely correct. I continued to gaze at the plover, wanting to prove him wrong. I could not.

A birder familiar with the species can judge with relative ease whether a standing plover is an American Golden-Plover or a Black-bellied Plover. The American Golden-Plover is smaller, with a broader, more marked eyeline and a daintier bill. The greatest differences between these two species are revealed in flight. Black-bellied Plover show dark axillaries or "armpits" and a bright white rump; American Golden-Plover show smoky gray axillaries and a dark rump. My lack of familiarity with American Golden-Plover meant that I needed to see a bird fly to be sure of my identification.

Ten minutes passed before the man spoke to me again. "Want to see a Thayer's Gull?" he said.

Thayer's Gull is a rare bird, a Texas Review Species, and a tough identification to make with confidence on nonadult birds. It is closely related to the Herring Gull, and many birders have misidentified other gull species as Thayer's Gull.

"Sure, I'd love to see a Thayer's Gull." It was the truth, of course.

"Then take a look in my scope," he said. "It's standing there next to a couple Herring Gulls." He waved vaguely in the direction of the sandbar. "I've seen thousands of Thayer's Gulls. No doubt about this bird."

I looked through his scope. The bird at field center was certainly something different, with Thayer's Gull being a real possibility. While concentrating on the gull's image in the scope, I realized that I might know this man, not personally but by reputation. I studied the gull for as long as possible, fearing it might fly before I was confident of its identity. Then I took my eye away from the scope and introduced myself.

"I'm Guy," the man said, shaking my hand.

I considered this response for a minute. I was fairly certain I had seen his photograph in one or more birding publications. "You're Guy McCaskie, aren't you?" I said.

"Yes, I am."

"Good to meet you." I forgave his gruff dismissal of my American Golden-Plover dreams. Guy McCaskie has been an active birder in California for decades and is one of that state's birding pioneers. We enjoyed the cooperative Thayer's Gull for a long time and showed it to many others, including a British tour group I had encountered several times over the weekend.

MY LAST MORNING ON THE COAST, Tuesday, April 18, dawned foggy, too. On two previous visits to the Willows at Anahuac NWR, I had failed to locate a Palm Warbler that had been seen by many others. But persistence is a key ingredient of a Big Year. With the fog, it would not be possible to search shortgrass fields for American Golden-Plover, Upland Sandpiper, or anything likely to be more distant than a few tens of feet.

So I began my day at the Willows. After walking half of this small patch of habitat, I found a Palm Warbler foraging in the trees, merrily pumping its tail, as individuals of this species often do. The bird was an individual of the "Western" subspecies of Palm Warbler, with a whitish streaked midsection, quite different from the solid yellow of a spring "Yellow" Palm Warbler.

As I was departing Anahuac NWR, at the intersection of FM 1985 and the refuge's entry road, a rare white rainbow, or fogbow, adorned the western sky. The lack of color in a fogbow is caused by the very small diameter of the water drops in a fog, generally less than a thousandth of an inch.

Later, in the afternoon, as I headed west toward Houston's Hobby Airport and my flight home, I was cheered by the results of my first spring coast trip: sixty-two new species in just three full and two partial birding days.

MY DAUGHTER JENNIFER sang with the community choir at a sunrise service on the grounds of the Fort Davis National Historic Site on Easter Sunday, April 23. After the service and a magnificent breakfast, I drove to the Davis Mountains Preserve, twenty-six

Prothonotary Warbler. Drawing by Kelly B. Bryan.

miles north of Fort Davis, where I had arranged to meet my friend Kelly Bryan. We wanted to determine whether the Buff-breasted Flycatcher had returned to its Road Canyon haunts of the previous year.

On May 3, 1999, West Texas Nature Conservancy biologist John Karges and a group visiting from Oregon had discovered a single male Buff-breasted Flycatcher in Wolf Den Canyon, adjacent to Road Canyon. After Kelly and I and others relocated the bird on May 5, it had been lost until Kelly, Greg Lasley, and Ro Wauer rediscovered the bird and its nest in June in Road Canyon. This was the first Buff-breasted Flycatcher to nest in Texas, and the first photographed record of this species for the state, elevating the species from the TBRC's Presumptive List to the official Texas State List.

On Easter morning, I reached Road Canyon and found a note telling me that Kelly had indeed found a Buff-breasted Flycatcher near the territory and nest of the previous breeding season. Thrilled by the news, I hiked in to look for myself.

Buff-breasted Flycatcher is a small, active bird, the easiest *Empidonax* flycatcher to identify, with whitish wing bars, pale buff on the throat and the breast, grayish white undertail coverts and belly, and a fairly narrow, small bill, uniformly light orange underneath. A half hour of increasingly anxious searching finally resulted in my finding a singing adult male Buff-breasted Flycatcher.

I caught up to Kelly at the entrance to Tobe Canyon. We bushwhacked up-canyon through a dense woodland and encountered a diverse foraging flock of migrants and breeders, adding Western Tanager, Hepatic Tanager, Hermit Warbler, Townsend's Warbler, and Cassin's Vireo (#368) to my year list in one quick sweep.

With spring's help, my Big Year was progressing well.

## chapter 12

The Road to Four
Hundred Species

Multiple spring trips to the coast had always been part of my plan. Though migration continues from late March through mid-May, the species mix varies considerably over these weeks. If I concentrated all my coastal effort into just one or two weeks, I would miss many species. Yellow-throated Warbler, for example, is most likely to be seen early in spring migration, but Bay-breasted Warbler travels across the coast later.

I was home for only eight days before I left again for the coast. Since this trip would cover more than two thousand miles, and I did not need off-road capability, I drove a new, comfortable minivan. I departed the observatory on Wednesday morning, April 26, with a pile of compact discs and cassette tapes, steeled for hours of driving but looking forward to more than a week of birding.

My first day was spent traveling to the Hill Country, stopping only to see a Black-capped Vireo in a canyon east of Fort Lancaster on Texas 290 in Crockett County. My final destination was the Lost Canyon resort, owned and operated by Tom and Judy Taylor, whom I had met on a Big Bend birding seminar the previous fall. The Taylors had offered to put me up for the night if I would do an astronomy program for local students. I readily agreed.

My evening program was attended by two dozen enthusiastic young people full of questions about science in general and astronomy in particular. Happily, I did not get to sleep until nearly midnight.

Tom and Judy gave me a unique place to stay: "Treetops," a well-appointed cabin nestled against and anchored to the trunk of a colossal tree. My cabin's floor was a dozen feet above the ground, and its window views looked out on the surrounding canopy. In this marvelous place, I awoke at three in the morning and lay in bed enjoying the nighttime sounds filtering through the open windows. A good fraction of the nocturnal voices I heard belonged to Chuck-will's-widows.

Golden-cheeked Warbler. Drawing by Kelly B. Bryan.

A visit to Garner State Park the following morning and a scramble up a steep slope clothed in junipers brought another highly sought Texas prize: a singing male Golden-cheeked Warbler.

NEW YEAR BIRDS sometimes dropped into my lap, so to speak, at odd places and times. The next afternoon, I roamed the backroads of Central Texas on my way to Corpus Christi. Fifteen miles south of Sabinal, near the Uvalde-Zavala County border, I stopped at a temporary red light on Ranch Road 187. The next half mile of RR 187 was under construction. The light controlled traffic through a single-lane construction zone.

But the construction equipment was parked. Not a soul was in sight. No other cars were on the road. As I dutifully waited for the light to turn green, a cowbird perched atop the red light. Even without binoculars, its silhouette told me it was not a Brown-headed Cowbird. Rather, it was my year's first Bronzed Cowbird.

Eventually, both the Bronzed Cowbird and I tired of the unnecessary wait. The cowbird departed skyward; I drove through the red light.

My first stop in Corpus Christi was Packery Channel, a county park and housing development located on Padre Island. Packery Channel does not look promising, and the roar of traffic from the nearby four-lane highway is omnipresent. But one can scan the Intracoastal Waterway for shorebirds and waders and bird the remnant coastal oak mottes around the houses. During migration, Packery Channel can be stunning.

I started at an oak motte adjacent to the visitors' information center along the highway. Local birders had permission to run a long hose from an outside spigot at the center into a natural depression in the motte. With the availability of water, this depression became a small pond and a favored stopping point for migrants. On Thursday afternoon, I entered the motte alone and found three low, comfortable chairs that had been left at an ideal viewing location near the pond. I chose a seat and waited.

An adult male Blackpoll Warbler—solid black cap, white cheeks, streaked white underparts—stopped for a bath. Continued patience also yielded several minutes during which three of the four normally occurring migrant thrushes (Swainson's Thrush, Wood Thrush, Veery) were simultaneously in sight.

As the day waned, the woods were increasingly busy with birds. Several species were just beginning to reach Texas in numbers. I spied a magnificent male Magnolia Warbler, and a female Bay-breasted Warbler hopped into view at the pond's edge.

THE CENTERPIECE OF THIS TRIP was a long weekend on the Kenedy Ranch, sixty miles south of Corpus Christi. Thousands of acres in extent, the ranch's habitat includes artesian wells that create wetlands among the grassy plains, sand dunes, open grass prairie and live oak mottes. In previous springs these mottes had yielded the best migratory birding I had experienced, with warblers, thrushes, vireos, and flycatchers swarming through the trees. In addition to migrants, Kenedy Ranch features several hard-to-find Texas breeding birds: Botteri's Sparrow, Audubon's Oriole, Tropical Parula, Ferruginous Pygmy-Owl, and Northern Beardless-Tyrannulet.

Jim and Phoebe Lou Sealy of Dallas, architect and artist, had organized this three-day weekend. In 1998, through Brush Freeman, I had stumbled into an association with Jim and Phoebe Lou's annual spring trips to the Kenedy Ranch, a bit of good fortune. As on my previous Sealy outings, Brush Freeman and Petra Hockey, who had surveyed much of this land over the years, were our guides.

At midmorning our group assembled at the ranch's Turcotte gate, south of Sarita and a busy northbound Border Patrol checkpoint on Texas 77. After signing in with ranch security, Brush and Petra led us down a dirt and caliche road toward our camp. Along the way, our caravan stopped to scan flocks of migrating shorebirds and waterfowl.

Halfway to camp Brush and Petra slowed, then stopped, having heard a singing Botteri's Sparrow, a plain-breasted, relatively large sparrow. In Texas, this species is a bird of the coastal plain. During breeding season, territorial males often sit in low bushes or trees while vocalizing. Their distinctive song with its "bouncing ball" lilt carries well. Out of our cars, we soon heard the sparrow's musical notes, but it took several minutes to find the bird, even with twenty eager and expert pairs of eyes searching with binoculars. Not surprisingly, the sparrow was finally spotted sitting in a low bush.

San Pedro Camp, our comfortable home for the weekend, was originally built in the nineteenth century, before the ranch was purchased by Captain Mifflin Kenedy. We spent little time at camp, though, simply dumping our bags into our assigned rooms before organizing ourselves into the minimum number of vehicles.

As in previous springs at the ranch, I joined Jimmy Sealy and others in the back of Brush's pickup truck. Several advantages accrued from my choice of seat. Brush's pickup would always be the first vehicle in our caravan. We would inevitably see some birds that would disappear before those behind us could see them. Also, since Brush and Petra knew the ranch intimately and rode in the cab, those of us riding with them had continual access to our guides.

I could also enjoy the irreverent boys-in-the-woods atmosphere of Brush's truck bed. Jimmy Sealy, for example, was always upbeat and entertaining, an unapologetic, effusive American male progressing from midlife toward retirement. In an e-mail to trip participants prior to our arrival at the ranch, Jimmy described himself to those who had yet to meet him: "I'm short, fat, look like Boss Hog, have a full white beard, and will be wearing the best looking gimme cap you have ever seen. I'll have some Zeiss binoculars hanging around my neck, will most likely be looking over your shoulder for birds, and my right hand will be slightly cupped, as though there should be a beer in it, and there may be."

Hurricane Bret had hammered many of the Kenedy Ranch oak mottes the previous August. Bret had formed in the southern Gulf of Mexico, then moved slowly north along the Mexican coast, rapidly intensifying into a powerful hurricane. Landfall occurred on August 22, 1999, at the Kenedy Ranch. Winds of 125 miles per hour lashed the land, uprooting large and small trees. It was now difficult to walk through many wooded areas that had once been accessible.

By late April, Ferruginous Pygmy-Owls have completed their breeding cycle and are not very vocal. At two oak mottes Brush employed a taped call, working to elicit a response so that we could find the owl.

But no calls broke the silence. Later, at what Brush had described as our "last chance" site, a Ferruginous Pygmy-Owl responded. The group found the owl being tormented by a Northern Mockingbird near the top of a half-dead tree.

On Saturday we spent every sunlit hour ranging from our camp to the Laguna Madre, where brilliant white salt pans hurt our eyes at midday. Snowy Plovers called these salt pans home, and we saw several chicks.

We stopped for lunch at an oak motte that had always been productive, especially for warblers. During lunch, Ernst Jasek found a Canada Warbler, a beautiful adult male. Though I expected to see more before leaving the ranch, as we had in past years, I did not. I saw but one more during my Big Year, in late September, also on the Kenedy Ranch.

In the afternoon, while birding in a mesquite and oak habitat bounded by towering sand dunes, Brush called to me: "Mark, get over here! Black-billed Cuckoo!" I had yet to encounter this species, a relatively rare Texas migrant. Eric Carpenter, Brush, and I surrounded the tree where the cuckoo had been sighted, approaching slowly. Over the next several minutes, we realized that it had somehow vanished. This was my closest encounter with the species all year. On this occasion, I had been no more than seventy-five feet from one. But that was not good enough to count it!

Our Kenedy Ranch weekend produced many migrants and all of the expected specialties except Tropical Parula, which I would have to find elsewhere. After departing the ranch on Sunday afternoon, I returned to the upper Texas coast.

ON TUESDAY, MAY 2, I awoke at 4:30 A.M. to thunder and heavy rain. Since rain showers would clearly prevail on the upper coast throughout much of the day, I modified my plans and targeted a shorebird species in which annual migration spans a good fraction of the southern and northern hemispheres: Hudsonian Godwit.

On the way to their arctic breeding grounds, Hudsonian Godwits migrate across the central and eastern Great Plains of North America. The visibility window for this species in Texas is restricted to late April and the first two weeks of May. After breeding, almost the entire Hudsonian Godwit population (ten thousand birds) gathers along Canada's South Hudson and James bays, then flies nonstop to South America over the western Atlantic to winter in Argentina. Given their fall migration route, a spring miss would likely be a year miss.

The East Bayou tract at Anahuac National Wildlife Refuge seemed a suitable place to search for a Hudsonian Godwit. Most of the land held shallow water, fine shorebird habitat. The rain had not eased, the wind was blowing, and the air was uncomfortably cool. An elevated metal-roofed shelter built for birders at East Bayou kept me reasonably dry, though it was impossible to avoid the wind-blown precipitation. The conditions argued for steaming hot chocolate, a good book, and a warm room, but I stayed at my outdoor post.

After forty minutes of watching the usual suspects, I saw a tall, darkish bird land sixty yards to my left. In my scope I saw a finely barred chestnut belly and breast and a curved, bicolored bill: Hudsonian Godwit! Another soon arrived, a female, flight exposing her white uppertail coverts. They still had a long journey ahead of them, but they had made my day by spending a few minutes with me in the rain at Anahuac.

AS DAWN STRUGGLED THROUGH a low gray overcast on Wednesday morning, my feet were the first on High Island's Smith Oaks trails. Heavy rain showers again accompanied me. Few people did. The birding hordes that had descended upon High Island on every April weekday and weekend were largely gone. Many birders apparently believe that the first day of May brings down the curtain on the spectacle of spring migration, though much remained to pass.

Given the successes of this and earlier trips, my focus shifted from migrating warblers, thrushes, and vireos to flycatchers of the genus *Empidonax*, several of which were not yet on my year list. These flycatchers, often referred to simply as "empids," are a headache to most observers since they are difficult to identify reliably to species. All empids are relatively drab. Much of their plumage is gray, tinted with varying amounts of olive, brown, or yellow. Their wingbars can be bold or weak, depending on wear and molt. Many show eye-rings that can deceive as easily as they can help with an identification.

Nine empid species might appear on a Texas year list: Acadian, Alder, Willow, Least, Hammond's, Dusky, Gray, Yellow-bellied, and Cordilleran Flycatcher. The three *Empidonax* flycatchers that breed in numbers in Texas—Acadian, Gray, and Cordilleran—are the easiest to identify. They can be found singing on territories in appropriate habitat. I had already discovered a wintering Gray Flycatcher in mid-January in the Big Bend Ranch State Park. Adding Cordilleran Flycatcher would require a hike into a western mountain canyon between mid-May and early September. This would be straightforward. And our Kenedy Ranch group had discovered two migrating Acadian Flycatchers on April 29, perhaps en route to suitable East Texas breeding territories.

The remaining six empids—Alder, Willow, Least, Hammond's, Dusky, and Yellow-bellied—can be seen in Texas only as nonsinging migrants. Their identification demands a careful accumulation of evidence. It cannot rely on any one trait. The best source for learning *Empidonax* flycatcher identification is chapter 24, "The Empidonax Flycatchers," in Kenn Kaufman's *A Field Guide to Advanced Birding* (Boston: Houghton Mifflin, 1990). I carry a reduced copy of this chapter with me in the field when empids are likely to be about.

Kaufman counsels observers to note the following characteristics of a migrating empid: (1) bill size and shape; (2) the color and pattern on the underside of the bill; that is, on the lower mandible; (3) the distance that the bird's primary flight feathers extend beyond the other wing feathers when the bird is at rest; that is, the "primary extension;" (4) the shape and width of the bird's eye-ring; and (5) any vocalization.

Until the 1970s, Alder and Willow flycatchers were considered one species: Traill's Flycatcher. They are visually identical, and even when the details described can be seen well, it is still impossible to separate Alder and Willow flycatchers by sight alone. Their voices, however, are distinctive. Voice is the ingredient that permits migrant *Empidonax* flycatchers to be identified. With few exceptions, migrants do not sing.

But they sometimes respond with call notes when prompted by a recording of their species' songs or calls.

Success with this method varies from day to day and bird to bird. That Wednesday morning at Smith Oaks, I encountered a dozen empids. Because of their pale, wide lower mandibles, indistinct eye-rings, and long primary extensions, several of these were clearly Traill's Flycatchers. I played Alder and Willow Flycatcher songs and calls for each of these birds, but they refused to respond. Finally, near lunch, an empid agreed to a short conversation, replying to my tape's exhortations with an Alder's loud "pip" and generously repeating this note three times.

After sunset, as I left the Smith Oaks parking lot, I spotted an Olive-sided Flycatcher perched on a wire. With this bird, on May 3, I reached the first goal I had contemplated for my Big Year. This flycatcher was the four hundredth species I had seen in Texas in the year 2000.

MEANWHILE, AS DUSK APPROACHED on May 2, Charles Brower had discovered a Black-whiskered Vireo, a Texas Review Species, at the Quintana Neotropical Bird Sanctuary near Freeport, along the coast. Several birders searched for this rare vireo the next day. Some saw it; some did not. I toyed with the idea of heading south to Quintana, though the Galveston traffic was unpredictable and might cost me a lot of time.

I had fared well through spring migration, but my Big Year lacked several nonmigrants that could be found in East Texas: Louisiana Waterthrush, Prairie Warbler, and Swallow-tailed Kite. Since the Black-whiskered Vireo's previous Texas visits had almost invariably been short, investing time in a trip to Quintana did not seem likely to yield a look at this vireo. After much debate with myself, I opted to go after the warbler, waterthrush, and kite. Though they would be in Texas until at least mid-July, it was unlikely that I could return to East Texas before then.

To further complicate my next move, another Review Species, Mangrove Cuckoo, was discovered in a Corpus Christi yard on

Wednesday, May 3. And I absolutely had to be home by Friday night May 5.

DESPITE ITS NAME, Prairie Warbler nests in young second-growth scrub, such as pine stands that are regenerating after clear-cuts. At dawn on Thursday morning I was at the south end of Fire Tower Road, near Silsbee, north of the coast and Beaumont. A singing male Prairie Warbler greeted me at the first regenerating pine cut I visited. This instant success was cheering and allowed me to move on immediately to my next target.

Swallow-tailed Kite is a majestic North American bird with graceful flight, a deeply forked dark tail, black and white wings, and white head and body. These kites migrate in small numbers across all parts of the state except the Panhandle and the Trans-Pecos. In 1994 and 1995, a pair nested in East Texas, in Tyler County, the first documented Texas nesting record since 1911.

In 2000, an apparent Swallow-tailed Kite pair had been seen in and around the town of Liberty, north and east of Houston. I had visited Liberty twice during my mid-April upper Texas coast trip but had failed to see any Swallow-tailed Kites. Several people had reported seeing them from a Wal-Mart parking lot in Liberty, my next stop. Here my gaze alternated between the sky, watching for the kites, and my surroundings, monitoring manic consumers who might run me over as they charged around the parking lot in their hefty sport utility vehicles and pickup trucks.

Thirty minutes at Wal-Mart yielded nothing. Two other suggested sites—the parking lot of a Mormon Church a few blocks north of Wal-Mart and the stretch of U.S. 90 between Liberty and Dayton—also failed me, though I added Mississippi Kite at the U.S. 90 bridge spanning the Trinity River.

At noon I returned to the Liberty Mormon Church site for the third time that day. I was standing outside my car eating a spartan lunch when a Swallow-tailed Kite, unmistakable even to the naked eye, crested a line of trees to the north, providing a one-minute window of opportunity. Less than ten minutes later, two Swallow-tailed Kites soared above the same line of trees, chasing each other.

ON THURSDAY EVENING I faced a decision. Should I stay around High Island for more migration birding, perhaps finding a Black-billed Cuckoo or a Bobolink? Or should I chase the Quintana Black-whiskered Vireo or the Corpus Christi Mangrove Cuckoo? The time seemed ripe for a roll of the dice. A check of my Texas road atlas clinched the decision. Quintana was closer than I thought. If everything went perfectly, I might yet see the vireo that evening, which would allow me to continue south to Corpus Christi and try for the Mangrove Cuckoo on Friday morning.

Despite a wait for the ferry to Galveston and a minor traffic jam near Freeport, I was at the Quintana sanctuary looking for the vireo at 5:30 P.M. Surprisingly, the only birders present were an elderly couple. The woman related to me, multiple times, how she had seen the vireo near the sanctuary's fountain just twenty minutes before I had appeared. While she sat calmly on a bench, her husband and I searched every nook and cranny of this small site. But the Black-whiskered Vireo would not cooperate. The elderly couple left; I persevered, without success, until it was too dark to see.

On the phone that evening, Brush Freeman told me about his multiple failed attempts to see a Black-whiskered Vireo in Texas. This was not encouraging. I considered giving up on the vireo, trying for the cuckoo.

But at dawn I returned to the Quintana sanctuary. Texas birders John Gee and Carol Edwards, and Ron Weeks, a local, were already there. Before too long, we heard the Black-whiskered Vireo singing its simple four-note song. This buoyed my spirits. John saw the vireo first, at head height. We chased it through low shrubs for several minutes before managing to see it well. With just a quick glance, one could easily mistake a Black-whiskered Vireo for a Red-eyed Vireo. But there was no doubting this individual: its diagnostic malar (chin) stripe was dark and bold.

I had to pass on an attempt for the Mangrove Cuckoo, a tough decision, but I could not delay my return home. John and Carol had seen this bird the previous evening. I would later learn that they were the last persons to see this rarity. A 654-mile driving marathon brought me to my front door at 10:30 P.M. on Friday night, May 5. I dropped into my bed and was soon lost to the world.

## chapter 13

West Texas Bounty

The Davis Mountains are perhaps the best kept hummingbird secret in the United States. The hummingbird diversity in these remote West Texas mountains competes favorably with that of southeastern Arizona. Nine species are seen annually in the Davis Mountains: Black-chinned (breeder), Broad-tailed (breeder), Magnificent (probable breeder), Blue-throated (probable breeder), Lucifer's (probable breeder), Rufous (migrant), Calliope (migrant), Anna's (migrant), and Ruby-throated (migrant). The peak fall hummingbird migration months of July and August are the best time to sample the region's riches. In addition, each year brings multiple rarities such as Costa's, Broad-billed, White-eared, or Berylline hummingbirds.

An efficient way to study these gems is to spend time at someone's hummingbird feeders. A couple of hours at well-tended feeders will yield more detailed hummingbird views than an observer could possibly accumulate in a year's field work. Watching at feeders is the best way, for example, to learn the subtleties of female and immature hummingbird identification, especially in late summer when most adult males have left the United States.

On May 18, Rex Barrick and I took comfortable seats on the porch of his McDonald Observatory home, at the base of Mount Locke, to census the hummingbirds visiting his feeders. In previous years, I had kept as many as seven hummingbird feeders at my house. But my Big Year had taken a toll on these habits. Rex, however, had been religious about his feeders, keeping them clean and full. The hummingbirds repaid his diligence by visiting en masse. Hordes of Black-chinned Hummingbirds fought for access to the nectar he provided, mixed according to the usual prescription: four cups of water to every cup of sugar. A dozen or more Broad-tailed Hummingbirds insisted on taking their turns, too, the adult males advertising their arrival with high-pitched wing whistles. Rex had recently seen an adult male Magnificent Hummingbird at his feeders, but this large, dark hummer did not show.

Two adult male Lucifer's Hummingbirds zoomed in for several tastes of sugar water. With their flaring purple gorgets, forked tails, and curved bills (which ornithologists insist on calling "decurved"), they are hard to miss. For decades, this hummingbird was considered very rare in the Davis Mountains, a specialty of the Big Bend. But over the past several years, Lucifer's Hummingbird sightings have become routine in the Davis Mountains from mid-May through mid-September. This change in status probably reflects an increase in the number of feeders and observers rather than a change in this hummingbird's range.

Rex and I tried to estimate how many birds were visiting his feeders. Each of his five feeders had six feeder ports. There were spans of several minutes when all thirty ports were occupied, with additional birds in the nearby trees, impatiently waiting.

In August, 1998, Brent Ortego gave me a lesson in estimating bird numbers at feeders when he visited my observatory home to band hummingbirds. I had told Brent that my hummingbird feeders were hosting perhaps ten birds total. Brent assured me that my estimate was conservative. In a morning's work, Brent and his assistant banded twenty-six hummingbirds at my feeders, and they could have banded more.

IN THE YEAR 2000, as he had done several times in past years, Ro Wauer organized a census of Big Bend National Park's most famous bird, the Colima Warbler. By mid-April, these rather drab gray warblers arrive in the high Chisos from Mexico. They settle into breeding by mid-May, when the census is conducted.

Up well before the sun, I drove to Big Bend NP on Friday, May 19. Mark Elwonger and I were assigned to census lower Pine Canyon. The first 1.4 miles of the trail through this canyon follow an old Jeep road through a healthy, mid-elevation desert grassland dotted with numerous sotol. The Jeep road becomes a hiking trail that then enters a pine-oak woodland. After 0.6 of a mile, the trail ends at a tall cliff wall. A thin stream of water flows over this cliff from upper Pine Canyon for a good fraction of the year, nourishing the pocket of woodland habitat where the Colima Warbler thrives.

The standard "Death March" route for those seeking the Colima Warbler in Big Bend is a two-thousand-foot ascent from the Chisos Basin to Boot Canyon, where the warbler is nearly guaranteed from mid-April through early September. This seven- to ten-mile round-trip endurance test requires much sweating, huffing, puffing, and grunting and has exhausted many hikers.

Few birders realize that the Colima Warbler can be reliably found in lower Pine Canyon. Reaching this canyon's woodland requires a round-trip hike of barely four miles with little elevation change. Lower Pine Canyon's difficulty is not the hike, but reaching the trailhead. Though one expert Texas birder has driven his late-model Lincoln Continental to the Pine Canyon trailhead, this is not recommended. High clearance is always advisable for this six-mile-long, variably rough dirt and rock track: two miles of the Glenn Springs Road and four miles of the increasingly bumpy Pine Canyon Road. After summer thunderstorms, the road sometimes cannot be safely negotiated without four-wheel-drive.

On Friday morning at dawn, Mark Elwonger's vehicle, parked at the Pine Canyon trailhead campsite, was empty. I proceeded double-time across the desert grassland and caught up with him in the first bit of the woodland. We birded slowly, looking and listening for Colima Warblers. In our first pass through the woods, walking toward the pouroff, we found no Colima Warblers, a surprising result.

In the vicinity of the pouroff, we heard and then saw three Cordilleran Flycatchers, the park's only breeding *Empidonax* flycatcher. An adult male Varied Bunting foraged nearby, and several migrants were still moving through, including Wilson's and MacGillivray's warblers, Olive-sided Flycatchers, and several Dusky Flycatchers. Working our way back through the woodland to the desert grassland, we encountered two Colima Warbler pairs, a typical census result for lower Pine Canyon.

At his campsite, Mark made us lunch and advised me regarding the pursuit of two difficult Texas species: Long-eared Owl and Black Rail. After lunch, the desert warmth combined with our full stomachs and the after-effects of a couple beers to induce weariness. We both took a siesta, nodding out for an hour.

MY OBSERVATORY RESPONSIBILITIES had barely allowed me to escape for the Colima Warbler census. With little time to prepare, I had made no provision for camping or a motel room. So on Friday afternoon, after exiting Pine Canyon, I stopped at the park's Panther Junction Visitor Center and called ahead to the Chisos Mountains Lodge, hoping to reserve a room. There were no vacancies. This should not have surprised me. The Panther Junction parking lot was nearly filled with vehicles and tourists from states near and far.

After I hung up the pay phone, I started back to my car and saw Mark Flippo at the visitor center entrance. Mark is a park ranger and naturalist and the person who knows the most about the park's birds these days. I waved; Mark did not see me and went inside. I turned and followed, but once I was inside the center, I could not find Mark.

Every birder visiting Big Bend should stop at Panther Junction to check the recent sightings book. Visitors report bird, butterfly, black bear, and mountain lion sightings on three- by five-inch "Natural History Report" cards. Park personnel file these in plastic holders in a three-ring binder. Reports for the last month can be reviewed by asking for the binder, which is usually sitting on a shelf behind the counter.

Since I could not find Mark Flippo, and the registration and sales counter was mobbed, getting to the bird sightings book would take a while. So I passed, wanting to get on the road to Study Butte, a small town just outside the western entrance to the park, where I planned to find a room and take a shower. As I was about to get into my parked Jeep, my friends Marc and Maryann Eastman arrived in their truck, ready for the next day's Colima Warbler census. We visited then parted ways, the Eastmans heading into the visitor center as I set out for Study Butte.

The Eastmans found Mark Flippo behind the Panther Junction counter. He took Marc and Maryann into the garden behind the center and within seconds had showed them an astonishingly tame adult male Black-throated Blue Warbler. A rare bird everywhere in Texas and a very rare bird in the Big Bend, Black-throated Blue Warbler was a species that could elude me the entire year. This particular warbler, a late migrant, resided at Panther Junction from Thursday, May 18, through Sunday, May 21. I was within a few yards of this bird on several occasions but did not know of its presence.

Almost all of my fellow participants in the Colima Warbler census saw this Black-throated Blue Warbler, but I did not see any of them in the park after they had seen the warbler. Mark Flippo reported that the bird flew right into the visitor center once while chasing a moth. Park personnel had to chase it back outside! Ironically, the last Black-throated Blue Warbler reported in the park had been one I saw at the Window Trail trailhead on May 4, 1997.

ON SUNDAY, MAY 21, Kelly Bryan organized a hike onto the Nature Conservancy's Davis Mountains Preserve. Kelly's long-time friend Tony Gallucci was visiting West Texas with Erik Breden, a fellow Kerrville resident. We walked the trail to the Mount Livermore summit at 8,300 feet under partly cloudy skies, seeing and hearing many of the high elevation species we sought. As the day warmed, small cumulus puffs grew ever higher. Thunderstorms seemed inevitable. Near the summit, we rested and ate lunch, then started back down the trail.

While Mount Livermore's rocky cap, Baldy, still loomed directly above us, Kelly noticed an unusual flycatcher swooping in and out of a grove of gnarled, wind-bent oaks anchored in the talus slope. The bird's apparently large size, long tail, and peaked crest soon grabbed everyone's attention and had us all thinking that it might be a Greater Pewee.

We moved closer without creating a disturbance. At twenty-five to thirty yards, Kelly prepared to play a tape of the Greater Pewee's song, hoping to encourage vocalization of this species' well-known "José Maria" song. But the bird darted out of the oaks one last time and disappeared over the Mount Livermore summit to the west or southwest. We hurried around to the far west side of the trail but could not relocate the bird.

Greater Pewee is a fairly common resident in the wooded southern mountains of Arizona. It is widespread in the Mexican highlands but is a Review Species in Texas. Each year, a few individuals are found in the Chisos or the Davis mountains, normally during migration.

Increasingly threatening weather and our exposed position curtailed our search. A nonvocalizing Greater Pewee observation of relatively short duration is tricky. As we hiked down, I studied the abundant Western Wood-Pewees at observer-to-bird distances similar to those we had encountered with the putative Greater Pewee. Based on these observations and a length of six inches for a Western Wood-Pewee, I estimated our interesting flycatcher at 7.5 to 8.0 inches in length.

The bird's head, face, nape, back, and wings were moderate to dark gray, paler at the throat and on the lower belly. The bird lacked wingbars and sported a notable crest. It had a fairly large bill, broad at the base. My one good but short view of the bill had revealed a dark upper mandible and, most important, a fairly bright orange or orange-yellow lower mandible without a dark tip or base. After much discussion, Kelly, Tony, Erik, and I concluded this bird had indeed been a Greater Pewee.

Many rare birds have been recorded on the Davis Mountains Preserve over the past several years. Everyone visiting the preserve enters with the hope that something rare will come their way. It often does. Erik, Tony, Kelly, and I were elated to have seen a Greater Pewee.

MY FRIEND MARYANN EASTMAN called me at home during lunch on Thursday, May 25, with the thrilling news that a Berylline

Hummingbird was at their Davis Mountains feeders, the first record of this species in Texas in the spring. I hurriedly left the house with my camera and binoculars.

Berylline Hummingbird is a fairly common resident in the western and southern highlands of Mexico, El Salvador, and Honduras. Its first recorded appearance in the United States occurred in 1964. Since then, individuals have been discovered almost every year in the mountains of southeastern Arizona, where it has even nested on several occasions.

A single sight record from August 8, 1991, by a reliable observer in Big Bend National Park's lower Juniper Canyon placed this species on the TBRC's Presumptive Species List. Since no photographs were obtained, however, Berylline Hummingbird could not be on the official Texas State List until such documentation, or a specimen, was obtained from a later record. Kelly Bryan and others photographed a Berylline Hummingbird that visited the Eastmans' feeders from August 17 until September 4, 1997. These photographs elevated Berylline Hummingbird to the official Texas State List.

After I arrived at the Eastmans' home on May 25, 2000, Marc, Maryann, and I saw no sign of the Berylline Hummingbird for more than an hour. We stationed ourselves at strategic points around the porch and kept a continuous watch. We feared the bird might have left. But then, at 2:20 P.M., it returned to a feeder directly in front of me: a striking medium-sized hummingbird, somewhat larger than the Broad-tailed and Black-chinned hummingbirds but smaller than a Magnificent Hummingbird. The Berylline Hummingbird displayed a gorgeous emerald green throat, upper belly, upper back, and head. The dull dirty brown on its lower belly and flanks transitioned to mottled gray-white at the undertail coverts. In full sun, the wings showed a bright rusty brown hue. The slightly curved bill was mostly black with a bit of dull red at its base.

The Berylline Hummingbird visited Marc and Maryann's feeders throughout the afternoon, though at widely varying intervals. Sometimes it was in view for several minutes, perching quietly on a nearby bare tree branch in between quick visits to a feeder for sips of nectar. At other times, we saw the bird only for a few moments as it swiftly arrived, sipped briefly, and zoomed off. A male Broad-tailed Hummingbird fought it for feeder access on several occasions. Though I obtained several good color slides of the Berylline Hummingbird, these birds are so quick that I also obtained several fine shots of empty feeders.

## chapter 14

Late Spring in the Rio Grande Valley

On Friday, May 26, I drove my daughter to a late morning hair appointment in Alpine, forty miles from the observatory, then attended her eighth grade graduation in Fort Davis. After the graduation reception, I sped to the Midland Airport and flew to Harlingen and the Lower Rio Grande Valley. Madge Lindsay, who had hosted the Hedges and me in early January, was visiting family in California and had given me use of her Weslaco home for the Memorial Day weekend.

I had not visited the Valley since early January. Though that trip had been fruitful, it had been impossible to see every Rio Grande Valley specialty in just two full and two partial days in the field.

Ornithologist Tim Brush had offered to meet me at 6:30 on Saturday morning at the Santa Ana National Wildlife Refuge. Tim moved from New Jersey to the Lower Rio Grande Valley in 1991 to take a faculty position at University of Texas–Pan American. His research interests are the birds that use the riparian forest, thorn scrub, and aquatic habitats along the Lower Rio Grande. Fortunately for me and others, Tim has always enjoyed the interaction between amateurs and professionals in field ornithology.

My alarm buzzed me from slumber on Saturday morning, but the previous long day had taken its toll. I inadvertently fell back asleep for a few minutes, eventually leaping out of bed with little time left. On my way to Santa Ana, I missed the turn into the refuge because of my haste and unfamiliarity with the area. When I finally rolled into the refuge's parking lot at 6:50 A.M., I was relieved to find Tim still there, calm and unworried. After I apologized for my tardiness, we headed through the entrance on a warm, cloudy, humid morning. A slight breeze ruffled the lush subtropical foliage.

The first order of the day was a search for the Gray-crowned Yellowthroat that had been a resident at Santa Ana since April 13. This species is widespread in Mexico and Central America. Until the end of the nineteenth century, Gray-crowned Yellowthroat had been resident and fairly common in the Rio Grande Valley of extreme South Texas, near Brownsville. Now it is very rare, a Texas Review Species. Its substantial decline is attributable to habitat changes caused by agriculture and overgrazing.

I expected others to be searching for the yellowthroat, but our only companions were an elderly couple from the United Kingdom who had no knowledge of this rarity's presence. Tim first heard the yellowthroat singing across the small pond to our southeast. The bird's warble resembled that of a Blue Grosbeak. We tracked its musical offerings as the bird worked around the north side of the pond, staying out of sight. Then we spotted the yellowthroat, tossing brilliant notes into the air from a swaying perch in the upper branches of a retama at the pond's edge.

The yellowthroat's cooperative nature permitted unhurried study. It had, of course, a yellow throat. Narrow gray-white crescents framed its eyes. In addition to its song, dark black lores marked this bird as a lonely male, hopeful of attracting female companionship.

As with other cooperative Review Species I had chased, I hated to leave this bird, still in plain sight twenty minutes after we had first laid eyes on it. But Santa Ana's richness called to us. Though our remaining time at the refuge yielded no additional birds for my year list, I could not fail to be impressed by White-tipped Doves strutting barely beyond arm's reach; a Clay-colored Robin seated on its nest; a Least

Bittern standing pole-like at the edge of the Willow Pond reeds; and brilliant orange-yellow Hooded Orioles decorating the trees bordering the parking lot.

TROPICAL PARULA BREEDS from along the United States–Mexico border far into South America and is thus one of the most widespread Neotropical warblers. In Texas, however, the species is very rare. I had hoped to see one or more on the Kenedy Ranch in late April, but we had been unable to find any, our only notable miss of that banner weekend. I had been seeking a Plan B for this species since that time. Since several birders had recently reported Tropical Parula from Anzalduas County Park, west of Santa Ana NWR, Tim and I went there next.

We had been in the park only a few minutes when the buzzy trill of a singing male Tropical Parula welcomed us from the higher reaches of the trees. We searched for this petite bird among the dense, moss-draped oaks it favors. The parula suddenly showed itself in an unorthodox manner, dropping to the ground from an oak, taking time out from its song program for a bath in a puddle not ten yards from Tim and me. The late spring light showed the Tropical Parula's most distinctive features well: the dark facial mask; the yellow throat; the pale reddish breast band; and the two bold white wingbars. The Tropical's lack of a white eye ring distinguishes it from the much more common Northern Parula, a migrant through the Valley but a breeder in parts of East Texas.

After this show, Tim toured me around the park, pointing out nesting locations that had been used by Rose-throated Becards, another Texas Review Species and an occasional visitor from Mexico. A becard had spent several weeks in the Valley in late winter and early spring, but we could find no sign of it on this late May morning.

My last stop of the day was the desolate McAllen sewage ponds. They held few birds. But several breeding Black-bellied Whistling Ducks were tending chicks. I studied these carefully. Black-bellied Whistling Duck chicks bear an uncanny resemblance to female Masked Ducks and have undoubtedly been reported as Masked Ducks on several occasions. This was a mistake I did not want to make.

The reclusive Masked Duck is one of the possible treasures that a birder might discover in the Valley. This tropical duck periodically invades the region, but its reluctance to swim on open water makes it a difficult species to see. Masked Duck's preference for thick marsh habitat also makes its abundance hard to gauge.

BECAUSE IT WAS A LONG DRIVE from Weslaco west to the town of Zapata, I was on the road well before sunrise on Sunday, May 28. This was my day for chasing the White-collared Seedeaters that had eluded the Hedges and me in early January.

There was little joy in searching the reed-filled pond behind the Zapata Library, an oft-visited site for birders seeking White-collared Seedeaters. Clouds of ravenous mosquitoes descended on me, undeterred by the thick layer of repellent I had lathered on my skin and clothes. Men and women were already prowling the neighboring golf course. Since the library pond seemed within range of a duffer's errant iron or wood, my attention was divided between looking for a seedeater and monitoring the progress of the numerous amateurs on the adjacent fairways. Unfortunately, the seedeaters were no-shows.

I abandoned Zapata and drove west for thirty minutes to San Ygnacio, where I explored the reeds and trees below Washington Street. Birding alone along any part of the U.S.–Mexico border can be unnerving, given the border realities of drug trafficking and illegal immigration. But everything was peaceful that morning, and my efforts soon paid dividends. An adult male White-collared Seedeater flew past, then clung to a sapling's branch. It allowed me ample time to admire its black cap, the broad crescent of white beneath its eye, its white wingbars, and its short, conical seed-eating bill. As I slowly worked my way back up to Washington Street, a drabber adult female stared back at me from the reeds.

Since I was already in the Valley's western reaches, I drove the short distance from San Ygnacio to the Falcon Dam to access a vantage point high above the Rio Grande. From a parking lot that overlooked the dam's spillway, the eastern view along the river was spectacular. A large group of black-and-white-winged birds swirled high above the river in a slow, loose spiral. Before I managed to get binoculars on them, I

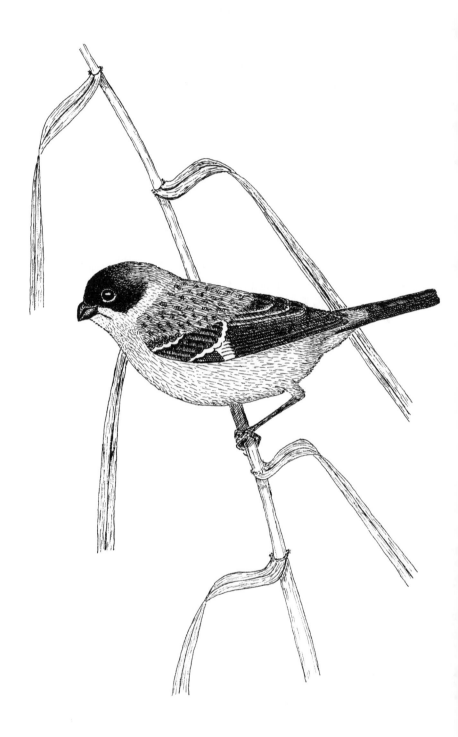

White-collared Seedeater. Drawing by Kelly B. Bryan.

guessed they were American White Pelicans. A little magnification showed this guess to be wrong. These were Wood Storks, postbreeding visitors in the Valley, generally seen in August or September. Their arrival in such numbers in late May was unusual.

At the spillway, I invested two hours in watching the Rio Grande for a flying Muscovy Duck, a raucous Brown Jay, or a soaring Hook-billed Kite, but I eventually left without having seen any of these Valley specialties.

ON MEMORIAL DAY, I passed the entrance to the sleepy El Rio RV Park at Chapeño and continued to a right turn and a dirt ramp to the Rio Grande. The Hedges and I had scouted here in January. I parked at the top of the hill that led to the river. The rest of the ramp was rutted and looked to be an "iffy" proposition for my rental car.

At the river's shoreline, near dawn, I waited for something interesting to happen. The common thread to the advice I had received about finding wild Muscovy Duck boiled down to a need for patience: a willingness to sit along the Rio Grande in the early morning or late evening and wait for a Muscovy to fly past. The unimpressive, domesticated versions of the Muscovy Duck are widespread across North America, occupy many barnyards, and are unlikely to ever be seen flying. The wild Muscovy is a different beast, a strong flyer and a wary native of the American tropics that favors wooded rivers and swamps.

Remarkably little patience was required of me, as it turned out. Ten minutes into a mostly sunny morning, two heavy, darkish, fast-flying ducks zoomed past, heading downstream to some urgent appointment. The Muscovy's white upper and lower wing patches and greenish purple gloss above made for a memorable sight.

After this fine start, I adjourned to the El Rio RV Park, seeking Brown Jays. Never numerous on the U.S. side of the border, Brown Jays had been especially rare in South Texas for many months. These large, dull jays are common in Mexico and first crossed into Texas in the 1970s. The former settlement at Chapeño, a remote spot along the river and a mile downstream from Falcon Dam, was one of the few locations where these jays were being seen with any regularity.

The folks who operate the El Rio RV Park maintained several platform feeders. The caretaker, nicknamed Nacho, was a silver-haired man with a ponytail (I never learned his real name). He told me that two or three Brown Jays visited his feeders most mornings. This was not as many jays as he had seen during the winter, but one was all I needed.

I paid my two-dollar entry fee and feed was added to the platforms by my newfound friend. I stationed myself a suitable distance from the feeders and watched. Not long after eight o'clock, an adult Brown Jay landed on one of the platforms. This bird stayed a few minutes, then departed down the hill toward the river. A half hour later, two Brown Jays (one adult, one immature) visited a nearby feeder for several minutes. Between these jay encounters, Nacho and I spotted a Great Horned Owl resting in a nearby bare tree, and we studied an occupied Barn Owl nest in the steep wall of an eroded culvert.

There remained plenty of daylight to search for a Hook-billed Kite. To maximize my chances of seeing one, I chose a spot with an unobstructed view. A mass of exposed rock extended out from the El Rio shoreline into the river. Walking out on these rocks gave me a clear view upstream and downstream.

Five birders from the Middle Atlantic states joined me in my Hook-billed Kite vigil. While we waited, another Muscovy Duck flapped past us, going downstream. Green Jays, a Green Kingfisher, a Ringed Kingfisher, and several Altamira Orioles kept us amused. Our patience was eventually rewarded when an adult male and female Hook-billed Kite (#435) soared into view. They circled and played above us for several minutes, demonstrating their flight skills and attachment to each other. Then the kites crossed the river and dropped into the trees.

My Rio Grande birding day had barely started, and I had already seen all three of the Valley specialty species remaining on my target list: two lifers, Muscovy Duck and Hook-billed Kite, and one personal first Texas record, the Brown Jay.

## chapter 15

Strategies and Surprises

he birding pace I had sustained through the first five months of my Texas Big Year resulted in a level of accomplishment that far exceeded my expectations. With the list at 435 species by the end of May and seven months left in the year 2000, I adjusted my year-end goal from 450 to 475 species. Meeting this new goal meant seeing just another forty species during the months of June through December.

It sounded almost trivial. But adding these last forty species would require an effort as great as that which had yielded more than ten times that many species in the early months. Through May, field days had often produced multiple new year birds. But from June 1 on, any day that brought me something new would be an achievement, and only extraordinary days would add more than one new species. With about 90 percent of my likely year-end total seen and spring migration completed, the remaining months called for different strategies.

In early June, I made and reviewed a list of the regularly occurring Texas birds I had yet to see. It was a short list of forty-seven species. For each of these, I considered when and where it was mostly likely to be found and how much time and travel would be needed. Some I could confidently find myself. Others would require research and consultation with more knowledgeable birders. I built several two- to four-day birding trips into my schedule for the remainder of the year, each with the goal of adding one or more species. This became my "strategic plan." I maintained it on a spreadsheet on my personal computer, updating it whenever new information presented itself.

A few of the remaining species would be straightforward, a simple matter of traveling to appropriate habitat at the proper time. Whooping Crane, for example, required a trip to the Aransas National Wildlife Refuge any day after the wintering flock's arrival in mid- to late October. Seeing a Rough-legged Hawk meant a trip to the Panhandle. It would be hard to miss seeing one during a day's birding north of Amarillo after November 1.

For most other species, however, the plan could not be so exact. Black-throated Blue Warbler, for instance, is never predictable at a given location on a given date, though it is easier to find one in the fall than in the spring. A trip to the upper Texas coast in October or November would be the best bet but was no guarantee.

For some of the species I had yet to see, I lacked information and experience. Though I understood which part of the state would likely yield an American Woodcock sighting (East and Northeast Texas after mid-October), I did not know of a specific area, park, or field I should hike to seek one. I needed to do some research on this and other unfamiliar species, including Purple Finch and Long-eared and Short-eared owls.

To achieve a large year list, I also needed to pursue as many Texas Review Species as possible. Since they are the rarest Texas birds, predicting their appearance is impossible. They require flexibility, not planning. I would need to stay in close contact with birders around the state and carefully monitor rare bird reports posted on TEXBIRDS. The trick would be catching reports as soon as they appeared and deciding which Review Species it was realistic to chase.

I hoped to take a pelagic birding trip as well. Offshore excursions into the Gulf, in the company of birders, offer opportunities to see species unobservable from land. When the Brownsville birding festival announced a July 14 pelagic trip, I immediately signed up (chapter 17).

Careful planning to see the remaining regularly occurring species, attention to Review Species, and finding a pelagic opportunity: these were the linchpins of my strategy for the remaining seven months of 2000. There were very few "easy" birds remaining on my list. I would work hard for most new birds I would see through the end of the year, crisscrossing the state multiple times.

SINCE LATE APRIL, a Dusky-capped Flycatcher pair had been reliably reported from the lower portion of the Laguna Meadows Trail in Big Bend National Park. This species is common in the woodlands throughout Mexico and south to El Salvador and Nicaragua; it reaches its northern limit in the summer in Arizona and New Mexico. Since it is a great rarity anywhere in Texas, Dusky-capped Flycatcher is a Review Species in the state.

Throughout May, everyone who looked carefully had seen the Chisos Mountains Dusky-capped Flycatchers. I decided to try and see them too. Chasing these birds avoided having to gamble on a future Dusky-capped Flycatcher being found in the Davis Mountains. In retrospect, this was a wise decision. Though Dusky-capped Flycatchers had been discovered nearly every summer in the Davis Mountains, only one was briefly seen and heard during my Big Year.

Dusky-capped Flycatcher is a member of the genus *Myiarchus,* a group of birds that includes more than twenty widespread species of the American tropics. Four other *Myiarchus* flycatchers can be observed in the United States in the summer. Great Crested, Brown-crested, and Ash-throated flycatchers are common summer residents in the eastern half of Texas, the Lower Rio Grande Valley, and West Texas, respectively. Nutting's Flycatcher has strayed north twice from Mexico into Arizona and once into California but has never been documented in Texas.

The *Myiarchus* genus presents major identification problems to North American birders and is regarded by many as even more difficult to master than the dreaded *Empidonax* flycatchers. All of the *Myiarchus* flycatchers are visually similar: fairly slender, medium-sized birds with some yellow on the underparts, reddish brown in the wings or tail, and a relatively large head with a peaked or crested nape. Though size is notoriously difficult to judge on individual birds and could not be the basis for identifying a Dusky-capped Flycatcher, this is the smallest *Myiarchus* in the United States.

As with the empids, *Myiarchus* flycatcher vocalizations are sometimes the only reliable means to identify a bird clearly to species. This is especially important for an out-of-range individual, such as a Dusky-capped Flycatcher in Big Bend or the Davis Mountains.

In planning for this chase, I learned that my friends David and Linda Hedges were game for a quick trip to Big Bend. We departed from their home, not far from the observatory, at an abominably early hour. Three hours later, we started up the Laguna Meadow Trail in Big Bend National Park in the embrace of a cool and cloudy dawn. We marched briskly up the trail from the Chisos Basin, hopeful that our target lay only forty-five to fifty minutes of moderate-paced hiking ahead. Familiar woodland birds greeted us: Mexican Jay, Tufted Titmouse, Rufous-crowned Sparrow, Black-headed Grosbeak, Black-chinned Sparrow, and others.

The Dusky-capped Flycatchers had been repeatedly seen near the first set of switchbacks, before the trail started ascending to higher elevations. As we approached this area, Linda heard a Dusky-capped call in the distance. Its mournful whistle, a plaintive, drawn-out, descending "wheeeu" or "peeeu," was readily separable from the calls and songs of other species in this habitat.

We proceeded a few feet at a time, listening and watching. After a minute or two, near the spot where others had seen the Dusky-capped Flycatcher, I noticed a tranquil, seemingly small *Myiarchus* flycatcher in the top of an alligator juniper just thirty feet distant. Whether this bird had been there or had just flown in unnoticed was not clear. It was barely above eye level as I stood on a higher portion of the trail.

After five minutes of regarding us in silence, it called twice—"peeeu, peeeu"—confirming its identity as a Dusky-capped Flycatcher. We studied the plumage details of this bird, checking that its tail was dark brown and that its secondaries showed rufous edges. Over the next half hour, we located a second Dusky-capped Flycatcher, as had other observers. This apparent pair entertained us, chasing each other around the tops of nearby pinyon pines.

We celebrated our victory back at the Chisos Lodge with a breakfast of sinfully high cholesterol and caloric content, then drove home. Three weeks later, Brush Freeman and Petra Hockey confirmed that this Laguna Meadow Trail pair of Dusky-capped Flycatchers were breeding, marking the first official Texas nesting record for this species.

DURING EACH OF THE PAST SEVERAL breeding seasons, a small group of ornithologists and birders had gathered to conduct a week-long survey on the Nature Conservancy's Davis Mountains Preserve. I was privileged to be a part of this group in June, 2000.

Our team consisted of several professional biologists and a similar number of amateur naturalists and birders. John Karges was the survey leader. John's professional responsibilities included biological oversight for all of the Nature Conservancy's West Texas properties. He is intimately familiar with the preserve. His professional collaborators included Kelly Bryan, Roland Wauer, and Chuck Sexton, a Texas ornithologist employed by the U.S. Fish and Wildlife Service. Texas birders and amateur naturalists Brush Freeman, Petra Hockey, Marc Eastman, Dick Eales, and I rounded out the team. During the period June 18–25, we surveyed key bird and butterfly territories all across the preserve's twelve thousand acres.

Early on Wednesday, June 21, we grunted up the steep trail that cuts through the pine forest at 7,300 feet elevation, near Bridge Gap, to higher elevations. Our point of departure from the trail was Pucker Switchback, a locally infamous sharp turn on the rock-strewn road that caused trouble for vehicles in years past, when this road was still driven.

At the switchback, the group divided. Kelly, Ro, and Chuck went on to the Mount Livermore summit via the usual path. The rest of us bushwhacked, at approximately constant elevation, across the steep mountainside to Pewee Canyon, a narrow cut in the high Davis Mountains, and Pewee Springs, where water oozes reliably from the ground and attracts wildlife. Both places are named for a Greater Pewee that visited for four days in late June of 1998.

As we hiked into the canyon, we crossed paths with Pygmy Nuthatches, Grace's and Virginia's warblers, a Green-tailed Towhee, Canyon Wrens, Bushtits, and Hepatic and Western tanagers. At midmorning, we stopped for a break among the relict quaking aspens that thrive in Pewee Canyon, almost directly beneath Mount Livermore.

After a rest, we began to bird again, retracing our path to Bridge Gap. As we passed near Pewee Springs, a warbler's song came from somewhere on the precipitous slope above us. Petra spied the bird first. Everyone soon had it in binoculars. The group emitted a collective gasp as everyone realized it was a redstart. *And it had no white in its wings.* Thus it was not a Painted Redstart, which would have been thrilling enough. Rather, it was a Slate-throated Redstart, which was extraordinary!

The redstart foraged in a Gambel's oak grove, singing, trying to attract a mate. Brush scrambled up the slope to photograph this rarity. During the five minutes we had the bird in sight, we excitedly recorded its plumage details, behavior, and songs.

In hopes of sharing this wonder with others and to photograph it myself, I returned to Pewee Canyon on June 25 in the company of Mike Overton and David and Linda Hedges. We descended into the canyon along a faster but much steeper route from the trail to Mount Livermore, concentrating so that we would not lose our footing on the severe slope. A tumble would have been long and painful.

We soon heard the Slate-throated Redstart's song below us. Clambering lower allowed us to find the bird again. After everyone had seen their fill, I slid down a ledge to a precarious perch within thirty feet of the redstart. My camera shutter clicked numerous times while the redstart periodically threw back its head and belted out its song. While foraging, it fanned its worn, white-edged tail.

Slate-throated Redstart is a fairly common bird of the high Mexican mountains and ranges as far south as Venezuela and northern Bolivia. Though it breeds within 150 miles of the U.S.–Mexico border, it has rarely strayed into the United States. This was only the third Texas record. The first was a bird that resided at Big Bend NP's Boot Spring from April 26 to May 15, 1990. The second dated from August 4, 1997, also near Pewee Springs.

Our June 25 appointment with this redstart was its last of the season. Others searched hard for the bird on July 2, but it had apparently tired of its failure to find a suitable breeding companion. It was gone.

On Thursday morning, June 22, our survey group—John, Kelly, Ro, Brush, Petra, Chuck, and I—undertook the bumpy ride across the northern shoulder of Brown Mountain to the base of 7,700-foot Pine Peak. We parked at the edge of a broad grassy field punctuated by an old dirt tank dredged years ago. While we removed our hiking gear from the vehicles, Steller's Jays screeched from the pines, objecting to our intrusion into their territory. Hepatic Tanagers and Plumbeous Vireos sang. Titmice and Bushtits roamed the woodland edge.

After shouldering day packs, we descended through dense, serene forest along an old closed Jeep trail. After a half mile, we dodged to the right, off the trail and into the woods, crossing a downed fenceline. We followed a rock-filled arroyo to Pine Peak Spring. It was slow going. Fallen trees clogged the narrow cleft that seasonal water flows had carved into the ground over decades. After much scrambling, some of it over damp, lichen-covered rocks, we reached the spring. A small pool of water was still being captured by the remnants of a 1920s era concrete and stone spring box.

At the spring, we discussed our options. A portion of the group— John, Petra, Chuck and myself—elected to continue trailblazing and exploring down Elbow Canyon. The other team members decided to climb back up from the spring to survey around Pine Peak.

An hour after we had split up, having worked around and over many more obstacles, we heard Steller's Jays scolding. Jays can get excited about almost anything. They might be annoyed about a snake, a mountain lion, or an owl. John, Petra, and I moved forward to investigate. Chuck trailed behind.

Another hundred yards brought us alongside a cliff face fifty to seventy feet high, fractured by several deep, wide fissures. Crests erect, the jays squawked and jumped around in the trees that grew at the base of the cliff. We scanned the ground and the sky and peered into the trees for the cause of the jays' agitation.

"Spotted Owl!" John whispered. He moved ahead, anxious for a better view. Petra and I followed. Suddenly we saw not one but two

Spotted Owls. We watched as they flew into and then, a few minutes later, out of the fissures in the cliff. Two whitewashed rock ledges were visible in the cliff fissures, probably favored owl perches. Later we saw both Spotted Owls sitting quietly on the same branch, close enough to fit in the same binocular field of view.

In Texas, Spotted Owl is a rare and local resident of wooded canyons in the Davis and Guadalupe mountains. Other than a single bird seen in Pewee Canyon in August, 1997, Spotted Owls had last been reported in the Davis Mountains in the 1970s. The standard route to see this species in Texas is an arduous hike in the Guadalupe Mountains to the forest above Devil's Hall, where at least one pair has nested in recent years.

At midafternoon, we hiked the final, flat couple miles out of Elbow Canyon to our rendezvous with Ro Wauer and my Jeep. The sky darkened and light rain showers began to fall. Precipitation is always welcome in the Trans-Pecos. Hiking through this gentle rain was pleasurable. And having seen Spotted Owls (#440) meant nothing could dampen my good mood.

## chapter 16

Big Year Nemesis Number Two

Louisiana Waterthrush

The tail-bobbing Louisiana Waterthrush is one of the first warbler species to return to North America each spring. Presumed migrants have been recorded in Florida as early as mid-February. By the second and third weeks of March, they arrive in numbers along the Gulf Coast from Florida to Texas. Their movement across the coast is essentially complete by mid-April. Though they are unlikely to be confused with any other species, Northern and Louisiana Waterthrush are often mistaken for each other.

Owing to my March 23–April 2 business trip to Germany, I was out of the country and unable to visit the Texas coast when Louisiana Waterthrush is a fairly common migrant. Though I had been successful with nearly every migrant warbler species I had hoped to see in spring, I had not seen a Louisiana Waterthrush.

Plan B was to find an individual of this species on its breeding territory. Louisiana Waterthrush is a rare to uncommon summer resident in the eastern third of Texas, settling in areas where streams flow through woodlands, particularly creeks with sandy or gravel bottoms.

I felt confident that a breeding Louisiana Waterthrush could be located in the Big Creek Scenic Area of the Sam Houston National Forest or at Boykin Springs in the Angelina National Forest. But business crowded my schedule, and other species had first call on my birding time in late May and June.

Since business took me to Austin at least once per month, I consulted with several Texas birders about the possibility of seeing Louisiana Waterthrush within a reasonable distance of the city, at places that would be reachable early in the morning or in the evening. As usual, several persons tried to help, sending directions to sites near Austin where they had sometimes seen Louisiana Waterthrush.

On Wednesday morning, May 31, I arrived at one of these places, an old bridge spanning a creek on winding two-lane Lower Elgin Road in Bastrop County. But an extensive search here and at other creek crossings on Upper Elgin Road over the next two and a half hours produced no Louisiana Waterthrush. The following morning, I revisited the Lower and Upper Elgin Road sites but had no luck then either.

A couple of birders suggested I check the small creek crossings in Bastrop State Park. The year had been a dry one, however. These crossings were virtually nonexistent, and no Louisiana Waterthrushes were present.

I also visited Alum Creek, a fair-sized watercourse that crosses Park Road 1C between Bastrop and Buescher state parks. It looked promising. There was good, strong, clean water flow under the roadway. Gravel and sand coated the creek bottom. I pulled off onto the shoulder of Park Road 1C and traipsed up and down and through the creek for more than an hour, looking and listening; but to no avail.

On these two mornings, I invested nearly six hours in my Louisiana Waterthrush search. I was frustrated by my failure but knew that another month would have to pass before my concern should become worry.

Somehow, the month of June vanished.

On July 1, this species was still not on my year list, promoting it to the status of nemesis in my mind's eye. Since this bird is among the first warblers to depart after breeding, the calendar urged me to make finding one a priority. Though Louisiana Waterthrush is recorded as a migrant through early and mid-July, it would be difficult to locate after July 15. Time was running out, and there was no escaping the fact that it would be downright embarrassing to miss Louisiana Waterthrush during my Texas Big Year.

Not wanting to give up on the thoughtful recommendations of people I trusted, I revisited the Upper Elgin Road, Lower Elgin Road, and Alum Creek sites again on the morning of Monday, July 3. While on Upper Elgin Road, I thought I heard a Louisiana Waterthrush at a stream crossing but could not locate it visually. Though I was desperate to record this species, I did not count this bird because of my lack of experience with Louisiana Waterthrush vocalizations and the similarity of its songs and calls to those of other warblers.

On July 3, I traveled to Port O'Connor and the coast, where Brush Freeman and Petra Hockey helped me see Glossy Ibis and a Barred Owl and hear two calling Black Rails. These finds reinvigorated me for yet another try at seeing a Louisiana Waterthrush.

Business brought me back from the coast. On the morning of July 6, before going in to work at the University of Texas campus in Austin, I drove to the now familiar Lower Elgin Road bridge at dawn. Brush was able to join me. Along Alum Creek, a singing warbler brought us hope, for it sounded like my nemesis. Once we saw the bird, though, we discovered that it was not a waterthrush, but a Hooded Warbler! Though we could not find our target species, we did locate two Swainson's Warblers, a rare bird in Bastrop County.

When I returned to West Texas and relayed my tale of waterthrush woe to Kelly Bryan, he told me that Louisiana Waterthrush bred in a canyon behind the home of his friend John Gee, who lived in Dripping Springs, near Austin. I had met John during my Black-whiskered Vireo chase at Quintana (chapter 12), so I e-mailed him. Might Louisiana Waterthrush still be found near his home and, if so, would he permit me to search for the birds?

John's reply contained the exciting news that my target had nested near his house for at least sixteen years, including the year 2000. He had not spent much time looking for Louisiana Waterthrush recently, but he had occasionally heard or glimpsed at least one pair. He was optimistic we could find one, and he invited me to try.

I FLEW TO AUSTIN on the evening of July 10 and made the forty-five-minute drive south and west to Dripping Springs the next morning. John fortified me with coffee, toast, and peach preserves, then we set out birding on his property and along Dead Man's Creek, which flowed through a narrow wooded canyon directly behind John's home.

We hiked a third of a mile upstream to a wide, still pool and natural rock formation known as Dead Man's Hole. This beautiful place cheered me. I was appreciative of the chance to see it, whether or not we found my nemesis.

From Dead Man's Hole we retraced our steps, birding back downstream to and past John's house. Ninety minutes into our day, halfway to the Pedernales River, John thought he heard a faint but appropriate chip note. Then a splendid Louisiana Waterthrush (#445) jumped up from the tangles along the creek and started singing. It was a glorious moment. This bird would likely be headed south within a few days.

We continued along Dead Man's Creek, sighting a second Louisiana Waterthrush, possibly the first bird's mate. I relished the morning and the other birds that joined us, including calling Acadian Flycatchers and Yellow-throated, Red-eyed, and White-eyed vireos. Now that the burden of chasing this species had been lifted from me, I imagined that my year's greatest challenge had been met. Little did I know what awaited me.

## chapter 17

Into the Gulf of Mexico

To see species that are rarely, if ever, visible from land, a birder must venture far enough offshore to enter truly pelagic waters, traveling beyond the continental shelf to places where the ocean depth is six hundred feet or more. To reach pelagic waters from Texas ports along the central and southern coast, from Port O'Connor to Brownsville, a boat must motor forty-five to fifty-five nautical miles, a journey of three to four hours. North of Port O'Connor, the continental shelf is too wide to allow single day trips.

Additional difficulties intrude on the Texas birding community's desire for pelagic trips. The season for such excursions is May through September, when the greatest concentration of bird species is present offshore, and the Gulf waters are typically calm. Unfortunately, these same months are the heart of the offshore fishing season. The demand for fishing boats and the revenue generated by persons interested in offshore fishing far exceeds the demand for and revenue possibilities of pelagic birding. These facts conspire to limit the availability of suitable seagoing craft for pelagic birding.

Until mid-May, it seemed there would be no opportunities to go offshore in Texas waters in the company of birders in the year 2000. Then, as mentioned, the Brownsville birding festival announced a pelagic birding expedition for July 14, departing from Port Isabel on

South Padre Island. I had sent in my registration form and fee without hesitation and was elated by the possibilities this trip opened.

Birding with no land under my feet would be a novel experience, though I was no landlubber. My father and I had spent innumerable days and nights fishing for striped bass in the Chesapeake Bay when I was a child. When I lived in Florida, I fished inland lakes for largemouth bass and had occasionally gone far offshore with friends who owned boats worthy of the Atlantic Ocean.

The pelagic possibilities offshore from Texas cannot compete in numbers of species and individual birds with the richer waters off the Pacific and Atlantic coasts and accessible from ports such as Monterey, California, and Cape Hatteras, North Carolina. The usual reward for venturing offshore in Texas is two to six pelagic species. Nonetheless, every pelagic species I recorded would be new to my Big Year. I could hardly wait for July 14.

MANY BIRDERS AVOID PELAGIC TRIPS, fearing that they will become seasick. No one wants to be forced to lean over the boat's rail and heave ungracefully into the sea in front of friends and strangers. Some people are more susceptible to seasickness than others, but everyone can minimize the chances of succumbing to this misery.

A decent night's sleep is a good start toward preventing seasickness. Since pelagic trips leave the dock before dawn, getting sufficient sleep often requires adjusting one's normal sleeping patterns, beginning as much as a week prior to the trip. What you eat immediately before and during the trip is important. Every pelagic birder should avoid greasy foods the night before and the morning of the trip. It would be folly to feast on bacon and eggs at a diner before boarding a boat headed for the Gulf's swells. Many find that munching on crackers in the morning gets one's stomach off to the right start.

Over-the-counter medications such as Dramamine or Bonine can be effective for short trips, such as one-day pelagic outings. For longer overnight trips, or for those who are more adversely affected, a prescription medication called transdermal scopolamine is available as a patch that is worn behind the ear. Some medical studies have indicated that ginger root can be effective against seasickness. Other persons swear by "seasickness bands," simple elastic straps worn around the wrists and pressing an acupressure point, preventing motion sickness. I saw all of these being used on the Port Isabel pelagic trip. I opted for a single Dramamine.

SINCE THE GOAL WAS TO RECORD unfamiliar birds that cannot be seen from shore, being prepared was critical. I reviewed species lists from previous Texas pelagic trips and studied these birds in multiple references, including my National Geographic Society field guide and specialized volumes such as Peter Harrison's *Seabirds of the World* (Princeton: Princeton University Press, 1987). Almost every possible species we might see would be new to me: Cory's and Audubon's shearwaters; Pomarine, Long-tailed, and Parasitic jaegers; Masked Booby; Band-rumped and Leach's storm-petrels; Bridled and Sooty terns. I also prepared for possible rarities such as Sooty and Greater shearwater, Brown Booby, Black-capped Petrel, Red-tailed Tropicbird, and Arctic Tern.

Our departure from the Port Isabel dock was scheduled for 5:45 A.M. I arrived at the marina with almost an hour's cushion. Our boat, the *Osprey II,* pleased me: a sixty-five foot blue and white craft with plenty of outside deck space and a well-cared-for appearance. This vessel and its sister ship ply the Gulf waters year-round, drift fishing for kingfish, shark, and dorado, and bottom fishing for red snapper, grouper, and amberjack.

By the time all forty birders and our guides—Dwight Peake, Mike Overton, and Brad McKinney—were on the boat, and the three-person crew was ready for departure, it was 6:15 A.M. As we headed for the deep water, the reddened sun rose into a clear sky. The trip out and back from pelagic waters would take three hours each way. The weather forecast was excellent: sunny skies, warm temperatures and, most important, light winds. The Gulf of Mexico would be calm, and few if any passengers would be tormented by seasickness.

Most guests were outside throughout the trip, standing or seated, scanning the skies. Laughing Gulls, Royal Terns, and Sandwich Terns were still with us ten miles from shore. An hour from the dock, we scored our first pelagic success. Two jaegers flew behind and around the boat.

All three species of jaegers—Pomarine, Parasitic, and Long-tailed— breed in the arctic and spend the rest of the year far out at sea. Jaegers are seen only rarely from the coast. Confused migrants, usually young birds, visit inland reservoirs on very rare occasions. Jaegers are swift flyers and aggressive predators, often harassing other birds, forcing them to give up their food.

Jaegers can be difficult to identify to species, owing to the complexity of their plumages and the subtle nonbreeding plumage differences among the three species. One of the advantages of a pelagic trip is that the boat is filled with knowledgeable birders. Identifying individual birds can be a group effort. When a trip is dedicated to birding, and if the birds permit, the boat can follow them as they fly. The guides and crew also periodically dump chum into the boat's wake to attract pelagic species and keep them close to the boat.

We studied our jaegers for several minutes. Their identification as Pomarine (#446), the largest of the three jaegers, was unanimous.

Having never been on a pelagic trip, I was unprepared for the difficulty of centering a bird in my binoculars, focusing and following a moving target from a semi-randomly bobbing platform. Though the Gulf surface was tranquil, with no more than gentle three-foot swells, it was still a formidable challenge to get a solid look at a bird. I slowly adapted.

An hour later, a second pelagic species, Masked Booby, investigated us. Three of these birds flew around the boat several times, like the jaegers, curious as to our mission and the possibilities of being fed. Long ago, sailors chose the unflattering name of boobies for these birds because they showed little fear of humans, which to the sailors was a clear sign of stupidity. Six species of boobies occur worldwide, but only the Masked Booby is routinely encountered in summer and in migration in Texas waters.

The feeding behavior of boobies and their relatives the gannets makes for remarkable outdoor theater. Starting from high above the waves, they fold their wings against their bodies, turn downward,

Masked Booby. Drawing by Kelly B. Bryan.

then plunge at high velocity toward and through the ocean surface like a missile, seeking fish.

Another three-quarters of an hour passed before the next new arrival flew near the boat: Band-rumped Storm-Petrel. By the end of the day, we had counted at least sixty of these birds, some flying, some floating. The experienced birders on board said they had never seen so many on a single outing. Until the late 1970s, Band-rumped Storm-Petrel was considered a very rare visitor to the waters around North America. Over the last two decades, as pelagic trips explored deeper waters, it has become clear that this species, and the related Leach's Storm-Petrel, are more numerous than had been thought.

The storm-petrels were entertaining, flying maniacally just above the swells, their wings madly flapping. These are true seabirds, coming to land only to breed or when driven off the ocean by huge storms, such as hurricanes. Some storm-petrels bounce their feet off the water while flying, and their name originates with this habit. "Petrel" is a diminutive of "Peter," the apostle whose walk on water is recounted in the Bible's New Testament.

As days offshore often do, our pelagic day featured long periods of birdlessness punctuated by frantic minutes of action whenever a bird appeared. As the day wore on, my early start made itself felt as my energy level dropped. The sun seemed hotter, the day's stillness more oppressive. I persevered, though an increasing number of birders retired to the air-conditioned cabin.

Our fourth and final pelagic species teased us. Thirty miles from land, we spied a dark-backed sea tern flying in the moderate distance. Our captain maneuvered the boat closer to it, trying to place the bird in good light. But its intentions were counter to ours. Though we nudged closer, the sun angle was never any better than fair. Everyone aboard agreed that this bird was either an immature Bridled Tern or an immature Sooty Tern. Most favored Bridled Tern, but some were vehement in their assertion that Sooty Tern was the correct identification.

I sided with those who felt that Bridled Tern was more likely correct. But since none of us could be certain, this bird went into my Big Year list as "Bridled/Sooty Tern." If I had seen either a definite Bridled

Tern or a Sooty Tern at any other time during my Big Year, then this Bridled/Sooty Tern record would have been replaced in my year list by the bird identified to species. Since I saw no other individuals of either species, however, this Bridled/Sooty Tern counted as one new bird for my Big Year (#449).

The four pelagic species seen on this trip were a reward as large as I had expected and better than it might have been. Everyone appreciated the unruffled Gulf waters; no one was afflicted with seasickness. Those who had taken many trips into the Gulf over the years counseled the neophytes, including myself, that we had been fortunate. The Gulf is rarely so toothless.

My one mistake was carelessness about sunblock. I wore shorts the entire day we were at sea, owing to the heat. Though I covered and protected my head, neck, and arms, I failed to put sunblock on my exposed legs. The vicious offshore sun exacted a price for this error. My legs were warm for several days and long pants were uncomfortable for nearly a week.

chapter 18

Among Butterflies
and Friends

B y the end of July, many bird species have completed their nesting activity for the year. Some wander widely during the postnesting period, improving the odds that a birder will come across an unusual, out-of-range bird. Since I had observed almost every available regularly occurring Texas species that could be seen during the warm months, rarities were my focus for the remainder of the summer.

On Saturday, July 22, three of my good friends—Marc and Maryann Eastman and Rex Barrick—joined me for a hike into Big Bend National Park's lower Pine Canyon, one of my favorite places. I had no specific target species in mind. Rather, I was hoping that this canyon would live up to its reputation as a productive locale for postnesting rarities. In recent years, the Pine Canyon woodland in the Chisos Mountains had been a temporary home for nomadic Flame-colored Tanager, Red-faced Warbler, Painted Redstart, Sulphur-bellied Flycatcher, and other goodies.

Driving from the Davis Mountains, our group reached the Pine Canyon trailhead as the sun crested the horizon on a promising summer day with scattered inconsequential clouds, good visibility across the desert to the Sierra del Carmen, pleasant temperatures, and the slightest breeze.

In the sotol grassland, a few of the usual suspects still sang: Cactus Wrens, Blue Grosbeaks, Rufous-crowned and Black-throated sparrows, and Scott's Orioles. Turkey Vultures lumbered into the sky from their roosts. In the early part of our hike, our greatest excitement came when Marc nearly stepped on a western diamondback rattlesnake. The snake lay coiled in the path, soaking up warmth. Marc was leading and looking skyward for birds. He almost did not see the snake. Fortunately, it rattled at him before he was within striking distance. Rattlesnakes are fairly common in the Big Bend. I had had a similar experience in August, 1997, while hiking this same trail with Ro Wauer. I came within two strides of placing my boot on a rattlesnake because I was watching for birds, ignoring the trail.

In less than a hour, we crossed the mile and a half of sotol grassland and entered the canyon habitat of oaks, junipers, pinyon and ponderosa pines, and Texas madrones. In the woodland an astonishing sight greeted us: thousands of inch-long green caterpillars slowly descended toward the ground, dropping on fine strands at about an inch per second. The pitter-patter of so many caterpillars striking the leaf litter mimicked the sound of a sparse rain shower.

The woodland birding mirrored the earlier unimpressive results of our trek through the grassland. We heard and saw a few Spotted Towhees. Noisy Mexican Jays expressed their displeasure with our arrival. Canyon Wrens sang from the tall cliffs above us. Acorn Woodpeckers called from across the canyon. No rarities crossed our path.

But an enormous number of butterflies fluttered about the trees as the sun warmed the air. Thousands of medium-sized, pale green Lyside Sulphurs and hundreds of dull brown American Snouts crowded the canyon. Amidst these dominant species, we spied other sumptuous butterflies: rust-red and black Question Marks, numerous bright Orange Sulphurs, a single Viceroy, a couple of Giant Swallowtails, and several Red-spotted Purples, the blue of their open wings electric. Hardly a year before, I would have noted this majestic butterfly display but could not have named any of these creatures.

FOR THE FIRST FOUR YEARS that I pursued birding, I carried and used an inexpensive pair of binoculars. Their limits were obvious to me as an astronomer, especially in nonoptimal conditions such as heavy cloud cover, dense woods, or low light at the beginning or end of a day. By the summer of 1999, my interest in birding had grown to the point that an investment in better optics was in order. In July that year, I bought a pair of optically fine close-focus binoculars. These benefited my birding immeasurably. I saw everything better and with more light. And the close-focus capability fostered my newfound fascination with butterflies.

A few years before, my friend Ro Wauer had become an avid butterflier. My attendance at two of Ro's Big Bend butterfly seminars infected me with his enthusiasm for the subject. As with birds, I discovered an entire biological sphere that I had somehow missed, similar to but also different from that of birding.

Butterflies have become increasingly popular with birders of all ages and skill levels, partly because the pursuit of butterflies complements birding. Birds are most active in the mornings. Needing warmth for function, butterflies start their day later. It is generally a waste of time to look for butterflies before nine or ten in the morning. Peak butterfly activity occurs in the early to midafternoon, when bird activity has waned. Many amateur naturalists, like myself, enjoy a morning of birding that seamlessly segues into a late morning and afternoon of butterflying.

The advent and availability of close-focus binoculars has also played a role in turning birders into butterfliers. One rarely observes a bird from a distance of less than twenty or thirty feet. But butterflies are more approachable, and many are tiny, creating a need for optics that can focus at distances of just five or six feet. Close-focus binoculars have also largely eliminated the need for amateurs to collect butterflies for identification purposes.

AT THE PINE CANYON TRAIL'S END, hundreds of butterflies were attracted to the trickle of water tumbling over the pouroff. Reaching the ground as widely scattered drops after a fall of two hundred feet, this precious moisture dampened the ground and the rocks at the base of the pouroff, attracting a diverse butterfly mob. Two dark Funereal Duskywings stood on the mud, in the company of tiny Reakirt's and Marine blues and a fresh, recently emerged Golden-banded Skipper. Brilliant yellow Two-tailed Swallowtails patrolled the canyon, occasionally joined by a more subtly marked black and yellow Giant Swallowtail or a gaudy orange-spotted California Sister.

Others in the woodland benefited from this butterfly show, too. A hefty crevice spiny lizard sat on the rocks in a patch of sun, unmoving except for occasional lunges that snatched unsuspecting butterflies from the air as they careened past, oblivious to their peril.

After lunch, on our way back to the grassland, two Zebra (Heliconian) butterflies glided gracefully through the woods, easily identified by their elongate wings with yellow and black stripes. Common in south Florida, the West Indies, South Texas, and south to Ecuador, Zebras are rare strays in the Big Bend.

This unanticipated spectacle continued as we emerged from the woodland back into the grassland. In the noon desert heat, thirty to fifty butterflies occupied each blooming sotol. At one flower, two individuals of a striking medium-sized species puzzled us. We eventually deduced that they were metalmarks. These butterflies, as one might guess, have metallic marks on their wings.

We walked completely around the sotol blooms to gain every viewing advantage. Our unknown butterflies stayed put at the rich nectar source they had discovered. After several minutes of study, we concluded that they were Chisos Metalmarks, closely related to but distinct from Nais Metalmarks. These two geographically isolated species are distinguished by small differences in the orange coloration and black spots on the underside of their hindwings. Many butterfliers pursue the Chisos Metalmark, but few find it.

One additional rarity came our way, also at sotol blooms in the grassland: three Poling's Hairstreaks—medium-sized, mostly gray butterflies with a touch of orange and blue underneath. This butterfly is another denizen of the Chihuahuan Desert borderland, with a range restricted to far West Texas and south-central New Mexico. Like the Chisos Metalmark, it is not easy to find.

Every field day contains expected elements and, most pleasurably, a bit of the unknown. We knew there would be plenty of Mexican Jays and their comrades in the woodland and that Cactus Wrens and their ilk would still be singing in the grassland. Though we had expected a few, we had had no idea that the butterflies would be so spectacular or that we might have an opportunity to find and study Chisos Metalmarks and Poling's Hairstreaks. Though the day in Pine Canyon had no impact on the results of my Big Year, it was as memorable as any other, a great day spent outdoors in an appealing place with good friends.

## chapter 19

Red Birds in August

On the first Sunday in August, Kelly Bryan and I had permission to bird the Nature Conservancy's Davis Mountains Preserve. Our plan for the day had been to hike the fairly steep one-and-a-half mile trail from Bridge Gap to the 8,300-foot summit of Mount Livermore, searching the highest reaches of the Davis Mountains for rarities. But when we met at the preserve's lower elevation bunkhouse, ten miles north of the observatory, the morning was cloudy and cool with intermittent rain showers.

We waited out the weather at the bunkhouse, content to sit on the covered porch and watch hummingbirds at several feeders hanging in the trees. The hummers did a good job of keeping us amused. Large numbers of the common residents, Black-chinned and Broad-tailed hummingbirds, crowded around the feeders, continually jostling each other. Fair numbers of migrants, primarily Rufous and a sprinkling of Calliope hummingbirds, were present, too. Representatives of the area's two monster hummingbird species, Magnificent and Blue-throated, visited at irregular intervals.

After forty-five minutes under the shelter of the porch, the sky lightened. There seemed little threat of more rain. Kelly and I decided to head up Madera Canyon in his pickup truck, stopping whenever we saw or heard birds.

The woods were quiet. Only a few of the expected residents and migrants, such as Rufous Hummingbirds and *Empidonax* flycatchers, crossed our path. At one stop, a single Olive-sided Flycatcher watched us from a high ponderosa snag. The sparse birdlife meant that we progressed rapidly along the road. A hundred yards below Bridge Gap, eight miles from the bunkhouse, a fair-sized foraging flock moved through and called from the pine-oak woodland below us. We stopped Kelly's truck again and got out to locate the birds. A snatch of Western Screech-Owl tape encouraged them closer.

For perhaps five minutes, we patiently sorted through and watched Tufted Titmice, Hutton's Vireos, Mountain Chickadees, Bushtits, White-breasted Nuthatches, and Western and Hepatic tanagers. Then I saw a different shape hop up onto a nearby low ponderosa branch. I aimed my binoculars and could hardly believe my eyes. The unmistakable features of a splendid Red-faced Warbler (#453) stared back at me: a long-tailed warbler with a bright red and black face and dull red throat and upper breast. Its black crown extended to the upper nape and down behind the eye through the auriculars, and there was a white patch between the black on the nape and the bird's dark gray back.

I yelled to Kelly: "Red-faced Warbler!" I knew this was a first record for this species in the Davis Mountains.

Many Texas birders had been expecting a Red-faced Warbler to be found eventually in migration, and perhaps even as a breeder, in the Davis Mountains. Though this warbler is principally a species of northwestern Mexico, some individuals move north in summer to medium and high elevation breeding sites in Arizona and New Mexico. Breeding pairs occupy heavily wooded mountain slopes and canyons that include a mixture of conifers and oaks. In the winter, these warblers withdraw to the highlands of western and central Mexico, from Sinaloa to Oaxaca and from Chiapas through Guatemala, Honduras, and El Salvador.

Red-faced Warbler is a Review Species in Texas. Most records are from the Chisos Mountains during a narrow window of two or three weeks in August. The species has also been seen on a handful of occasions outside montane habitat, with records from El Paso, Bastrop County (near Austin), Laguna Atascosa National Wildlife Refuge on the lower Texas coast, and Matagorda Island off the central Texas coast.

After my initial sighting, we lost the Red-faced Warbler for several minutes. With an intense search we relocated it, bounding about in low shrubs at a distance of just twenty feet. While I kept the bird in sight, Kelly ran back to his truck, a short distance down the dirt road, to retrieve his camera and long focal length lens. We then tracked the warbler and its friends through the woods. Kelly struggled with the poor lighting and steep rocky terrain, but he succeeded in capturing a fine photographic image of this Red-faced Warbler, a marvelous souvenir of one of my year's most exciting finds.

FALL MIGRATION WAS UNDER WAY but still distant from its mid- to late September peak. Many of the regularly occurring Texas species I had yet to see were winter residents and would not arrive for two months or more. Fortunately, this late summer lull was broken on the afternoon of Wednesday, August 23, when Tom Johnson, the superintendent at Balmorhea State Park, called with the news that a Red Crossbill was enjoying his backyard feeders.

Readily identified by their odd bill shape, Red Crossbills are rare and irregular summer residents of the Trans-Pecos mountains. They are also rare and irregular winter visitors in many parts of the state. In "invasion years" (see chapter 21), they can occur in numbers over a wide area. But in most years, seeing a Red Crossbill requires long hikes to the high country of the Davis or Guadalupe mountains, with no guarantee that any of the birds will be seen on a given day. Their presence or absence is related to the availability of cone crops. Crossbills use their unique bills to pry open the cones of evergreen trees and extract seeds. In years with an abundance of seed-bearing cones, crossbills can be abundant; in years with few seed-bearing cones, these birds can be absent from Texas altogether.

Throughout the previous months, my frequent hikes into the Davis Mountains and occasional forays into the Chisos had not turned up any crossbills. I wanted to see the bird in Tom's backyard. On the day he called, I had to be in Fort Davis for a few minutes of personal business at 5:30 P.M. and again at 7:30 P.M. Between these appointments, I drove to Balmorhea State Park, a round-trip of seventy-two miles; a minor detour by West Texas standards.

When I arrived at Tom's house, I sat in a comfortable outdoor chair near his feeders and waited impatiently. Twenty anxious minutes later, a molting juvenile Red Crossbill (#454) appeared in Tom's peach tree and preened.

I stood slowly and crept closer. The crossbill flew up. I thought it was leaving Tom's yard. Instead, it made a sharp turn and hurtled toward me, landing at a shallow six-inch-wide water basin suspended by a chain from the lower branches of a sprawling cottonwood. The basin was just two feet from my right shoulder. I stood still, moving only my eyes. The crossbill drank, not at all concerned about my proximity. It eventually returned to the peach tree and its preening.

Where did this bird come from? I cannot be certain, but most likely it flew to Balmorhea State Park from the Davis Mountains high country. The young of the year are especially prone to wandering.

THROUGHOUT THE JULY-TO-OCTOBER shorebird migration window, I periodically checked several West Texas reservoirs, hoping for a rarity among the migrants that crowded the muddy flats. On Saturday, August 26, I visited nearby Lake Balmorhea, as I had many times during the year.

Over the course of several hours, I accumulated a day list of more than fifty species, logging fair numbers of migrants and one real surprise: Fulvous Whistling-Duck. Eight of these tawny and black ducks rested together on the south side of the lake. There were only three previous observations of this species in the Trans-Pecos: single birds seen in 1965 and 1985 and a 1940 specimen from El Paso County. Though I had already recorded them in my Big Year, this find was a highlight of my late summer birding.

Not unexpectedly, August was the slowest month of my Big Year, adding just two red-themed species—Red-faced Warbler and Red Crossbill—to my year list. Big Year or not, Red-faced Warbler was an excellent and enjoyable bird to find. And seeing the Red Crossbill so easily saved me at least one long day's hike into the high country of the Chisos, Davis, or Guadalupe mountains.

## chapter 20

Adventures while Chasing a Long-tailed Jaeger

On the last day of August, Bob Johnson discovered a wayward Long-tailed Jaeger in El Paso at the Fort Bliss sewage ponds, formally known as the Fred Hervey Water Reclamation Plant. Constructed in the midst of a stark Chihuahuan Desert landscape, these ponds are surrounded by willows, tamarisks, cottonwoods, and shrubby vegetation. They can provide banner birding days at any time of year but especially during migration.

Though he was initially uncertain as to which species he had found, Bob knew he had found something unusual. For assistance, he contacted his El Paso colleague Barry Zimmer, an international tour leader and expert birder. Once Barry arrived at the sewage ponds and studied the bird at length with Bob, Jim Paton, and others, the vagrant was identified with certainty as a Long-tailed Jaeger, an extraordinary rarity and a Texas Review Species.

Barry alerted me to the jaeger's presence via an e-mail that I read on Friday morning, September 1. I very much wanted to chase this bird. Since the Fort Bliss sewage ponds contained no fish, the jaeger was unlikely to linger. It would not be able to feed normally and perhaps not at all. The earliest possible departure for El Paso was necessary.

Two important Friday morning business telecons necessarily delayed me, but I wrapped up my work in the afternoon and sped away from the observatory just before 3:00 P.M.

Unfortunately, the three-hour drive to El Paso turned out to be more than half the fun. Along the remote forty-mile stretch of Texas 118 between my home at the observatory and Interstate 10, the sky clouded and it started to rain. I drove through fifteen miles of moderate to intense showers with just the bikini top on my Jeep. Time was precious. I did not want to stop and waste several minutes putting up the Jeep's complete soft top. A little rain was no problem.

Then thirteen miles east of Van Horn on I-10, only an hour into my trip, the metal strip that held the front edge of my Jeep top in place—the windshield channel—started working loose. When I noticed the windshield channel problem, I took my foot off the accelerator, put on my right blinker, and started slowing down. But before I could safely get off the highway, the entire six-foot-long metal strip blew off, arcing up and over the Jeep!

I stopped and searched the roadside and I-10 itself, but I could not find the part. I feared that this projectile had frightened or impaled an unsuspecting motorist, truck driver, or passenger, but no one jammed on brakes or pulled over to the side of the road to scream at me. Not wanting to waste any more time, I declared this bit of hardware a casualty of my Big Year, climbed back into the Jeep, and headed on west.

There was more trouble to come, however. A few miles from Sierra Blanca, a black and white highway patrol car appeared in my rearview mirror with its headlights and flashers on, urging me to pull over. Oops! Did I know I had been traveling at eighty miles per hour in a seventy-mile-per-hour zone? I received no mercy from the man. Twenty minutes later, I was again on my way to El Paso, $105 poorer. Angry with myself and worried that there would be too little daylight left in El Paso to search for the jaeger, I almost turned around and went home. But I persevered and continued west, though at the speed limit—well, almost.

Then while driving through the eastern side of El Paso, I took the wrong exit from the interstate and promptly got lost. After wandering aimlessly for a while, I found a policeman, sans radar gun, and he gave me the directions I needed. But I had lost *another* twenty minutes. I finally reached the Fort Bliss sewage ponds about ninety minutes before the sun would disappear behind the Franklin Mountains. Concerned that the birding gods were exacting some sort of retribution for my year's many successes, I was relieved to have made it at all.

Barry Zimmer had provided detailed directions to the pond where the jaeger had been seen the previous day. I stopped seventy-five yards south of this pond. With binoculars and naked eye, I scanned the water and the sky for a jaeger. Though these several acres of water hosted numerous birds, including migrant shorebirds such as Wilson's Phalaropes and Least and Western sandpipers, I did not see a jaeger.

My luck improved when tall, lean Jimmy Zabriskie pulled up in his car, saw my scope, got out, and introduced himself. An El Paso birder of great energy and skill, Jimmy had seen the Long-tailed Jaeger on this pond earlier in the afternoon. We drove slowly up the dirt levee on the pond's east side. An unusual, fairly large dark bird floated on the water near the east shore. Its size, proportions, coloration, and bill characteristics marked it as a jaeger, but identifying it to species was more difficult.

Though Jimmy, Barry, and others had already studied this bird from point-blank range, and I did not doubt their conclusion, I had to identify it to my own satisfaction. Fortunately, the bird's habits and location enabled me to study it in a scope at distances of twenty-five yards or less for nearly an hour, an uncommon opportunity with this species. This jaeger's throat was marred with dark streaks of what appeared to be oil or some similar thick black substance. Others had seen this bird working to remove some of the oil from its throat.

The jaeger's wings and back were dark sooty gray. Its coverts and scapulars had thin, fairly bright and distinctive whitish tips that contrasted strongly with the otherwise dark wings and back. The undertail coverts showed straight black and white barring that ran perpendicular to the body axis and continued up the flanks. The uppertail coverts were also barred black and white. The bird flew a short distance, giving me brief views of its extended wings. But these looks were important:

the primaries showed white shafts only on the outer two primaries and perhaps, more faintly, on the third. The head and nape were a lighter gray than the wings and back, with no strong facial pattern. Two central tail feathers with rounded ends extended an inch beyond the rest of the tail. The bill was large and moderately gray on its inner half, transitioning to black at its tip. The sum of these and other details added up to a Long-tailed Jaeger (#455).

An hour later, while I stalked this jaeger with my camera, Jimmy saw a second jaeger fly to the pond, an unexpected bonus. Since I was across the pond, intently following the first bird, I did not see this new arrival until Jimmy called to me. The second bird cooperated, too, permitting twenty minutes of study, more than enough to ascertain that it was also a Long-tailed Jaeger. Near sunset, it flew off to the southwest.

While observing the jaegers, I took a minute to scope a group of phalaropes and discovered a half-dozen Red-necked Phalaropes (#456) mingling with a larger group of the more common Wilson's Phalaropes. These were the first Red-necked Phalaropes anyone had seen in El Paso that fall season and a species I had hoped might come my way soon.

Jimmy, Marcie Scott (another experienced birder), and I stayed with the two jaegers until after sunset. As the sky darkened, we adjourned to a nearby restaurant for an inexpensive and pleasant celebratory dinner. With a stomach full of food and caffeine, I started my long haul back to the Davis Mountains. I had to pass through only one thunderstorm with absolutely no top on the Jeep, a mere five miles of moderate dampness, thirty miles east of El Paso. Since I was traveling at or (ever the adventurer) slightly above the speed limit, little rain found its way into the Jeep.

After midnight, driving south along Texas 118 from the fading town of Kent back to the observatory, I made several stops in the mountains. Only Western Screech-Owls responded to my taped and whistled calls. Weary but pleased, I trudged back through my front door at 2:30 A.M., grateful that lost Jeep hardware, a speeding ticket, rain showers, and my inability to exit I-10 at the right place had not prevented my seeing the Long-tailed Jaeger.

Several reliable observers worked hard but were unable to relocate either of the Long-tailed Jaegers on Saturday morning. Jimmy, Marcie, and I were the last people to see these birds in El Paso. Chasing the Long-tailed Jaeger on Friday rather than waiting for a more convenient Saturday attempt had been the right call. The birding gods had smiled on me after all.

## chapter 21

Welcoming the Invaders

In early September, my e-mail brought news that foreshadowed the remarkable events of the coming fall: a White-breasted Nuthatch was in Barry Zimmer's El Paso backyard. In his two and half decades of living in this West Texas border city, Barry had seen White-breasted Nuthatches only about once every five years. Considering this and August sightings of Red Crossbill and Pine Siskin, Barry speculated that West Texas might be in for some birding excitement in the fall and winter—a "montane invasion."

Invasions occur when food becomes scarce in a bird's normal range. Cone crops can fail or be scarce because of drought or disease. Such failures force species to become nomadic and "invade" territory they would not normally visit. A Red Crossbill, for example, ordinarily found in wooded mountains, might be driven into the Chihuahuan Desert around El Paso or into mountain ranges from which it is usually absent.

My first indication that Barry's speculation might be on the mark came on Tuesday, September 26. My Davis Mountains friends Marc and Maryann Eastman called near lunch time. An adult female Cassin's Finch was at their feeders. The cooperative Cassin's Finch (#459) was still downing sunflower seeds when I reached the Eastmans' porch.

Residents of the western mountains and conifer forests, Cassin's Finches consume seeds, buds, and berries. In Texas, they are rare and irregular winter visitors to the Trans-Pecos, the High Plains, and the western edge of the Edwards Plateau. Most years they are not present. The last Cassin's Finch invasion had occurred during the winter of 1996–97, when they were present in numbers for several months.

When Maryann and Marc called, we had no idea whether the lone bird at their feeders was a vagrant or the vanguard of many more to come. By late October, it was clear that the latter was the case. Cassin's Finches remained common at mid- to high elevations through mid-April 2001, when they finally withdrew.

SABINE'S GULL IS A SMALL GULL with a striking wing pattern that can be readily discerned even at long range. These gulls nest on the tundra of the high arctic and migrate south over the ocean, typically far offshore. Birds that breed in Siberia and Alaska migrate through the Pacific to wintering grounds off western South America. Individuals that breed in Canada and Greenland migrate across the Atlantic to winter off the southwest coast of Africa. A very few stray inland in the fall. These are almost always immature birds, unsure of their migration path. Until recently, Sabine's Gull had been a Texas Review Species. Study had demonstrated, however, that the frequency of its occurrence in Texas exceeded TBRC guidelines, so Sabine's Gull had been dropped from the Review Species list. Nonetheless, it was still a Texas rarity.

On September 22, Matt White told me that he and Bob Stone had located a Sabine's Gull at Lake Tawakoni. I went back and forth as to whether I should chase the bird. It was a long haul to Northeast Texas, and I might find one in West Texas. While I waffled about chasing the Lake Tawakoni Sabine's Gull, Matt found another at Cooper Lake. Using a boat, he was able to approach to within twenty yards of this bird. With the appearance of a second Sabine's Gull in Northeast Texas, it was definitely time to travel. The chase was on. The odds looked good for seeing a species I had never counted on as part of my Big Year.

On Friday morning, a week after the first Sabine's Gull had been spotted, I dragged myself out of bed at 3:15 A.M. for the lonely drive to Midland-Odessa and the earliest flight to Dallas. Bob Stone picked me up at the Dallas terminal, whisking me in his comfortable Lexus to Matt's home in Commerce. The three of us then made tracks for Cooper Lake. Along the way, I faded in and out of sleep.

At the lake, I learned that Matt had arranged for a boat to transport us to the favored roosting spot of the Sabine's Gull, a secluded beach distant from the available lakeshore observation points. We departed from a south shore dock at about eleven. Our sixteen-foot boat's outboard churned through a light chop for three and a half miles. Along the way, we crossed from Hopkins County into Delta County. Our destination was an eastward-pointing spit of land extending from a peninsula on the north shore. When we arrived, plenty of the usual winter fare was present: pelicans, terns, and gulls, some soaring high, others hovering and feeding low over the lake. To find our quarry, we undertook the tedious business of checking each gull.

For a quarter hour, there was no sign of the Sabine's Gull. Then Matt found it, sitting contentedly among a dense congregation of gulls. This juvenile's dark bill, relatively small size, and gray-brown nape, crown, and back contrasted with similar features on other gulls. Our Sabine's Gull (#460) eventually flew, showing its dark tail band, dark outer primary flight feathers, and a bright white V on the uppersides of its wings. We pulled the boat ashore so that we could savor this treasure in our scopes. The gull fed over the water at a distance of fifty to seventy yards.

Courtesy of an on-time return flight and an uneventful 160-mile drive from Midland, I was back in Fort Davis an hour before midnight, parked at the local high school, awaiting my cheerleader daughter's return from an away football game in distant McCamey. The game ran late. The athletes and cheerleaders did not reach Fort Davis until 2:30 A.M. With the twenty-five-minute drive home, I did not walk through my front door until three, another Big Year marathon at last complete.

PINYON JAYS HAD NOT BEEN in Texas for more than a decade, so I was startled by a report that a group had been seen in the
Davis Mountains on Wednesday, September 27. These powder-blue
jays are primarily residents of the Great Basin region. They are appro-
priately named: pinyon pine seeds are their major food source. If the
seed crop fails or is poor in their usual range, these jays wander far
afield, especially in fall and winter.

My first success with Pinyon Jays (#461) came on September 30: I
heard and then saw six birds in the Davis Mountains. I also saw flocks
of five, three, and fifty birds on the Davis Mountains Preserve on October 1; twenty-two noisy Pinyon Jays flew across Texas 118 near the
observatory on October 1; on October 12, a flock of twenty-five calling birds flapped alongside my Jeep for a hundred yards when I was
two miles north of Fort Davis; three Pinyon Jays screeched at me from
the scrub between the Frijole Ranch and the mountain foothills in the
Guadalupe Mountains National Park on October 14; and another large
flock greeted me at Frijole Ranch on October 17. The Pinyon Jays
remained fairly common in West Texas into the following spring.

On a October 1 hike to the highest reaches of the Davis Mountains
Preserve with Kelly Bryan, Brush Freeman, and Eric Carpenter,
Townsend's Solitaires (#462) were abundant. We saw at least three
dozen. Several small groups of these slender gray birds flew past, exposing their buff wing patches and white outer tail feathers to good
advantage. This species had been hard to find the previous winter.
Just a single bird had been recorded on the Davis Mountains Christmas Bird Count in December, 1999.

As noon neared, we progressed from the steep lower portions of
the trail to the flatter final half mile, nearing Baldy, the rocky cap of
Mount Livermore. Winter residents had arrived in the woods, including Golden-crowned Kinglets and Red-naped Sapsuckers. My mind
wandered, relaxed by this fine fall day among friends.

Suddenly a heavy gray bird with white outer tail feathers, jet-black
wings, and bold white patches at its rear wing edges flushed ahead of the
group. I knew this was a bird I had never seen. Before I could process
what I was seeing into a species name, Brush yelled, "Clark's Nutcracker!"

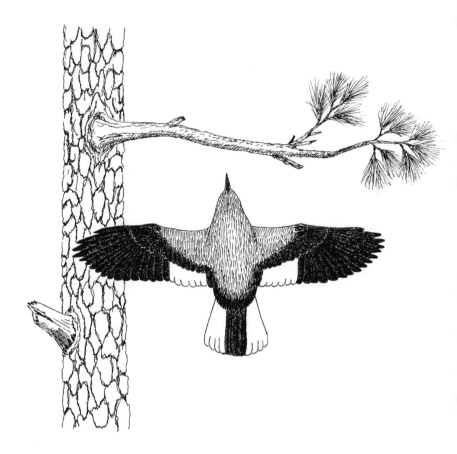

Clark's Nutcracker. Drawing by Kelly B. Bryan.

This unexpected apparition flew a short distance and perched. As we studied the bird, off it went again, disappearing. We walked up the trail to its last perch and played a short tape of Clark's Nutcracker calls. We sat down to minimize our profiles. The bird reappeared and watched us from a tree only fifty feet up the trail. Like the Pinyon Jay, Clark's Nutcracker (#463) was a species I had not anticipated seeing during my Big Year. Many of the state's best and most traveled observers had yet to see one in Texas. And though a Clark's Nutcracker had been reliably reported from near Mount Livermore on August 25, no one had seen it since.

Surprises like this are one of the reasons for birding on any given day. If what we would see in the field were perfectly predictable, some of the pleasure of birding would evaporate. Fortunately, birds will never permit this to happen.

OVER THE WEEKEND of October 6–8, I took a canoeing trip along the Rio Grande. I floated from La Linda, east of Big Bend National Park, downstream for eleven miles to Maravillas Creek in the Black Gap Wildlife Management Area. This adventure was an annual event for me, the outcome of a mutually beneficial business collaboration between the McDonald Observatory and Texas River and Jeep Expeditions. I provided the river trip with an astronomical theme, leading the guests on an exploration of the stupendously dark night sky in this remote area. In return, the company donated a portion of the trip revenues to the observatory.

Unfortunately, abysmal weather hounded us. On Friday, as we headed downriver, an early and incredibly cold "blue norther" swept through Texas. Low scudding clouds, persistent rain, and record cold temperatures made our two-day river trip unpleasant. The sun never shone; at night we saw only clouds; the wind blew relentlessly in our faces; and the temperature never climbed above fifty degrees. Bird carcasses littered the river. We made the best of it, seeing a face of the Big Bend that few ever see.

In the Davis Mountains, this powerful storm coated trees with thick layers of ice, bringing down many branches and even entire trees. Iced powerlines fell, too, leaving residents without electricity. When I emerged from the Big Bend wilderness late on Sunday afternoon, I called my family from Study Butte and learned that while I had been freezing on the Rio Grande on Saturday, Brush Freeman and Petra Hockey had found a Painted Redstart on a West Texas ranch near Valentine.

Jody and Clay Miller, the ranch owners, are from families with long histories in the Trans-Pecos. Both Jody and Clay pioneered bird study in the region. I called the Millers that evening. Happily, they had seen my nemesis, the Painted Redstart, outside their home's back door on

Sunday. They invited me to come and search for it. Monday was no better than Saturday or Sunday, though, with clouds, cold, and severe, gusty wind. The wet weather transformed the private roads connecting U.S. 90 to the Miller Ranch headquarters into a muddy bog. My vehicle slipped and slid, barely powering through several quagmires that nearly ended my mission.

Just before I arrived, Jody and Clay discovered a failing Flammulated Owl at their home's gate. This petite owl was alive when I walked through the gate, though it looked exceedingly weary. Later that afternoon, it died. I delivered this specimen and another victim of the unseasonable weather, a Western Wood-Pewee, to Kelly Bryan for preservation. Over the next week, more than two dozen dead Flammulated Owls were discovered in West Texas. The deep cold had struck at the peak of their southward migration, and these owls had been devastated. Thousands likely perished.

After hellos and catching up, Jody and Clay told me that they had not seen the Painted Redstart since the previous evening. Not about to admit defeat, I spent hours outside. The wind cut through my clothes and made every tree and shrub in their yard dance to its wild tune. Muffled in layers, with thick gloves and a wool cap, I nevertheless found my face going numb, my legs and arms chilled. I yearned for warmth.

The Miller home is an island of green in an otherwise brown desert landscape, nestled in a few acres of tall trees at the base of the Sierra Vieja. Throughout the day, migrating birds struggled to survive, their lives seriously at risk because of the weather. Warblers were abundant, with Wilson's, Nashville, Yellow-rumped, Black-and-white and Orange-crowned present near the house. Two Cassin's Vireos, Indigo and Lazuli buntings, Pine Siskins, Red Crossbills, Cassin's Finches, *Empidonax* flycatchers, a Western Wood-Pewee, and several Gray Catbirds ranged the Millers' yard.

Most of the warblers and flycatchers fed on the ground, foraging in and among the grasses as though they were sparrows. Their desperate focus on survival left them caring little about my business. I walked to within two or three feet of several birds. Some appeared especially weak, landing limply on the ground, lying pathetically still, their wings sloppily unfolded.

At noon, Jody and Clay invited me to a lunch of thick, hot soup and delicious sandwiches shared with them and their ranch hands. Thinking that this was my last chance for a Painted Redstart, though, I was soon outside again.

This West Texas fallout was incredibly sad to witness. As is always the case, the severe weather that yields fallouts provides opportunities for birders but is a life-threatening situation for migratory birds. And I never did see the Painted Redstart. After its two-day stay with the Millers, it had either high-tailed south to escape or had died in the cold.

WITH RED CROSSBILLS, Pinyon Jays, Cassin's Finches, and Clark's Nutcracker in the Trans-Pecos, an invasion was clearly under way. Birders speculated as to which species might show up next in Texas. The answer came on October 11 when my friend Dale Ohl informed me that Evening Grosbeaks had been seen at midafternoon at a private feeder in Alpine, forty miles from the observatory. Not long before sunset, I was parked along the residential street Dale had described. The ubiquitous White-winged Doves and House Sparrows held court outside several homes. A nearly empty feeder hung in a front yard.

As I debated whether I was at the right place, two female Evening Grosbeaks (#464) flew into the yard with the feeder and started pecking at seed scattered on the ground. These heavyset, large-billed finches, like many of the other invaders, are irregular winter Texans, absent in most years. I was very glad to welcome them in 2000.

AS OF MID-OCTOBER, I had yet to look for a Juniper Titmouse, an uncommon resident of the Guadalupe and Delaware Mountains of West Texas, near the New Mexico border. My research indicated that Frijole Ranch, in the Guadalupe Mountains National Park, was prime territory for this species.

The area around Frijole Ranch has been settled for centuries. Mescalero Apache thrived here. Five springs—Pine, Juniper, Smith, Manzanita, and Frijole—lie within a small area and have nourished generations. The Walcott family initiated ranching here in the 1860s. This tradition continued until J. C. Hunter, Jr., sold the sixty-seven thousand acres of his Guadalupe Mountain Ranch to the National Park Service in 1966. The Frijole Ranch House opened as a history museum in 1992.

I visited the museum on Saturday morning, October 14, then turned my attention to finding a Juniper Titmouse. It took only twenty-five minutes to locate a family group of four headed down a narrow, steep-sided arroyo near the ranch house. The trees that frame and protect the house held a mixture of winter residents and fall migrants. Cassin's Finches and Townsend's Solitaires were common. A late migrant Cassin's Vireo joined a surprising number and variety of eastern migrants, including two Gray Catbirds and a male-female pair of Rose-breasted Grosbeaks.

As I about to leave, a mammoth accipiter perched nearby and increased my pulse. Northern Goshawk? The bird obliged my efforts to study it with my scope, remaining still and perched. But I was disappointed. The bird was an especially large immature female Cooper's Hawk.

Since my mid-May miss of the tame male Black-throated Blue Warbler at Panther Junction in Big Bend NP (chapter 13), I had been watching for an opportunity to recoup this species. Black-throated Blue Warbler is always rare in Texas but is more likely to be encountered in the fall than in the spring, a characteristic it shares with Mourning Warbler, and the inverse of the relative spring-fall migration frequency of almost every other warbler.

Earlier in the week, in response to a Big Year update I had e-mailed to numerous birders, Midland resident Rose Marie Stortz had startled me with the news that an adult male Black-throated Blue Warbler was in the city. Now, after tracking down the Juniper Titmouse, I called Rose Marie from the Guadalupe Mountains NP. She had relocated the warbler that morning and offered to help me search for it that afternoon. I hopped into my Jeep for the three-hour drive to Midland.

At the residence where the warbler had made its home for the past week, Forrest Roweland and Jaymie Arnold joined Rose Marie and me. From an alley between two rows of well-kept homes, we searched backyards and trees that hung over fences. After an unproductive hour, I started worrying. Rose Marie mentioned that yet another Black-throated Blue Warbler had been recently seen, only a few miles from our current location. I considered giving up on this first bird and trying for the other.

Then Forrest whispered that he heard the warbler chipping from somewhere in a row of low shrubs, less than four feet from where we stood. I thought he was kidding. But then I heard it, too: "tik, tik, tik."

We turned and cocked our ears toward the warbler's chip notes. And then there it was, on the ground in full view, a splendid adult male Black-throated Blue Warbler (#466). How it had gotten into the shrub row without our seeing it was a mystery. Once in view, the warbler allowed prolonged views from close range in fine light. It looked plump and healthy after several days of rest and feasting in Midland.

I returned to the observatory a happy fellow. I had seen Juniper Titmouse and had remedied my maddening spring miss of the Panther Junction Black-throated Blue Warbler without traveling to the coast. The day's odyssey had encompassed 530 miles. There would be several more like it over the coming weeks.

Just three days after this first Frijole Ranch trip, I was on my way back. Chief Park Ranger Jan Wobbenhorst alerted me that Jimmy Jackson of Beeville, Texas, and Billy Sandifer of Padre Island had discovered a Lewis's Woodpecker at Frijole. First catalogued during the Lewis and Clark expedition (1804–1806) to the northwestern United States, Lewis's Woodpecker is yet another rare and irregular winter West Texas visitor. Jimmy and Billy had found the woodpecker in the immense pecan trees growing alongside the old ranch house.

After arriving at Frijole Ranch on Tuesday morning, October 17, I spied the Lewis's Woodpecker (#467) in less than a half hour. The broad, rounded wings of this woodpecker furnished a distinctive silhouette. Its green, silver, and pink coloration and flycatcher-like feeding style, catching insects in flight, are unusual among woodpeckers. This bird was fond of high perches. It was also possessive, repeatedly chasing an Acorn Woodpecker away from the pecans. As a bonus, fifteen Pinyon Jays flew into some low trees while the Lewis's

Woodpecker was nearby, furnishing a rare chance to see these two invaders in Texas in the same binocular field of view.

In the span of less than a month, September 26 through October 17, the fall invasion added Cassin's Finch, Pinyon Jay, Clark's Nutcracker, Evening Grosbeak, and Lewis's Woodpecker to my year list. It would be entirely normal to undertake a Big Year in Texas, work hard at it, and see none of these birds. I welcomed the invaders.

## chapter 22

Studies in Pain

American Golden-Plover and Yellow Rail

With the clock running down on my Big Year, I had several key questions to consider and answer. How much time could I devote to birding from late October through December? Barring unforeseeable problems at work or home, I could spend quite a bit of time in the field. I still had a considerable cache of vacation and compensatory time with my employer and the flexibility to use it.

How many regularly occurring, nonpelagic species had I not yet seen? I had been tracking this number since early June. Now there were only twenty-seven such species. Some of these would present little challenge: Whooping Crane (Aransas NWR), Rough-legged Hawk (Panhandle), Northern Gannet (upper or central Texas coast), Sprague's Pipit (fairly common winter resident over much of Texas), and Grasshopper Sparrow (winter resident at many locations).

Some other species that remained were unfamiliar. Locating them meant more research, correspondence with expert observers, and perhaps many field hours, though eventual success seemed likely. This group included Purple Finch (East Texas or Panhandle), American Woodcock (East Texas), Short-eared Owl (several possible locations), and American Tree Sparrow (Panhandle). Only Bobolink was definitely lost for the year. Painted Redstart and Black-billed Cuckoo were highly improbable after mid-October, but a handful of such records existed. The mathematician in me assigned a probability of success to each species—for example, 100 percent for Whooping Crane, 75 percent for American Woodcock, 50 percent for Yellow Rail, and 0 percent for Bobolink. Combining the odds for individual species allowed me to estimate that I would most likely find, by the end of the year, another eighteen regularly occurring species.

How many trips would be needed? Many.

Which locations would I need to visit? If possible, I should revisit each major Texas region outside my Trans-Pecos home at least once: the Panhandle, Northeast Texas, East Texas, the Hill Country, the Rio Grande Valley.

How many Review Species might I see? In nine and a half months, I had successfully chased or discovered nineteen Review Species, an average of exactly two per month. With two and a half months remaining, the odds favored my seeing another five Review Species.

Since my current year total was 464 species, another eighteen regularly occurring species and an additional five Review Species would yield a year-end total of 487 species. I would achieve the goal of 475 species I had set for myself in June, and amassing 485 or more species seemed within reach.

Looking for outside counsel, I e-mailed sixty active Texas birders regarding how I should manage my year's last few weeks. Many of these people had already helped me, and they rallied for me again, unanimously encouraging and cajoling me to continue to bird hard through the end of the year. They recognized the magnitude of my investment to date. I would welcome the December 31 finish line. But until then, I was determined to make use of every possible resource, maximize my Texas Big Year results, and have fun doing so.

Having conquered my Louisiana Waterthrush nemesis in mid-July, the one serious remaining piece of unfinished business from spring migration was American Golden-Plover. As with the waterthrush, I had been out of the United States at the best time to see this bird in Texas. The American Golden-Plover begins its northward migration from South America in late February via an inland route to Central America. It continues north by land or by crossing the Gulf of Mexico. Either route leads into Texas and thence north to arctic tundra breeding grounds. The American Golden-Plover is fairly common in Texas in late March, especially in the eastern parts of the state.

After breeding, most individuals migrate over the western Atlantic to southern South America, a flight of exceptional dimensions. A very few southbound juveniles migrate over the Great Plains. Thus, American Golden-Plover is a rare fall migrant in Texas between late August and early November. A handful of exceptional records extend into early December.

This species is usually seen in shortgrass prairies, flooded pastures, and plowed fields and, much less often, on mudflats and beaches. Throughout the late summer and fall, across the state, I searched suitable habitat for an American Golden-Plover. Occasional reports teased me. Biologist Glenn Perrigo saw several in the plowed fields east of Riviera, on the lower Texas coast, in early to mid-September. Matt White saw small groups of American Golden-Plover on two occasions in early and mid-September, near Lake Tawakoni in Northeast Texas. Brush Freeman located a single American Golden-Plover at the Hornsby Bend Wastewater Treatment Plant near Austin on October 12.

My searching along the central and lower Texas coasts, in Northeast Texas, in the Trans-Pecos, and in Central Texas failed to produce any American Golden-Plover. On September 24, for example, I spent five hours along the backroads east of Riviera, hoping to strike the same gold that Glenn Perrigo had found. I checked field after field with naked eye, binoculars, and scope, but no golden-plover appeared. By the end of October I was anxiety-ridden about this species. My chances for seeing one were approaching zero. The species seemed destined to be an embarrassing miss.

In early November, I spent a long weekend on the upper Texas coast with American Golden-Plover as a primary target. The weather forecast was poor, but any further delay seemed unwise. The morning of Friday, November 3, was mostly cloudy, warm, and humid, with passing rain showers. My day began in fine American Golden-Plover habitat at the plowed fields along FM 1941, Pear Orchard Road, and FM 1985 and the East Bayou Tract of Anahuac NWR. But a morning of staring through my scope yielded only Black-bellied Plover.

Frustrated, I broke for lunch. In High Island, I purchased a soda and a prepackaged, preservative-soaked sandwich at a convenience store. The town that had been warm and bustling with traffic and birders during spring migration was now wet, much colder, and almost entirely deserted.

Food in hand and with the rain temporarily on hold, I chose the Boy Scout Woods as my lunch site. A single car was parked outside the gate. Two elderly Houston birders were my only companions at the damp, leaf-littered bleachers. The incredible hordes of spring birders were months in the past and future. A sparse population of late migrants and winter residents entertained us while we munched: a couple of Orange-crowned Warblers, a single Gray Catbird, several "Myrtle" Yellow-rumped Warblers, single Black-and-white and Wilson's warblers, noisy White-eyed Vireos, Eastern Phoebes, Bewick's Wrens, and chattering Ruby-crowned Kinglets. I was midway through my turkey and Swiss when a surprising female Black-throated Blue Warbler came into view, foraging nearby at about head height.

From High Island, I wandered south along the Bolivar Peninsula, checking the beach and the fields across Texas 87 for plovers, scanning far out into the Gulf for gannets and scoters, finding nothing new. Rollover Pass and Yacht Basin Road held birds but no golden-plover. Fort Travis Seashore Park, at the peninsula's southern end, hosted only numerous Black-bellied Plover on its grassy lawn.

Turning back north, I parked as close as I could to the North Jetty, a mile-long finger of rock marking the southern boundary of the Bolivar Flats. As I walked out onto the jetty, a strong storm drifted over the Gulf, moving slowly inland. The first raindrops pelted me when I was only a hundred yards from shore. Thousands of birds roosted in the sanctuary's shallow water and mud flats: immense concentrations of Black-bellied Plover, Black Skimmer, American Avocet, and Least and Western sandpipers, along with a few Piping, Snowy, and Semipalmated plovers. As I started to study these birds, the storm's march brought a wall of water across the jetty. I retreated.

Seated in my rental car, damp and cold, I considered leaving. It was after 4:00 P.M.; the day was about to expire. I pondered trying to outrun the storm but elected to wait it out, reasoning that what little remained of the day was best spent studying the birds on the Bolivar Flats rather than driving.

After twenty minutes, the rain eased then ended as the storm tracked off to the north and west. With my scope and tripod balanced on my shoulder, I returned to the jetty, walking out as far as the pavement permitted. From the jetty sidewalk's terminus, I scoped every plover I could see, paying particular attention whenever one leapt into the sky. Unfortunately, every flying bird showed the dark black axillaries and white wingbars and rump of the Black-bellied Plover.

I eventually noticed two plover, standing together, that seemed a bit smaller than those that I had confidently identified as Black-bellied Plover. As I watched, one of these birds decided to preen, lifting its right wing, exposing its axillaries. They were gray, not black!

A nervous quarter hour passed. I never took my right eye from my scope's eyepiece, fearful that I would lose these birds, that they would fly when I was not looking. I had not adjusted the height of my scope, so I was stooped, my neck bent. As my vigil began to turn painful, Black Skimmmers came to my aid, flying just a couple feet above my putative American Golden-Plover. The skimmers flushed fifteen or twenty shorebirds, including my two suspects. As they flew, I had them in the center of my scope's field of view. Both definitely had gray, not black axillaries; neither had a white wingbar; neither had a white rump. Sheer persistence and a dose of good luck had at last brought me the American Golden-Plover (#472).

ALL RAILS ARE SECRETIVE, but Yellow Rails are especially so. A single person might walk through the damp, tangled marsh grasses favored by Yellow Rails for hours or days without seeing one, even if a dense population were present. These birds navigate the marsh without showing themselves. They can practically run between your legs and remain invisible.

My quest to see a Yellow Rail had begun in March of my Big Year.

At that time, as I pondered how I might find this elusive species, an interesting TEXBIRDS post about rails caught my eye. It was authored by Matt Whitbeck, a young U.S. Fish and Wildlife Service employee at the Anahuac NWR. I privately e-mailed Matt with some questions. He responded generously, even offering to instruct me about how to locate a Yellow Rail.

Two months after our March e-mail exchange, late on the afternoon of Monday, May 1, I took Matt up on his offer of help. We met at the Anahuac NWR. The probability that we would see a Yellow Rail in Texas on the first day of May was vanishingly small. Yellow Rails are winter Texans. After mid-April, they are rarely found even in prime habitat. But simply learning how to look for one would be valuable. From the refuge's check-in station, Matt and I bumped along four miles of dirt road to the Yellow Rail Prairie, an extensive marsh.

Groups of birders sometimes search for Yellow Rails using a technique known as "dragging," which briefly flushes the birds from the marsh. For my lesson in dragging, Matt and I donned wading boots. Marching across the prairie, we each held one end of a long section of common rope. A one-gallon plastic milk or water jug was knotted into the rope every three feet. Each jug held several handfuls of rocks.

We jiggled the rope as we walked, erratically yanking it up and down and sideways. The rock-filled jugs bounced noisily along and through the grasses. Moving the rope and the jugs and the rocks up and down was easy. Walking through the marsh without nose-diving into the sharp-edged, wet grass was not so easy. Every step demanded lifting my heavy boots high out of the grass. Walking through deep snow is similarly exhausting. Since the prairie grass was bunched and mounded, the location of terra firma was never clear. Sensing the sweat pouring from my body, hungry saltwater mosquitoes swarmed around my face, attacking without mercy. When Matt and I were a quarter mile out in the marsh, I broached the topic of snakes. Matt told me, "Don't worry." I then tried, with limited success, not to worry about snakes.

When we were only ten minutes into this ordeal, my legs screamed for a rest. But I pressed on, determined to keep up with my younger, fitter teacher. When I could not take the suffering any more, I requested a time-out. As we rested, Matt told me about his research on the Seaside Sparrows that make their homes in this prairie. After oxygen started flowing to my legs again, we continued. We dragged the prairie for a bit more than an hour, by which time I feared Matt might have to drag me out of the prairie. We flushed fair numbers of Seaside Sparrows and Sedge Wrens, and one Sora. But as expected, we saw no Yellow Rails.

MUCH LATER IN MY BIG YEAR, I returned to the problem of finding a Yellow Rail. Early on Saturday morning, November 4, I met Houston birder David Sarkozi, his fiancée Cheryl, Rice University student and birder Nick Block, and his friend Tim at the Anahuac NWR registration shack. I would put my spring dragging lessons to good use.

David knows the Anahuac prairie as well as anyone. He has successfully found Yellow Rails for many birders. Every spring, David leads tours into the Anahuac marsh for rails. We made the four-mile drive to the scene of my May dragging lessons, donned our boots, grabbed another rope festooned with milk jugs and rocks, and headed out into the prairie.

Once again, I was impressed by the amount of work involved. As in May, an hour's slogging around the Yellow Rail Prairie gained me nothing more than sore legs, ragged breathing, a sweaty body, and an elevated pulse rate. It was a good workout.

We took a break and drove backroads, searching for rice being harvested. Combines flush birds, including rails, from the fields more effectively than do a few humans with rope and rock-filled milk jugs. But we could find no working combines, despite miles of driving.

After a midday rest, our team of masochists returned to the Anahuac Yellow Rail Prairie at midafternoon, ready for another round of self-inflicted torture. As we prepared to walk out into the prairie, it started to rain hard. We tried to ignore this, pulling waterproof hoods over our heads as we steeled ourselves for more suffering in quest of the Yellow Rail. Another hour of high-stepping and dragging in the marsh wore us out. The rain never relented. Tired, muddy, and wet, we admitted defeat.

Anahuac NWR held its annual volunteer appreciation dinner and reception that evening. David and Cheryl kindly invited me to join them at this event. During an excellent meal among friendly people, David and I discussed Plan B possibilities for Yellow Rail. I wondered if I would ever see one.

The next morning I had the Bolivar Flats to myself. Birdwise, an adult Lesser Black-backed Gull spiced my morning, but I could not find any scoters on the Gulf. The visibility dropped at midmorning as the weather turned inclement. Near Rollover Pass, I watched shrimp boats drift near shore, mere ghosts behind the curtains of rain. By late morning there seemed little hope that the storms would end within the next few hours, so I left early for the Houston airport, still without a Yellow Rail.

## chapter 23

Two West Texas Gifts

On the second Friday in November, I unsuccessfully chased an immature Black-legged Kittiwake, a one-day wonder that had been sighted at Pecos County's Imperial Reservoir the previous afternoon by Eric Carpenter. I spent the next morning at the far West Texas reservoirs at McNary, Tornillo, and Fort Hancock, then devoted my afternoon to a jaunt along the remote dirt roads that parallel the Rio Grande south of the Quitman Mountains, seventy miles east of El Paso.

On Sunday, worn by the previous day's 380-mile trek, I moved at a slower pace. An hour before noon, I roused myself to check e-mail. My energy level rose as I read a TEXBIRDS post by Canadian Alan Wormington. On the previous afternoon, he had discovered an Olive Warbler, a Texas Review species, at Hueco Tanks State Historical Park, thirty-two miles northeast of El Paso.

Hueco translates from Spanish as "hollows in the rock" and refers to the park's natural basins that trap and hold rainwater. Birding can be good at Hueco Tanks SHP, though the park is best known for some two thousand pictographs and its high granite cliffs, which are popular with rock climbers.

Unfortunately, Alan's TEXBIRDS post was sketchy. He had seen the bird in an area not open to the public, but his post did not even hint at where he had been in the park. It might not be possible to gain access to the place where he had seen the warbler. I pondered my options, gauging the odds that I could relocate this Olive Warbler. They seemed slim. Among my other problems, I had never visited Hueco Tanks SHP. However, owing to work pressures, it would be the following weekend before I could consider leaving the observatory again. By then, according to the weather forecast, a cold front would have swept across West Texas. The warbler might soon fly south. Thus, though I was exhausted, I needed to act.

I phoned my friend Kelly Bryan. As a Texas Parks and Wildlife employee, he knew Hueco Tanks and its staff. Kelly graciously called the park on my behalf. He spoke with Marcia Wheatley, a volunteer host, explaining my interest in the Olive Warbler. Marcia offered to have someone escort me into the area where Alan had seen the bird. I called Marcia next and confirmed that I could pursue the Olive Warbler that afternoon. As soon as I was off the phone, I assembled my binoculars, camera, film, and notebook and roared out of my driveway.

Once on the road, I realized that in my haste I had neglected to ask Marcia some key questions. I did not know how long my hike would be. It was also unclear how well the park staff understood the bird's location. I had to trust the resolution of these details to fate. Alan, Kelly, and Marcia had given me what I needed most: allies and an opportunity.

I met Marcia at the park headquarters. She introduced me to Wanda Olszewski, a Texas Parks and Wildlife staff member who had talked to Alan and ascertained the essential information. Alan had seen the Olive Warbler in Mescalero Canyon, near the concrete dam, in the East Mountain portion of the park. Other good news surfaced. The hike would be short—less than a mile.

Within a half hour, Marcia and her park host husband, John Fulton, were leading me down a well-trodden, level trail into Mescalero Canyon. They were as intrigued as I was by the possibility of seeing an Olive Warbler in Texas. Bird activity was minimal; not surprising, given the time of day. We soon stood at the base of a modest concrete dam.

To gain an overview of the area, we scrambled to the top of the dam, then assessed the habitat and bird activity in the canyon. The area above the dam was in shade and seemed devoid of birds. But the hackberry trees below the dam, a short distance back down the trail, sat in full sun. Ruby-crowned Kinglets, a Brown Creeper, a couple of Canyon Towhees, and a group of Dark-eyed Juncos were in these trees. We climbed down and started sorting through this active flock.

Marcia and I saw the Olive Warbler (#473) almost simultaneously, twelve feet above our heads in a sprawling hackberry. We both called out excitedly to John. Olive Warbler is a resident of the southwestern mountains. This bird was outside its usual high elevation pine, fir, and oak forest habitat. The species breeds from the mountains of central Arizona and southwest New Mexico south through the highlands of Mexico to northern Nicaragua. The northernmost populations, in the United States and Mexico, are partially migratory, with some or most breeders in these regions moving south in the winter. The Hueco Tanks SHP bird was likely one of these migrants.

Our Olive Warbler was a sumptuous sight with its moderately dark face mask, yellow-green-tinted face and head, bright white wingbars, and overall kingletlike wing pattern. It remained in the same hackberry for at least an hour, feeding among this tree's middle and high branches.

RAIN, SLEET, AND SNOW pummeled the Davis Mountains the following Saturday, with periodic fog. I foolishly tried to bird Lake Balmorhea. Predictably, I did not fare well. Snow fell on Saturday night at the observatory, an inch accumulating. Sunday dawned sunny, but with temperatures in the low twenties, I started my birding day at a later hour than usual.

Returning to Lake Balmorhea, I watched a Cooper's Hawk repeatedly dive at a Northern Harrier. In midair they seemed intent on locking their talons but broke off each time just before contact. An immature Reddish Egret, rare away from the coast and salt water, danced in the lake's shallows, wings spread. White-throated Swifts had drifted down from the mountains, as they often do in the winter. Thirty of these speedsters careened above the dam, calling shrilly. Given the wandering that so many species had shown this fall, I was not shocked by a Western Scrub-Jay in the trees on the lake's south shore.

Olive Warbler. Drawing by Kelly B. Bryan.

After two complete circuits of Lake Balmorhea, I was preparing to leave when I noticed a possible birder ahead. I drove over, introduced myself, and discovered that I knew this person through TEXBIRDS and mutual acquaintances, though we had never met. Raised in Dallas, Brian Gibbons had collaborated on ornithological research in several states, including Alaska, where he monitored Spectacled Eider nests and nestlings in the Prudhoe Bay area. In Texas, he had taken part in a Louisiana State University program studying the effects of offshore oil and gas platforms on migratory birds.

After we had exchanged recent observations and discussed the status of the montane invasion, Brian invited me to join him in birding Imperial Reservoir. Another eighty-five-mile drive had not been part of my day's itinerary, but I was receptive to the idea. The remoteness of Imperial Reservoir normally guarantees lonesome birding. To be there with another set of eyes would be a pleasure and an advantage. After stocking up on brisket burritos at the Balmorhea Grocery, we were on the road.

Once at the reservoir, we hurried around to the south via the sandy, bumpy lakeshore trail, wanting to make the most of the fine late afternoon light. We split up the scanning duty, with Brian checking the reservoir's surface from east to west and me working from west to east. I had hardly put my eye to my scope when Brian announced that he had a probable Little Gull.

I had already seen Little Gull in my Big Year, but that did not diminish the thrill of looking upon this Review Species for a second time. The gull was flying, providing clear looks at its dark wing undersides and trailing white wing edges. It approached to within forty yards, allowing me to snap numerous photographs.

We then drove and walked our way around to the north shore, continuing until the high winter water level stopped us. I was not about to risk getting stuck again (see chapter 10). Among the noteworthy birds we saw were five Common Loons, several Hooded Mergansers, a group of White-faced Ibis, a few Bonaparte's Gulls, and a Reddish Egret, which, like the Lake Balmorhea individual, had become a regular over the past year.

With the sun only a few degrees from the western horizon, we approached a group of gulls. Brian identified these while I examined the birds floating on and flying over the water. The gulls standing on the beach were all Ring-billed Gulls of various ages, Brian said. Except one. His next statement, that the exception might be a Mew Gull, another Texas Review Species, brought my attention instantly back to the shoreline.

Mew Gulls breed in Alaska and northwestern Canada and are common in winter on the Pacific Coast. Other subspecies live in Europe and Asia, and a few stray each winter to the Atlantic Coast. Mew Gull identification can be tricky. There are few accepted Texas records. One must avoid being confused by runt Ring-billed Gulls, for example.

We edged closer, seeking details. Scope comparisons of the possible Mew Gull with the nearby Ring-billed Gulls showed that its body length was 10 to 15 percent smaller. Its bill was shorter and slimmer, and it was two-toned, pale green-yellow with a dark black tip. Our suspect's mantle was a slightly darker shade of gray than that of the Ring-billed Gulls. Its head was rounder, streaked with pale brown. Its legs were gray-green. Its iris was dark brown or black. The odds seemed good that Brian's initial call had been correct, but we sought certainty.

At a range of less than thirty yards, our gull filled a sizable fraction of the field of view in a scope. In the sun's last rays, the gull unfolded its wings and took flight. The black at the wingtips extended inward several primaries but not to the secondaries. The outer two primaries displayed white spots or "mirrors." The upper wing surface was fairly uniform gray, like the mantle. The trailing edge on the upper wings was a narrow ribbon of white at the secondaries. The bird's rump and uppertail coverts gleamed white. The tail lacked a band. In sum, these features added up to a second-winter Mew Gull (#474).

At home, I consulted *Birds of the Trans-Pecos* by Jim Peterson and Barry Zimmer, curious as to how many previous records there were for Little Gull and Mew Gull in the region. Little Gull was unmentioned. And there were just three winter Mew Gull records: two from Hudspeth County (1988, 1993) and the third from El Paso County (1998). If the TBRC concurred, Brian and I had just established the first Trans-Pecos record for Little Gull and added one of the region's few Mew Gull records. Not a bad afternoon's work. Having two sets of eyes had made a real difference.

## chapter 24

Of Owls and Cranes

S ince they are primarily nocturnal creatures, owls can be frustratingly difficult to see. Nonetheless, my first observation dates for having seen or unambiguously heard most Texas owls were quite early in the year: Barn Owl (February 6), Barred Owl (July 4), Burrowing Owl (April 3), Eastern Screech-Owl (February 3), Elf Owl (May 7), Ferruginous Pygmy-Owl (April 28), Flammulated Owl (May 21), Great Horned Owl (April 29), Spotted Owl (June 22), and Western Screech-Owl (May 7). By mid-November, only the "eared" species remained elusive, Short-eared Owl and Long-eared Owl.

My first good chance to see a Short-eared Owl came near Thanksgiving. Tim Fennell, a friend and avid birder who lives in Round Rock, north of Austin, saw a Short-eared Owl on the evening of November 16 along Williamson County Road 110, a place where he had seen one the previous winter, too. Since I was in Austin for business the week of Thanksgiving, Tim met me at the intersection of CR 110 and Park Road 945 on Tuesday, November 21. The time to see the owl was just before it became too dark to see anything at all.

I drove away from the University of Texas campus at 4:40 P.M. with what I thought was an ample margin to reach CR 110 at the agreed-upon time. The distance I needed navigate was only seventeen miles of Interstate 35 and another few miles of secondary road.

I was incredibly naive about Austin traffic. My northward progress on I-35 was an intermittent crawl. Start and stop, start and stop. Horns honked. Drivers made rude gestures at each other. Cars made slow-motion lane changes for no reason or effect. Traveling seventeen miles consumed eighty minutes. It was dark when I exited I-35, pulled into a gas station, and called Tim on his cell phone, apologizing for missing our meeting. Tim gave me the depressing news that he and Mike Creese, an active birder from San Antonio, had briefly seen the Short-eared Owl just before six.

The next afternoon, I left the university at 3:10 P.M., reaching CR 110 ninety minutes later, well before dark. I waited patiently for the owl, but it never showed.

In the predawn of Thanksgiving day, I unsuccessfully searched another potential Short-eared Owl location, this one east of Austin. I also visited a residential pond where Brush Freeman had recently encountered a Long-tailed Duck. But that bird was gone or hiding, too.

BARELY AWAKE, I left my Austin motel's parking lot at three on the Friday morning after Thanksgiving, destined for the coast. Southeast of Goliad, along Texas 239, deer crossed the highway and grazed at the roadside in frightening numbers. One weighty doe bolted from the shoulder, forcing me to swerve to the right and off the road at the last minute, brakes locked.

Ten miles farther along this deserted, dark highway, a medium-sized owl, too small to be a Great Horned Owl, flushed from a fence post. I worked to keep the fleeing owl in my high beams. If a highway patrolman had seen me—driving slowly, partly on the road, partly off the road, turning left, right, then left again—I would undoubtedly have received a ticket. And these foolish automotive lunges were for naught. Given the habitat, the owl was probably a Short-eared, but it disappeared before I could sort out its identity.

As dawn colored the eastern sky, I paused at an area along U.S. 77 where Brush Freeman and Petra Hockey had seen Short-eared Owls in previous winters. No owls were out and about.

Soon after dawn, I joined my friend Ro Wauer for breakfast at a quiet, past-its-prime diner in Tivoli. After gulping our food and coffee, we headed for the fifty-five thousand acres of the Aransas National Wildlife Refuge on the Blackjack Peninsula, winter home to the world's one remaining wild Whooping Crane flock.

The wind blew hard as Ro and I searched the Heron Flats, where the cranes sometimes feed. Two tall white long-necked birds in the distance vexed us momentarily, but we soon determined that they were Great Egrets, not Whooping Cranes. We adjourned to the refuge's high observation tower along the Tour Loop Drive. The atmosphere was breathtakingly transparent, every distant detail crisp. Patience yielded excellent views of a Whooping Crane family: two stately, red-capped, black-and-white-winged adults and a smaller juvenile, tawny and white. These were my first views of this regal bird, a species that had come back from the verge of extinction over the past half century. Ro and I shared our find and optics with others who had climbed the tower's many steps and braved the stiff breeze.

With this victory, my Big Year list reached the 475-species milestone, the higher goal I had set in June. With five weeks left in the year, there was time to stretch further. How far? Could I reach the record? How much energy did I have left? I thought about these and other questions on the return trip to Austin.

A glutton for punishment, I detoured to Williamson County for another try on CR 110 and PR 945. The raw evening chill and scouring wind were distracting. To keep me humble, the Short-eared Owl again declined to appear. At dark, having covered 490 miles from Austin to the coast and back, with the detour to Williamson County, I was worn out.

Tim Fennell and I tried one last time for the Williamson County Short-eared Owl, on the evening of November 30. Chestnut-collared Longspurs and Double-crested Cormorants flew over, an unusual juxtaposition of species. We heard a Burrowing Owl as darkness encroached, and we found it perched on a fence pole. It flew and was soon joined by two others. As they hovered above the field, all three fit in my binocular field of view. But there was no sign of the Short-eared Owl.

## chapter 25

Frantic December Days

December began with business, a Board of Directors meeting in Austin for the observatory's new Hobby-Eberly Telescope. After the meeting's conclusion on Saturday afternoon, December 2, I flew to Dallas and drove northeast to Greenville, looking forward to more field time with Matt White.

At dawn on Sunday we hustled to Lake Tawakoni, where Matt had found a Long-tailed Duck among a raft of Common Goldeneyes two days before. Situated on the Sabine River and with a surface area of twenty thousand acres, Lake Tawakoni is operated by the Sabine River Authority for municipal water, industrial use, and irrigation. The list of excellent finds that Matt and others have made at this lake includes Red-throated and Pacific loons, Red-necked Grebe, Harlequin Duck, Parasitic and Long-tailed jaegers, Black-headed and Sabine's gulls, Black-legged Kittiwake, Snow Bunting, and more.

Matt and I grunted up a steep grassy slope to the top of the Iron Bridge Dam. A sizable flock of Common Goldeneyes still floated along the dam. Sadly, there was no Long-tailed Duck among them. Principally a bird of the cold north, where it can be common, Long-tailed Duck is a rare winter visitor to Texas. It can appear almost anywhere in the state. Part of the difficulty of sighting one derives from this duck's habit of staying underwater for long periods. Though much of its feeding activity takes place within thirty feet of the surface, Long-tailed Duck has been documented diving to depths of two hundred feet, deeper than any other duck.

Hordes of Bonaparte's Gulls were at the lake, all of which Matt and I scrutinized, hoping for a Black-legged Kittiwake. While I was engrossed in this activity, Matt heard and then saw a single Smith's Long-spur fly high overhead. I momentarily saw this bird but not well enough to identify it.

All four North American longspurs usually winter in Texas: Chest-nut-collared, McCown's, Lapland, and Smith's. The name *longspur* derives from the long nails on their hind toes. Identifying them can be a frustrating winter exercise. They are the epitome of the "little brown birds" or LBBs that are the bane of many birders. Longspur nonbreeding plumages are dull and similar. Also, since wintering long-spurs travel in restive flocks, rarely perching, they are not approach-able. Even when they are on the ground, they are often invisible in their favored grassy habitat. Attention to their flight calls is key to discerning which species is present.

Though it is a regular winter visitor to north-central Texas between November and March, Smith's Longspur is the rarest longspur in the state. Very few Smith's Longspurs had been reported the previous winter, but in 2000 Matt had been hearing and seeing them regularly since late November.

A search of the fields near an old airstrip adjacent to the Sabine River Authority's offices resulted in an impromptu meeting with a flock of fifty Smith's Longspurs (#476). We heard their dry rattles before we saw them. As they streamed by, some stopped briefly. As in the Lapland Longspur, the white in the tail of a Smith's Longspur is restricted to the outer two feathers on each side of the tail. Even in winter, Smith's Longspurs remain fairly buffy underneath, and several showed the remnants of a white shoulder patch. Matt counseled me that our views had been "as good as it gets."

By noon, we had progressed to the western side of the lake, be-tween Duck Cove and Arrow Point. With scopes and ourselves perched precariously on the sloping shoreline, within a few feet of the traffic roaring past on FM 751, Matt and I scoured the lake surface. We had been at this for a while when Matt shouted: "Three Long-tailed Duck, flying right and fast!"

I looked to see where Matt's scope was pointed. Checking that direction with binoculars, I found the ducks and then got them in my scope. Three female Long-tailed Ducks (#477) flew past without pause, crossing the FM 751 bridge and heading off to the northeast. We watched them until they disappeared near Arrow Point. This species had been recorded several times from the Rains County portions of Lake Takawoni. But these three individuals provided a long overdue first record for Hunt County.

I said good-bye to Matt and then traveled east for a rendezvous with Guy Luneau in Kilgore, near the Louisiana border. Guy grew up in Arkansas liking birds, and this passion is also part of his adult life. He divides his time between his family, his work as a senior chemical engineer for the Eastman Chemical Company, and the study of birds. Guy has traveled extensively for birding. The only regular North American bird that has eluded him is Boreal Owl. Given my inability to see a Short-eared Owl, this miss was easy for me to understand.

Guy had offered to take me into the field as the day ended to try to find an American Woodcock, a hard-to-see winter resident. During a recent Texas Ornithological Society meeting in nearby Longview, Guy had led several field trips that had targeted and found this species.

By 4:30 P.M., he and I were bushwhacking through the damp, thorny, vine-choked woods near his home. Guy flushed our first woodcock. Its twittering wing whistle was a type of music my ears had never heard. I saw this first bird only as a fleeing silhouette in the dim winter light. Over the next half hour, though, we flushed two more woodcocks, one of which I saw well (#478).

After sunset, Guy monitored the ambient light. He described how once the light dimmed to a particular level at mid-twilight, American Woodcocks would fly for about five minutes. To be ready, we moved to where the trees were head height or lower, and less densely packed, a place that afforded a relatively unobstructed view of the sky.

"Any moment now," Guy said, looking upward.

Within sixty seconds, I heard the now familiar wing whistle and sighted the unmistakable silhouette of an American Woodcock—

chubby and long-billed, with broad, rounded wings—against the darkening dome of the sky. "There!" I said, louder than I had intended.

Soon another woodcock flew, well above the trees. A couple of Wood Ducks flew past. Less than thirty seconds later came another wing whistle and woodcock silhouette. A Brown Thrasher uttered its last call of the day.

"Another woodcock, heading away," Guy said.

Five minutes into our vigil, one last woodcock enticed me to twist my neck for a good look. I watched as it dropped into the woods.

I RETURNED TO KILGORE to watch Guy's busy backyard the next morning, hoping to see Purple Finches. A few had begun to infiltrate the area, as they do in most winters. Guy and his spouse, Joan, had seen two at their feeders on Sunday. But despite an investment of five hours, no Purple Finches came to the Luneaus' feeders on Monday morning.

A fast-food lunch in Longview prepared me for the two-hour highspeed haul back to Greenville to reunite with Matt White. I had originally planned to fly home that afternoon. But having sensed my frustration with Short-eared Owl, Matt had suggested we try to find one on Monday evening. Given how well my birding went whenever Matt stepped in to help, I changed my travel plans.

While waiting for dusk, Matt and I birded along country roads northwest of Greenville, then drove to Clymer Meadow, a hilly grassland owned by the Nature Conservancy near the town of Celeste. We set up our scopes along a serene roadside bordering Clymer Meadow and waited as daylight ebbed. I tried to be confident, but my searches for Short-eared Owl had been so frustrating that negative thoughts repeatedly entered my mind.

In regions where the two species occur jointly, the presence of Northern Harriers is a good indicator for Short-eared Owl. Northern Harriers thrive near large populations of voles and other rodents, and these same prey species are sought by Short-eared Owls. More than a dozen Northern Harriers patrolled Clymer Meadow in the late afternoon, a positive sign. One by one the harriers went to roost.

In twilight, a few minutes passed when none were visible. Then we saw a Short-eared Owl (#479). The bird flew low and lazily over the open terrain, back and forth across our line of sight. Marvelous!

MY FRIENDS ERIC AND LARRY CARPENTER, son and father, invited me to join them for a birding weekend in the Panhandle beginning December 8. Larry lives in the Woodlands, near Houston, with his wife, Carol. A lifelong birder, Larry has instilled his passion for the natural world, particularly birding, in his two sons, Eric and Scott. Larry began studying birds while growing up in New York and New Jersey. In the 1970s he moved to Texas, where he has continued to pursue his hobby.

Eric's first birding experiences were Saturday or Sunday trips to the Katy Prairie, west of Houston. His youthful interest in birds developed into an adult's passion. Eric travels extensively, especially around Texas. Several times each year, he undertakes the long drive from Austin to the Trans-Pecos, his favorite place to explore and bird.

A trip in the company of Eric and Larry was guaranteed to be productive and fun. I had not been to the Panhandle since early April and hoped to find at least two species from the shortlist of Rough-legged Hawk, American Tree Sparrow, Tundra Swan, Long-eared Owl, and Northern Shrike. Rarities were a possibility, too. Brant, for example, had been reported near Dalhart and Canadian.

I met Eric, Larry, and several Amarillo area birders—Rosemary Scott, Ed Kutac, Barrett Pierce, and others—on Friday morning, December 8, at the entrance to Palo Duro Canyon State Park. This sixteen-thousand-acre park preserves a dramatic portion of the western Caprock Escarpment, a land of deep, rugged canyons. Our morning brought no new species, though an *Empidonax* flycatcher was notable. Seeing this place, a natural wonder, was an experience worth having, with or without birds.

While driving from our lunch stop to Buffalo Lake National Wildlife Refuge, we halted along FM 1714 so that I could observe my first Rough-legged Hawk (#480) as it soared high above the land. At Buffalo Lake NWR, we struggled through a narrow tree- and shrub-filled draw

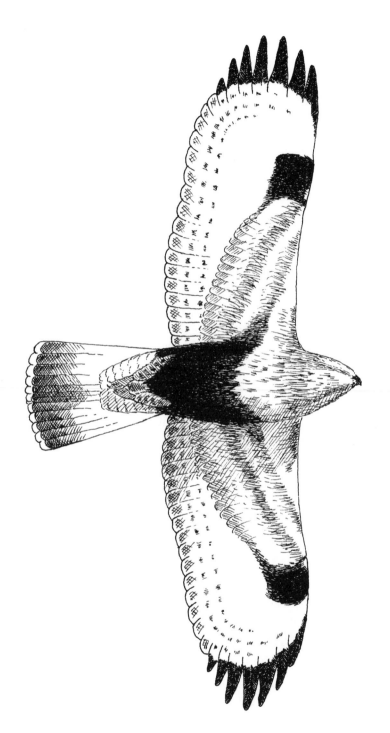

Rough-legged Hawk. Drawing by Kelly B. Bryan.

that had hosted a Long-eared Owl the previous year. But none was present for us.

When Larry, Eric, and I mentioned that swans were on our trip's target list, Barrett offered to see if a Sunday visit could be arranged to a private ranch where swans had recently been found. He believed that these birds were Trumpeter Swans, a Texas Review Species, seen far less often than Tundra Swans. This possibility greatly piqued our interest.

PHEASANT HUNTERS PACKED THE MOTELS and restaurants in Dalhart on Friday evening, something we had not anticipated. Breakfast in a local greasy spoon before sunrise the next morning was noisy, and we had to wait for a table, a rare occurrence at 5:30 A.M.

Eventually fed and caffeinated, we faced a cold, mostly cloudy Panhandle dawn, standing with our scopes and binoculars on a high bluff above Lake Rita Blanca, south of Dalhart. A Brant had been reported here, mixed in with the wintering geese. We had good optics and three trained sets of birding eyes. Still, our confidence dipped when we saw and heard the mob of geese carpeting the water: thousands of Canada Geese, hundreds of Snow and Ross's geese, and a handful of Greater White-fronted Geese.

We picked through this proverbial haystack for the needle, a Brant. A solid hour of checking one bird after another failed to reveal it. The Brant was either gone or lost amidst the riot of geese.

Nevertheless, these Lake Rita Blanca geese were a made-to-order laboratory to study Canada Goose variation. The length of individual Canada Geese varies widely, from twenty-seven to forty-five inches. This one species includes the largest and nearly the smallest goose in North America. Ornithologists recognize at least six different subspecies. At Lake Rita Blanca, we were most likely seeing individuals representing three of these subspecies, often side by side: the small-bodied, small-billed, and short-necked "Richardson's" Canada Goose; the intermediate-sized "Lesser" Canada Goose; and the large-bodied, long-necked, long-billed "Common" Canada Goose.

Eventually admitting failure with our Brant hunt, we departed for Texas' northwest corner and the Rita Blanca National Grassland, which encompasses 77,463 acres in Texas and another 15,860 adjacent acres in Oklahoma. Administered by the U.S. Forest Service, it is a dramatic landscape, offering solitude and long-distance vistas. The paved and unpaved roads we traveled were empty. The place was ours.

Along FM 1879, we pulled over at a nondescript spot where Eric had seen American Tree Sparrows two winters before. Remnants of farm machinery rusted on the north side of the road, alongside the only two trees to be seen for miles, both dead. Within sixty seconds, several American Tree Sparrows (#481) hopped up from the grass and into view on the bare gray limbs of the dead trees.

Near noon, we pulled into the Thompson Grove Recreation Area, a wooded site with picnic tables and restrooms. A wandering, invading Mountain Chickadee greeted us. Rows of cedar planted as windbreaks and isolated groves of tall trees provided opportunities to search for roosting owls. I hoped for a Long-eared Owl, but we found only a roosting Western Screech-Owl (rare for the region) and a single Great Horned Owl. We also thoroughly investigated the islands of trees at Area 18, a Long-eared Owl roost in past years, but Great Horned Owls were our sole find. As at Buffalo Lake, the more aggressive Great Horned Owls had likely run off the smaller Long-eared Owls.

TRAVELING SOUTH ON U.S. 83 on Sunday morning, we turned west onto Texas 281 to inspect yet another cedar windbreak, this one miles in length. As a strong cold front approached, we checked tree after tree for owls. The temperature dropped steadily, the cloud layer thickened and lowered, and the wind increased. We were not having fun. And there were no owls in the cedars.

Near Lake Marvin, twenty miles east of Canadian, we met Barrett and Carol Pierce as appointed. Raised in the Rio Grande Valley, Barrett had taken up birdwatching as an active hobby in the fall of 1999. Though only a recent convert to birding, he was impressively competent and sharp-eyed.

We drove onto the Oasis Creek Ranch in northeast Hemphill County as guests of the ranch owner, Bub Smith. Having hunted for much of his life, Barrett knew the Panhandle's publicly accessible land and many private ranches. Unfortunately, the weather progressed from fair to poor to abominable, with visibility of a hundred yards or less in fog, mist, and occasional sleet. Had we not had the generous assistance of ranch foreman Charlie Coffee, and had we been searching for anything more subtle than two outsized, blazingly white birds, our situation would have been hopeless. As it was, the odds for success were steadily dropping as the conditions deteriorated.

The pond where the swans had last been seen was empty. Disappointed, Barrett drove on through the worsening weather to a reed-filled few acres of water known as Trout Pond. As it came into view through the obscuring mist and rain, we saw two huge white birds sitting peacefully on the water.

We parked and exited the Pierces' SUV, careful not to spook the swans. Peering through three scopes, everyone came to the same conclusion: Trumpeter Swans! Neither of these birds bore a neck, leg, or wing band, and they were clearly wary of people. These were not escaped captives; they were wild Trumpeter Swans (#482). We admired them for as long as we could stand the weather, then beat a hasty retreat to the car.

CHRISTMAS BIRD COUNTS (CBCs) are the centerpieces of the holiday season for many birders. The counts are coordinated across the United States by the National Audubon Society, each CBC sampling the bird population within a fifteen-mile-diameter circle on a single day. Repeated year after year, CBCs provide a valuable long-term record of early winter bird populations.

Ornithologist Frank Chapman organized the first "Christmas Bird Census" in New England in the fall of 1900. Chapman hoped to replace the killing contests of that era, such as the "side-hunt," with a nonlethal alternative. The side-hunt was a Christmas day shooting spree, a tradition in parts of the United States whereby the team of armed men with the most dead creatures at day's end was declared the winner.

The census initiated by Chapman and twenty-seven birdwatchers in December, 1900, has succeeded and expanded beyond anyone's dreams. During the 101st Christmas Bird Count (December 14, 2000–January 5, 2001), more than 40,000 observers in the United States recorded 689 species and 51,657,566 individual birds across 1,553 count circles. Additional efforts by Bird Studies Canada and others resulted in 297 Canadian counts and 50 counts in the Caribbean, Latin America, South America, and the Pacific Islands.

In mid-December, Yellow Rail was still near the top of my "need to see" list. Two Christmas Bird Counts where this species might plausibly be found were to be held on December 15 (San Bernard NWR) and December 17 (Freeport).

To participate in the San Bernard CBC, I made my way to the central Texas coast near Lake Jackson, drawn by a TEXBIRDS call for volunteers from Ron Weeks. Organizers of CBCs are formally known as "compilers." Their duties include setting the date, finding participants, scouting and assigning territories, accumulating the required paperwork and data, and then submitting these to the National Audubon Society or Bird Studies Canada.

On Friday, December 15, I drove to the refuge headquarters with my car's windshield wipers working overtime. At the refuge, Ron Weeks and co-compiler Jennifer Wilson finalized the day's assignments, getting everyone into the field in short order.

Ron and Jennifer's partnership for this CBC is a fine example of the professional-amateur collaborations that have so benefited ornithology. A chemical engineer, Ron has been birding since he was fourteen years old. After moving to Texas in December, 1997, he became a well-known member of the state's birding community. Ron has undertaken several successful "Big Day" efforts and has volunteered at Brazoria and Aransas national wildlife refuges. Jennifer is a biologist for the Texas Mid-Coast National Wildlife Refuge Complex. Her duties encompass several coastal refuges, including San Bernard NWR and Brazoria NWR. Given the breadth of her professional responsibilities, she could not organize a scientifically interesting CBC without the assistance of a knowledgeable volunteer such as Ron.

In view of my focus on Yellow Rail, Ron assigned me to one of this count's two "marsh buggies." This would be a new experience for me. The tractorlike marsh buggies rode on large balloon tires and functioned well in bumpy, sloppy, off-road terrain. Each buggy had a high wooden bed that accommodated four to six birders behind the driver's cabin. Once the buggy entered the marsh, holding onto a waist-high railing was mandatory as the vehicle pitched and heaved on the uneven terrain. The count's two buggies drove in parallel across the marsh, dragging between them a long metal cable that flushed birds so that they could be counted. To minimize the disturbance to the habitat and the birds, this dragging occurs only once each year, during the CBC.

Throughout the morning, warm showers passed across the marsh. Whenever the buggy stopped, clouds of mosquitoes buzzed about our heads, undeterred by liberal applications of repellent and constant swatting. Though we saw Virginia and Clapper rails and Sora, and one buggy rider even spied a tiny Black Rail racing through the marsh, no Yellow Rails were detected. The buggies returned to headquarters at lunch. Since we had yet to find a Yellow Rail, we rode out again after our meal but returned with no different result.

By nightfall, more than fifty birders had recorded a remarkable 195 species for the count. I still had not seen a Yellow Rail, but it had been a memorable day. At the "countdown dinner," a CBC tradition, the volunteers and compilers convened to report and review the day's results, to discuss and document rarities, and to relax while enjoying a communal meal. Ron Bisbee and his assistants had spent the day preparing a magnificent seafood gumbo. In combination with the refuge's fine habitat and birdlife, word of mouth about this gumbo ensures that the San Bernard CBC will have large volunteer crews at future counts.

STRONG WINDS AND COLD battered me on Saturday near Freeport. I spent much of the day at the Quintana and Surfside jetties, scanning the Gulf. Braving the conditions on these jetties did add Northern Gannet (#483) to my Big Year, but I saw no scoters.

The afternoon brought warmer temperatures, but the wind howled, gusting to thirty miles per hour. On the Surfside Jetty, I momentarily stepped away from my scope to pick up a blowing styrofoam cup, a piece of litter. The wind chose that moment to gust, toppling my tripod and scope. My heart leapt into my throat. Miraculously, my uncovered optics and tripod escaped damage.

On Saturday night, I accomplished the trip's most important task. I waded into the throngs of people shopping at the Lake Jackson stores and purchased several Christmas presents for my family.

The Freeport CBC has always been one of the most productive and well-run. The area is blessed with excellent habitat and a diverse array of wintering and resident birds; each count lists two hundred or more species. Most important for me, the Brazoria NWR marsh census, north and east of the count center, has consistently recorded Yellow Rail.

At dawn on Sunday, I gathered with others at the refuge gate. Our day began with a "sparrow walk" in the fields near the headquarters, led by Houston birder P. D. Hulce. Crisp views of one of my personal favorites, Le Conte's Sparrow, pleased me. Each individual of this species sports a distinctive head and face pattern: a white central crown stripe squeezed between two black lateral crown stripes, and a buffy face with inset gray eye patches.

The refuge staff struggled to start the marsh buggies, vehicles similar to those I had ridden at the San Bernard NWR. I feared the rail search might be scrubbed. But dogged persistence won out, and both buggies eventually coughed to life. Riding atop the rear bed on these buggies was more comfortable than Friday's experience at San Bernard. Though it was cold, there was little wind. Bright sun dazzled us from a cloud-free azure sky. The flatter marsh with far fewer hillocks helped, too. There was much less lurching and listing.

We had spent only fifteen minutes in the marsh when a Yellow Rail (#484) flew between the two buggies. Over the next two hours, we recorded seven Yellow Rails, including one scurrying in the open no more than twenty feet from my perch. I savored my excellent views of this reclusive bird, delighted that I had persevered in my efforts to see it.

## chapter 26

Chasing to the End

B ack in my West Texas office, a TEXBIRDS post from Noreen Baker and George Saulnier caused me to emit a loud "Arrrgh!" On Tuesday, December 19, as I was traveling home from Austin, George and Noreen had discovered an adult winter-plumaged Red-necked Grebe, a Texas Review Species, along Lake Austin's Scenic Drive!

Thursday was the earliest I could travel again; I was worried that the Red-necked Grebe would disappear. The Austin weather forecast promised little help, with the wind predicted to be twenty to thirty miles per hour. But my Big Year's days were numbered, and the bird was seen by many birders on Wednesday, so I hit the road at 3:30 A.M. on Thursday, driving with bleary eyes. After the usual three-hour drive to Midland and one-hour flight to Austin, I made a beeline for Scenic Drive. Expensive homes lined the east shore waterfront, with pools, decks, docks, and sleek boats. My apprehension about using a scope in the midst of such affluence was trumped by my desire to see a Red-necked Grebe.

Two skilled young birders, Nicholas Block and Cameron Cox, arrived shortly after I did. Throughout the morning, the wind created waves on Lake Austin, making our job harder. After an hour and half of failed effort, we moved north, seeking other lake access. Mount

Bonnell's rocky crags overlook Lake Austin from a substantial height, offering views of a mile or more of this narrow body of water. From Mount Bonnell we enjoyed an unexpected bonus: watching from above, we could see through the transparent water to follow feeding birds, such as a Common Loon, through an entire dive sequence. But we found no Red-necked Grebe.

We continued north to Loop 360, crossing the high bridge that spans Lake Austin. From underneath the bridge, we checked up and down the lake but remained grebeless. Out of time, Nick and Cameron departed for home. My stomach grumbled, so I diverted away from the lake for a delicatessen lunch. After wolfing down a corned-beef sandwich, I returned to my day's starting point. Three more hours were available to me.

On Scenic Drive I met Mike Creese, an active San Antonio birder. He had not yet seen the grebe, either. Discouraged, I took a deep breath, pointed my scope at lake center, put my eye to the eyepiece, and started scanning again, trying to ignore the wind and waves. I had moved the scope only slightly to the right when I stumbled upon the Red-necked Grebe (#485), swimming 120 yards north of me. Larger-bodied and grayer than the Pied-billed Grebes, it sported a sizable yellow bill and a white crescent along the rear of its face. I shared my find and scope with Mike. The Red-necked Grebe divided its time between swimming and diving.

The afternoon turned into quite a social occasion, with Texas birders Lee Hoy, Ted Eubanks, Barbara and John Ribble, Judy Williamson, Jeff Hanson, and others arriving to see the grebe. The bird cooperatively remained in plain sight.

THE FOLLOWING SATURDAY MORNING I was again in Kilgore, staring at Guy and Joan Luneau's backyard feeders, hoping for a Purple Finch. This species is less common in Texas than it once was, having come up on the short side in its competition with the House Finch.

The Luneaus' feeders were aflutter with American Goldfinches, Carolina Chickadees, Dark-eyed Juncos, Northern Cardinals, and

White-throated Sparrows. A Pileated and a Downy Woodpecker patrolled the wooded yard, as did a finely plumaged Yellow-bellied Sapsucker. And among the crowd, I was thankful to see Carpodacus finches.

Care must be taken with the identification of the three *Carpodacus* species that can be seen in Texas: House, Cassin's, and Purple finches. The separation of House Finch from the other two species usually requires just a good look in decent light. But it is easy to confuse Purple Finch with Cassin's Finch, especially when looking at females and immatures. I used my scope to study the Luneaus' finches, noting the distinguishing field marks. There was a well-marked male and the rest were females and immatures. Within twenty minutes, I had convinced myself that all of these were Purple Finches (#486).

My plan for the homestretch, December 26–31, was to bird the Panhandle for two or three days, visit the upper and central Texas coasts, and finish my year in the Rio Grande Valley. In the Panhandle, I would seek Northern Shrike, Long-eared Owl, and Tundra Swan, hoping to see at least two of these three. There was reasonable hope that I would see these species, though each required a different pursuit strategy.

Northern Shrike is a rare Texas visitor. Unless someone else had already located one, I would cruise the backroads, scrutinizing every shrike sitting on a power line or a fence. All or almost all would be Loggerhead Shrikes. If I were lucky, a full day's effort might turn up one Northern Shrike. Long-eared Owl roosts are difficult to find. This species is nonvocal in the winter and strictly nocturnal. A few Tundra Swans drop into Panhandle ponds every winter. Since mid-December, for example, Tundra Swans had been seen with some regularity near Wichita Falls. Lake Marvin, near Canadian, was another spot worth checking.

On the coast, I hoped to see another two species among Whitewinged Scoter, Black Scoter, Glaucous Gull, and Black-legged Kittiwake. Patrolling the coast for these species, I would be spending time from Freeport north to High Island. Anything might show up in the Valley. A female Blue Bunting had been reported from the Trailer Loop at Bentsen–Rio Grande Valley State Park since mid-December. I was praying it would stay put, relishing the bulging seed feeders maintained by the winter Texans.

THOUGH I NEEDED A PLAN, flexibility and willingness to adjust my itinerary on short notice were equally critical. The importance of flexibility was demonstrated when a massive winter storm scrambled my end-of-year plans. At Christmas, monitoring the storm's progress via the Internet, it became obvious that the Panhandle would be inaccessible for two or three days. Snow and ice paralyzed not only the Panhandle but much of the Trans-Pecos and North Texas, too. It would be foolish to challenge deep snow, dangerously cold temperatures, and horrific wind chill. I reorganized my itinerary. Instead of traveling from the Panhandle to the coast to the Valley, I would bird the coast first, then the Panhandle, and end in the Valley.

For the next day, December 26, I planned a detour to Red Bluff Reservoir on my way to the Midland Airport. This reservoir, formed by damming the Pecos River, lies in the arid country along the New Mexico border and is rarely birded. Though visiting this remote place would be time-consuming, Red Bluff Reservoir has produced a disproportionate number of unusual records for the small amount of time birders have devoted to it.

From Red Bluff I planned to continue to Midland, where I would catch a flight to Houston. By evening of Christmas day, however, this plan also lay on the scrap heap, another winter storm victim. The roads north of Interstate 10 were icy. Midland and its airport were a mess. My only remaining option was to fly from El Paso, where it was warm enough for the airport to be open for flights to nonsnowy destinations, such as Houston.

I left for El Paso on December 26, traveling the lower elevation highways that hug the foothills of the Davis Mountains. Thirty miles from home, I realized my camera equipment was not in the car. I retraced my path and eventually departed the observatory a second time. This time I chose the shorter route north along Texas 118 toward Kent, traversing slightly higher elevations. This entailed some risk. But it was midday, snow had not fallen for several hours, and the roads were clear in the vicinity of the observatory.

The first twenty-five miles were fine, but I encountered snow flurries fifteen miles south of Interstate 10. A slim layer of snow soon coated the road. I dropped my speed to thirty-five miles per hour.

After another mile, my Jeep Wrangler slid a bit. I shifted into four-wheel-drive and slowed down some more.

Another quarter mile north, I suddenly lost control. The Jeep slid across the highway, angling forward and left. I wrenched the wheel in the direction I wanted to go, but the snow and ice would not permit the Jeep to respond. My vehicle rotated counterclockwise. The back end tried to overtake the front from the right. I crossed the left lane and went off the road onto the shoulder. Having turned three-quarters of a circle, the Jeep and I shuddered backwards down a steep embankment toward a rock wall several feet high. I thought my Big Year was going to end right there and then. A scary image flashed through my mind: the Jeep flipped, with me hanging upside down in a seatbelt for hours on remote, icy Texas 118 until help finally arrived.

But my Jeep did not flip. It rumbled down the rough, steeply angled shoulder, and finally finding some friction in the grass and stone underneath the mantle of snow and ice, it slowed and came to a stop. My heart raced. I did not move for a minute or two, recovering my senses, thanking the deity for my salvation and the fact that I was still upright. Neither the Jeep nor I seemed to be damaged.

I got out. Had the Jeep gone off the road just thirty feet farther north, it would have tumbled into a steep arroyo with significantly less benign consequences. I inspected the roadway. The layer against the ground was ice, dusted with a half inch to an inch of snow. It was only nine miles to the interstate. I eased the Jeep back onto the roadway in four-wheel-drive, but it was hopeless. The vehicle immediately started sliding again, no matter how slowly I proceeded.

Though it would be costly in time and might mean missing my planned El Paso to Houston flight, I backtracked south to U.S. 90 and Van Horn and turned onto I-10 heading west. These roads were free of snow and ice. Since I had intentionally scheduled myself on a flight arriving from a warm climate, Los Angeles, I eventually made it to Houston that evening. On the El Paso airport monitors, every flight to the Panhandle and North Texas was listed as "CANCELED."

Adding to the complexity of my race to the finish line, the computer server that handled all my e-mail malfunctioned, and I lost all electronic connectivity to the outside world. From December 26 through December 30, I had no access to TEXBIRDS or e-mail. This severely cramped my ability to track avian sightings around the state. Fortunately, Brush Freeman was willing to spend a portion of every evening with me on the phone. He filled in admirably as my source of day-to-day Texas birding information and news.

ON DECEMBER 16 the Houston CBC was held for the sixty-seventh time since 1913. Fifty-eight counters recorded 164 species despite high winds, cool temperatures, and choppy bay waters. P.D. Hulce reported the CBC results on TEXBIRDS, including a White-winged Scoter, a rare bird in Texas.

I contacted P.D., whom I had met at the San Bernard CBC a few days earlier, about this scoter. It had been found on private property at the cooling ponds of a Houston Lighting and Power plant. Gaining access to plant property for the CBC had meant an advance letter, phone calls, and liability waivers. P.D. said, "I'll see what I can do for you." But he was not optimistic.

Only a couple of days later, I learned that the scoter was still present on the utility's pond, and I might be allowed to see it. P.D. put me in contact with Breck Sacra, a biologist for Houston Lighting and Power. Breck graciously offered to escort me to the plant on Wednesday, December 27. At eight that morning, Breck and I rendezvoused at a fast-food restaurant along U.S. 59, southwest of Houston. The weather remained miserably wintry, with bone-chilling cold, a damp, incessant breeze, and intermittent rain showers that hovered on the verge of sleet.

After introductions and some much-needed coffee, I followed Breck along FM 762 to the power plant, a place of well-lit buildings and towering gray stacks. He escorted me past the entry gate, along a maze of internal roads and turns, and through a short, narrow tunnel. When we arrived at the pond, the sky was low and ominous. Wind whipped the five acres of water. These were far from ideal conditions. But at the far end of the pond, against a stand of reeds that afforded some protection from the wind, a raft of ducks floated. I jumped out and rapidly assembled my scope and tripod.

Through my wide-field eyepiece, I saw thirty or forty Lesser Scaup, several Canvasback and Redhead, twenty American Coots, and a handful of Green-winged Teal. It was a busy stretch of water. And there was an exquisite adult male White-winged Scoter (#487), too. The scoter was about the size of a Canvasback but predominantly jet black, its white secondaries a bright patch on the swimming bird. A crescent-shaped patch of white showed above and behind the eye. Shivering uncontrollably, I attached my camera and long focal-length lens to the tripod and snapped several photographs.

NOW MY MISSION WAS to search the coastal waters for Black Scoter and patrol the beaches and air for Glaucous Gull and other rarities, perhaps finding a Black-legged Kittiwake or a Greater Black-backed Gull. Finding Black Scoter, the rarest scoter in Texas, was a tall order. Small numbers are usually located on coastal Christmas Bird Counts, such as those at Galveston, the Bolivar Flats, and Sea Rim. But these birds are never easy to find. An investment of hours over a day or more might not yield any.

Through the afternoon of December 27, I birded along a forty-mile stretch of barrier island north from Quintana Jetty. I stopped at San Luis Pass County Park, various unnamed, deserted bits of Gulf and bayside beach, and Galveston's famous East Beach. Though the rain relented, the wind and chill remained nasty. By sunset I was exhausted and had nothing new to show for my efforts. With darkness, I checked into an inexpensive Galveston motel, flipped on the lights, and planned my next day.

Because a Black Scoter had recently been seen from Galveston's Flagship Hotel at 25th Street, I started there on Thursday morning, December 28. Built over the Gulf, the rear parking lot and jetty at this Galveston landmark provide a commanding high view of the water. But two hours of constant surveillance in good conditions yielded no Black Scoter.

A noontime call to local expert Richard Peake brought the recommendation that the odds would tilt in my favor if I concentrated my Black Scoter effort between Rollover Pass and Crystal Beach, a ten-mile stretch of the Bolivar Peninsula. I caught the Galveston ferry and was deposited on the peninsula at 1:00 P.M. With some care, much of the peninsula's beach can be driven. For the next three hours, I stopped every quarter mile, set up my scope, and checked every bird over and on the Gulf.

Ducks were numerous offshore, mostly Lesser Scaup with a few Greater Scaup. Cormorants were abundant. An occasional Northern Gannet wandered past. A few Eared Grebes and Red-breasted Mergansers bobbed in the waves. Birds were plentiful along the beach, especially Sanderlings, Willets, and Black-bellied Plovers. The expected gull species—Laughing, Ring-billed, Herring, and Bonaparte's—were common. Over the course of the day, I saw two Surf Scoters floating with ducks, including a striking male, but no Black Scoter.

On Friday morning, December 29, the dead calm Gulf waters provided excellent scoter hunting conditions at Rollover Pass. I returned to my tedious routine, stopping frequently along the beach, sometimes backtracking. Near nine o'clock, two miles south of Rollover Pass, I spied two promising birds flying north and parallel to the shore at a range of seventy-five yards. As they closed the distance between us, I became hopeful and excited. As they passed into better light, I could see that their bodies were entirely and unambiguously black. Flying just above the Gulf, both showed dark wing linings that contrasted with paler flight feathers. The finest lighting lasted for precious few seconds, but it was enough. I had at least succeeded in seeing Black Scoter (#488).

IN THE EVENING I CONSULTED by phone with several Texas birders. No new rarities were on the grapevine, probably due to the severe winter weather that blanketed the state. Many Panhandle homes remained without power. In the rural areas I had hoped to bird, such as the Rita Blanca National Grassland, the roads were impassable even with four-wheel-drive. However, a female Blue Bunting was still at Bentsen–Rio Grande Valley State Park. She was fickle, showing for only short periods each day. Many had failed to spot her. But lacking anything else to chase, and with the Panhandle still a frozen mess, I opted for the Valley.

My flight from Houston was delayed. Then, after a midnight arrival, I had to search for a motel room in McAllen. On Saturday morning, December 30, I arrived on the Trailer Loop at Bentsen in a sleep-deprived, crusty-eyed state. I shuffled over to site 23, the feeder location preferred by the Blue Bunting. Several other birders, intent on seeing the same bird, were already present. Four birders from Indiana had been chasing the Blue Bunting for four days! Since they seemed knowledge-able and competent, this troubled me. I did not have that kind of time.

While waiting for the Blue Bunting, we studied a "streak-backed" oriole, an individual well-known to the locals. Though it certainly had a streaked back, it was not, as some had suggested, a Streak-backed Oriole, a Mexican species. The black on the face, below the eyes, was too extensive; the streaking and back color were incorrect; and the bill curved too much. Locals believed this bird and another similar park denizen to be Audubon's–Altamira Oriole hybrids.

Discussion with fellow birders revealed that the fickle Blue Bunting's last brief appearance, the previous afternoon, had actually occurred at site 19, not site 23. Both sites were soon staked out by birders who remained in constant contact via walkie-talkies.

While waiting, I tried to plan. To have any hope of reaching the Panhandle that evening, I had to depart trailer site 23 no later than 11:30 A.M. As my watch ticked toward this time, I pondered what I would do if the Blue Bunting failed to show soon. Then suddenly the birders at site 19 screamed to everyone within hailing distance: "Blue Bunting! Blue Bunting!"

Those of us at site 23 rushed to cover the seemingly infinite fifty yards to site 19, straining to not flush the bird. "Look at feeder number two," someone said. The trailer resident at site 19 had several feeders hanging from the trees, and each feeder was labeled with a large black numeral. I was soon watching a calm female Blue Bunting (#489) through the clear plastic dome of feeder number two. The bird dined for four or five minutes, allowing detailed observation and comparison with two Indigo Buntings at the same feeder. Uniform cinnamon color separated the Blue Bunting from the streak-breasted Indigo Bunting females. Then the bird hopped off the feeder and disappeared into a shrubby tangle.

One of the four Indiana birders was in another part of the park when the Blue Bunting surfaced. This fellow returned a few minutes too late. His friends stopped smiling and broke the news to him gingerly. He sat down on a bench near feeder number two and stared. He was still there when I left.

The next day, Sunday, December 31, would be the last day of my Big Year. What should I do? Where should I go? During my Saturday morning at Bentsen, I had overheard two conversations about possible rarities that, if they were real, would be extraordinary birds worth chasing. Birders come to the Valley expecting great things, especially in the winter. Some become too eager, too ready to leap to an unlikely conclusion before adequately eliminating the likely possibilities.

The first conversation I overheard involved a possible female Garganey that might have been glimpsed at a Santa Ana NWR pond. Garganey is an Old World species, a very rare bird in Texas. A drake Garganey is striking and an easy call. But a female Blue-winged or Green-winged Teal could easily be misidentified as a female Garganey by an over-excited birder.

I also eavesdropped on a hushed discussion of a possible Common Greenshank. This Eurasian shorebird species had been noted as a rare spring and fall visitor to the Aleutian and Pribilof islands off Alaska and had been recorded very rarely in northeastern Canada. It had never been documented in Texas. Since it strongly resembles Greater Yellowlegs, a common Texas winter resident, caution was needed.

But I did not hear caution or a careful sifting of the observational facts in either conversation. My assessment was that neither of these potential rarities had been conclusively seen, so neither merited a chase, especially given how little time I had left. To my knowledge, these possible records were never reported, confirmed, or documented.

No other rarities seemed to be at hand in the Valley. A Roadside Hawk had made a brief appearance at Bentsen at midmonth but had not been seen for two weeks. Since the weather seemed to have improved in the southern portions of the Panhandle, I decided to travel to Lubbock to seek a Long-eared Owl. This seemed a reasonable bet. Local birders had given me two locations to check, each many acres in extent: the Lubbock Cemetery and the tree nursery adjacent to the

Texas Tech Medical Center. Each site had been known to harbor these owls in past years, and a Long-eared Owl had recently been reported from the cemetery.

AS I DROVE FROM the Lubbock Airport into the city after dark, deep snow still covered the ground. The city streets were messy. Few people were out, and the weather forecasters had suddenly turned more pessimistic about New Year's Eve. My companion the next day would most likely be freezing drizzle.

In my Lubbock motel, I was disheartened to learn that a Ruff had been discovered on Friday evening in Kenedy County on the lower Texas coast. This Review Species had also been seen on Saturday, when I had been in the Valley seeking the Blue Bunting. Unfortunately, no one at Bentsen had known about this discovery.

Ruff is the most likely Eurasian shorebird to be seen in North America. Though still a rare Texas visitor, it is most often seen in the fall in the state's southern regions. The landowners with the Ruff were allowing interested observers in to see and study the bird, though for a fee. Had I remained in the Valley, I certainly would have tried to see this bird. But having already traveled across most of Texas, and with just one day to go, I could not now return to the Valley, though I did consider it. Still, a Lubbock Long-eared Owl seemed a good bet.

Cold fog greeted me on the morning of New Year's Eve. Visibility was an eighth of a mile or less. I struggled to find the Texas Tech University Medical Center, eventually asking directions at a convenience store. It took another quarter hour to find the tree nursery, which was fenced. There was no gate that I could find. I eventually noticed a downed part of the fence and slipped in.

Long, neat, well-separated rows of trees, tens of evergreens, stood before me. I slogged through three to ten inches of ice-crusted snow, peering into tree after tree. I did this for three hours and never saw an owl.

After lunch, I drove across town to the Lubbock Cemetery. A lengthy, nearly unbroken line of full, tall evergreens trees marked the cemetery's border. A few more evergreens grew in the cemetery proper. I started in the southwest corner, an area I had been told the Long-eared Owl favored. A large, chunky black dog of uncertain ancestry was loose and had appointed himself guardian here. As I approached, he ran toward me, loud and lathering. I grabbed a hefty dead branch and brandished it. The dog stopped at a distance of ten yards and barked. Since he came no closer, I tried to ignore him. He eventually tired of me and trotted away. Peace returned to the cemetery.

By midafternoon, having worked three-quarters of the cemetery's promising but barren perimeter, I noticed a few short, dense, long-needled evergreens growing in the interior. Each had been trimmed to a smooth-surfaced sphere. Hoping that these might be the key to finding a Long-eared Owl, I approached one. As I peered into its tightly interwoven branches, there came a tremendous rustling from within. An owl burst from deep in the branches, near the trunk, and flew. Startled, I raised my binoculars, my intuition and naked eye already telling me that this bird was a Barn Owl, not my fervently hoped-for Long-eared Owl.

Four of these spherical evergreens held Barn Owls. Each time one flushed, my heart raced and my hopes momentarily soared with the thought that this must be my Long-eared Owl. But each rush of excitement was followed by disappointment. The Long-eared Owls of Lubbock eluded me. Very few species had managed to do so during the previous twelve months, but this owl was one.

## chapter 27

Reflections on a Texas Big Year

ightfall in Lubbock on New Year's Eve officially brought
down the curtain on my Texas Big Year. It had so consumed
my energy and time for all 366 days of the year 2000 that
it was hard for me to believe no more planning, organizing, research,
e-mail, consultations, phone calls, or traveling would be needed. I
could truly relax. I could stop worrying about how my family and my
job were faring while I was otherwise occupied. Relief washed over
me, though I also felt a touch of sadness. My year-long birding adventure was over. On my December 31 flight from Lubbock to Midland, I reviewed my Big Year from start to end in my mind and felt
satisfied. I had given it my all. I had accomplished more than I had
imagined possible when I began on January 1, 2000.

The primary goal of my Big Year, of any Big Year, had been achieved:
I had seen as many bird species as possible in a well-defined geographic
region—Texas, in this case—in one year. I had also achieved my personal objectives of getting to know people and places. I had come to
know many new people and now counted among my friends a series
of Texas birders whom I had known poorly before my Big Year started;
many names and e-mail addresses now evoked faces, voices, and per-

sonalities. I had wandered the Lone Star State widely, through urban, suburban, and rural environments, from the Trans-Pecos to the Panhandle, from the plains to the Pineywoods, from the upper, central, and lower Texas coast to the Rio Grande Valley.

Of the 489 species I observed in 2000, twenty-five were Texas Review Species. The remaining 464 species I observed were regularly occurring species for the state. Since I had begun the year with no thought of approaching the Freeman-Hockey record, I was pleased by my result of 489 species, tying with two very skilled and knowledgeable birders.

It was inevitable that I would miss some species. None of these misses was due to neglect. One person with a job and family simply cannot be everywhere at once, especially when the action is nonstop during spring migration. Over the course of the year, only eight regularly occurring Texas bird species escaped me: Tundra Swan, Glaucous Gull, Black-legged Kittiwake, Black-billed Cuckoo, Long-eared Owl, Northern Shrike, Painted Redstart, and Bobolink. I missed just 1.7 percent of this vast state's typical birds. Greater Prairie-Chicken is still formally considered a regularly occurring species in Texas, but its current status argues against this classification (see chapter 9).

Had the Panhandle weather been better in the week after Christmas, I would have made it to Wichita Falls and would probably have found the Tundra Swans that had been seen since mid-December and continued to be seen into the new year. Better Panhandle weather would also have given me at least an opportunity to search that region again for a Northern Shrike and a Long-eared Owl.

Had the Black-legged Kittiwake at Lake Balmorhea in December of 1999 lingered into 2000, it would have been a pleasure to greet. But it did not. I was constantly on the watch for this species, especially in winter, when individuals are most likely to appear. At least two immature kittiwakes were seen around the state in 2000. One was at the Lake Livingston Dam spillway in East Texas on December 10–11; and on November 10 I chased but could not find one that Eric Carpenter had located at Imperial Reservoir the previous day.

Glaucous Gull was always where I was not. A few were seen on or near the coast, their normal haunt. Most reports were from early in the year, when I thought I still had plenty of time to find this rare Texas visitor. A first-winter Glaucous Gull was at East Beach for about a week beginning on January 2. Petra Hockey found a first- or second-year Glaucous Gull at the Victoria landfill in early February. On December 15, Brian Gibbons discovered a first-winter Glaucous Gull at an unusual inland location, White Rock Lake near Dallas. I prepared to chase this individual, but it did not stay.

I was within seventy-five feet of a Black-billed Cuckoo on the Kenedy Ranch in late April (chapter 12). But this infrequent migrant and the rarer Bobolink both avoided me in 2000, though I searched specifically for them on the coast in late April and May. A very unusual fall migrant Black-billed Cuckoo that appeared in San Antonio's Brackenridge Park in mid-October chose not to stay for my arrival a day later. By contrast, in the spring of 2001, I saw *three* Black-billed Cuckoos on the Kenedy Ranch; and I saw a beautiful adult male Bobolink in West Texas, just twenty-five miles from Fort Davis, on May 8.

Unbeknownst to me, an approachable Long-eared Owl had roosted at Hueco Tanks in January and February, 2000. Just after the New Year, on January 6, 2001, a large roost of fourteen Long-eared Owls was discovered in Carrollton, near Fort Worth. Observers from all over the state monitored the roost until the birds dispersed in March. These owls were probably present in December, 2000.

Painted Redstart frustrated me. I chased and failed to see two migrants, one early in the year (mid-March), the other late (mid-October), and I missed another opportunity because of foreign travel (late March). Someday soon, I will see a Painted Redstart in Texas, though it did not happen in 2001.

What might I have done differently during my Big Year? Had business and personal obligations permitted, I would have taken more trips around the state. There is no substitute for getting out to as many locations as possible, as often as possible.

In addition to my two productive coastal trips, in April and early May, I could have saved much time and effort later in the year if I had also been on the coast in late March, at the beginning of spring migration, and in mid-May, as spring migration wound down. These additional trips would have permitted better sampling of the changing species mix during migration. A late March trip would have eliminated Louisiana Waterthrush (chapter 16) and American Golden-Plover (chapter 22) as serious problems that consumed substantial time and effort later. A mid-May trip would have given me a better shot at Bobolink and more time to find a Black-billed Cuckoo. Both of these trips would also have given me opportunities to chase more coastal rarities, such as two Green Violet-Ears that appeared sporadically in Corpus Christi.

My Big Year list contained four species from my single midsummer pelagic trip (chapter 17). Had I understood the potential of such outings better, I would have hopped aboard a deep-sea fishing boat out of Port O'Connor or Port Isabel at least once during the summer. These fishing trips do not cater to birders, but I might have added another pelagic species or two—a Cory's or Audubon's Shearwater, for example—had I been offshore in the Gulf at least one more time in summer.

Another winter trip around the Panhandle would likely have yielded some gain. I waited until after Christmas for my second cold-weather visit to this part of Texas, and the weather betrayed me. Earlier in the year, January through March, I had scheduled Panhandle trips on four different occasions, but each was postponed because of a weather forecast that seemed to guarantee high winds. In retrospect, I should have gone to the Panhandle, wind or no wind, as long as the roads were drivable. Wind is a fact of life in Texas. It is nearly inescapable through the winter and spring.

A considerable amount of good fortune accompanied me all year. There were no major personal or professional disruptions to my life. Such events could easily have derailed my Big Year at any point. My closest call was a set of business problems in mid-April. These delayed and almost canceled my second coastal trip. Had that trip not occurred, I might have halted my Big Year effort. Without a substantial spring birding push, a Big Year is hopelessly hobbled.

The year 2000 was a fine year for rarities in West Texas, my home region. The fall invasions of Evening Grosbeak, Lewis's Woodpecker, Clark's Nutcracker, Cassin's Finch, and Pinyon Jay could not have been expected. Until this montane invasion got under way in late

September, I never imagined that these wonderful species might grace my Big Year. Furthermore, the Trans-Pecos hosted, and I was able to see and study, Buff-breasted and Dusky-capped flycatchers, Slate-throated Redstart, Varied Thrush, Spotted Owl, Long-tailed Jaeger, Greater Pewee, Red-faced Warbler, and Berylline and Broad-billed hummingbirds. There is simply no way to earn such good fortune.

Some, including myself, were skeptical of my chances for a high tally during a Big Year because I lived well to the west, more than six hundred miles from the avian richness of the Texas coast. This proved to be a nonproblem. I had ample time to travel around the state, and throughout the year the Trans-Pecos proved to be a very good place for a Texas birder to be.

IN ADDITION TO THE 489 species I observed, approximately forty-two other species were reliably reported during the year (see appendix B). Thus my Texas Big Year list represents about 92.1 percent of the bird species reported in Texas in 2000. Other than the eight regularly occurring species mentioned in this chapter as misses for me, the birds I did not see were, of course, mostly Texas Review Species. A fair fraction of these were one-day wonders seen briefly by an individual or a group, birds that were at inaccessible locations, or birds that disappeared before anyone other than the observer realized they had been present.

I chased and failed to find a handful of Review Species. Hours of searching failed to locate the skulking, highly irregular Blue Mockingbird that had been in Weslaco, in the Rio Grande Valley, since November, 1999. This bird wandered in and out of the Frontera Audubon property, the Weslaco Cemetery, and nearby private yards, and it frustrated me on three separate occasions. A stunning Greater Flamingo remained for several weeks in the Intracoastal Waterway near Saint Joseph's Island. Seeing the bird required a boat. A couple of fishing guides eventually realized there was money to be made taking birders to see this rarity. But the bird disappeared four days before my scheduled trip with a guide and friends.

How much effort did it require to see 489 species in one year in

Texas? I spent an hour or more birding on 174 days, and on 111 of those days I saw at least one new year bird. I could have spent more time in the field only if I had been retired or unemployed. During the year, I traveled thirty thousand miles across Texas by car and another eighteen thousand miles by airplane. By the end of the year, my trip log listed three trips to East Texas, four to the Panhandle, nine to the coast, four to the Rio Grande Valley, three to north-central Texas, and nine to Central Texas. I estimate that my birding efforts in the year 2000 consumed 1,050 hours.

The ideal time of life to attempt a Big Year would seem to be the early years of retirement. Without a job or children to consider, major impediments to travel could be eliminated. Such flexibility is especially valuable for chasing rarities on short notice or for rushing to the coast when weather conditions create fallouts. One's financial resources would dictate whether this travel took place by plane, bus, train, recreational vehicle, or automobile. With sufficient travel funds and time, an unhindered, dedicated retiree could certainly achieve a Texas Big Year list of 500 or more species in a favorable year filled with rarities.

Was my Texas Big Year worth the time, money, and effort it cost me? Was it worth enduring the hassles of air and auto travel for the rewards of being in the field in interesting places with generous people?

Absolutely.

Throughout the writing of this book, I have often felt the excitement and fun of a Big Year pulling at me again, urging me to give it another go. I have read birding reports from around the state and felt drawn to my waiting Jeep. I want to travel even more, to sample again the wonderful places that I encountered only briefly in my Big Year, such as the Panhandle. I still have so much to learn. And I want to see again the many fine people whose paths crossed with mine during my Big Year.

It is likely that I will undertake a Big Year again, perhaps when I retire. But, for now, it is your turn. However you care to define your own Big Year, whatever you choose to observe, study and chase, and whether you choose as your Big Year's domain your yard, your county, several counties, or your entire state, may you learn as much as I have and be rewarded for your efforts as richly as I have been rewarded for mine.

Texas Big Year Species List

All 489 bird species I identified in Texas in the year 2000 are listed in the following table. They are on the official Texas state checklist and are presented in taxonomic order. I have also listed each identifiable subspecies or morph. Reddish Egret and Snow Goose, for example, each count as only a single species. But I also recorded red and white morph Reddish Egret and white and blue phase Snow Goose.

The left-hand column is a simple counter, progressing from 1 through 489. Subspecies are counted to the right of the decimal place. Two species in the list are coded NC in that column because they cannot be counted in any way: Aplomado Falcon and Lilac-crowned Parrot.

The next column gives the species names, with Texas Review Species capitalized. The symbol † after a species name indicates that this was the only date on which I recorded the species. Where the symbol § appears after a species name, I recorded only one individual of the species during my Big Year. The Elf Owl and Black Rail were heard only and not seen.

The remaining three columns give the detail of my first record of the species in the year 2000 — the first date when the species was seen (or heard, if heard only), the county where this occurred, and the specific location. Abbreviations used in the final column are CR = County Road; FM = Farm to Market Road; RR = Ranch Road; SP = State Park; NP = National Park; NWR = National Wildlife Refuge; WMA = Wildlife Management Area; TX = Texas state highway; Co. = County; and Rd = road.

#	Species Name	First Sighting Date	First Sighting County	First Sighting Location
1	RED-THROATED LOON	20 FEB	GRAYSON	LAKE TEXOMA
2	Pacific Loon	27 Feb	Angelina	Sam Rayburn Reservoir
3	Common Loon	30 Jan	Reeves	Lake Balmorhea
4	Least Grebe	6 Feb	Kenedy	Sarita
5	Pied-billed Grebe	2 Jan	Reeves	Lake Balmorhea
6	Horned Grebe	2 Jan	Reeves	Lake Balmorhea
7	RED-NECKED GREBE §	21 DEC	TRAVIS	LAKE AUSTIN
8	Eared Grebe	2 Jan	Reeves	Lake Balmorhea
9	Western Grebe	2 Jan	Reeves	Lake Balmorhea
10	Clark's Grebe	2 Jan	Reeves	Lake Balmorhea
11	Band-rumped Storm-Petrel †	14 Jul	Cameron	Port Isabel pelagic
12	Masked Booby †	14 Jul	Cameron	Port Isabel pelagic
13	Northern Gannet	16 Dec	Brazoria	Quintana Jetty
14	American White Pelican	2 Jan	Reeves	Lake Balmorhea
15	Brown Pelican	8 Jan	Cameron	Port Isabel
16	Double-crested Cormorant	2 Jan	Reeves	Lake Balmorhea
17	Neotropic Cormorant	7-Jan	Hidalgo	Santa Ana NWR
18	Anhinga	3 May	Galveston	High Island, Smith Oaks
19	Magnificent Frigatebird §	17 Apr	Galveston	Bolivar Peninsula, Frenchtown Rd
20	American Bittern	15 Apr	Jefferson	Sea Rim SP, Beach Unit
21	Least Bittern	15 Apr	Jefferson	Sea Rim SP, Beach Unit
22	Great Blue Heron	2 Jan	Reeves	Lake Balmorhea
23	Great Egret	2 Jan	Reeves	Lake Balmorhea

Species Name	First Sighting Date	First Sighting County	First Sighting Location
Snowy Egret	7 Jan	Hidalgo	Santa Ana NWR
Little Blue Heron	8 Jan	Cameron	Laguna Atascosa
Tri-colored Heron	7 Jan	Hidalgo	Santa Ana NWR
Reddish Egret (red morph)	2 Jan	Reeves	Lake Balmorhea
Reddish Egret (white morph)	8 Jan	Cameron	Laguna Atascosa
Cattle Egret	6 Feb	Kleberg	CR 2250
Green Heron	7 Jan	Hidalgo	Santa Ana NWR
Black-crowned Night-Heron	2 Jan	Reeves	Lake Balmorhea
Yellow-crowned Night-Heron	23 Jan	Lubbock	Lubbock, Clapp Park
White Ibis	8 Jan	Cameron	Laguna Atascosa
Glossy Ibis †	3 Jul	Calhoun	Aransas NWR, Whitmire Unit
White-faced Ibis	7 Feb	Victoria	DuPont wetland, Victoria
Roseate Spoonbill	8 Jan	Cameron	Laguna Atascosa
Wood Stork	28 May	Starr	Falcon Dam spillway
Black Vulture	6 Jan	Maverick	Eagle Pass
Turkey Vulture	6 Jan	Maverick	Normandy
Fulvous Whistling-Duck	16 Apr	Chambers	Anahuac NWR
Black-bellied Whistling-Duck	6 Feb	Kenedy	Sarita
Greater White-fronted Goose	6 Feb	Kleberg	FM 772
Snow Goose (white phase)	2 Jan	Reeves	Lake Balmorhea
Snow Goose (blue phase)	2 Jan	Reeves	Lake Balmorhea
Ross's Goose	6 Feb	Kleberg	FM 771
Canada Goose	2 Jan	Reeves	Lake Balmorhea
TRUMPETER SWAN †	10 DEC	HEMPHILL	OASIS CREEK RANCH
Muscovy Duck †	29 May	Starr	Chapeño
Wood Duck	4 Jul	Travis	Hornsby Bend, Austin
Gadwall	6 Jan	Starr	Salineño
American Wigeon	2 Jan	Reeves	Lake Balmorhea
Mottled Duck	8 Jan	Cameron	Laguna Atascosa
Mallard	2 Jan	Reeves	Lake Balmorhea
Blue-winged Teal	7 Jan	Hidalgo	Santa Ana NWR
Cinnamon Teal	6 Feb	Kenedy	Sarita
Northern Shoveler	7 Jan	Hidalgo	Santa Ana NWR
Northern Pintail	2 Jan	Reeves	Lake Balmorhea
Green-winged Teal	2 Jan	Reeves	Lake Balmorhea
Canvasback	2 Jan	Reeves	Lake Balmorhea
Redhead	8 Jan	Cameron	Port Isabel

#	Species Name	First Sighting Date	First Sighting County	First Sighting Location
59	Ring-necked Duck	2 Jan	Reeves	Lake Balmorhea
60	Greater Scaup †	5 Feb	Comal	Canyon Lake Park
61	Lesser Scaup	2 Jan	Reeves	Lake Balmorhea
62	Surf Scoter	29 Oct	Pecos	Imperial Reservoir
63	Black Scoter †	29 Dec	Galveston	Bolivar Peninsula
64	White-winged Scoter §	27 Dec	Fort Bend	Houston Lighting Power pond
65	Long-tailed Duck †	3 Dec	Hunt	Lake Tawakoni
66	Bufflehead	2 Jan	Reeves	Lake Balmorhea
67	Common Goldeneye	2 Jan	Reeves	Lake Balmorhea
68	Hooded Merganser	2 Jan	Reeves	Lake Balmorhea
69	Common Merganser	2 Jan	Reeves	Lake Balmorhea
70	Red-breasted Merganser	2 Jan	Reeves	Lake Balmorhea
71	Ruddy Duck	2 Jan	Reeves	Lake Balmorhea
72	Osprey	6 Jan	Maverick	Normandy resaca
73	Hook-billed Kite †	29 May	Starr	Chapeño
74	Swallow-tailed Kite †	4 May	Liberty	Liberty
75	White-tailed Kite	8 Jan	Cameron	TX 100
76	Mississippi Kite	4 May	Liberty	Trinity River
77	Bald Eagle	2 Jan	Reeves	Lake Balmorhea
78	Northern Harrier	2 Jan	Reeves	Lake Balmorhea
79	Sharp-shinned Hawk	2 Jan	Reeves	Lake Balmorhea
80	Cooper's Hawk	7 Feb	Victoria	DuPont wetland, Victoria
81	Gray Hawk	6 Jan	Zapata	San Ygnacio, Washington St
82	Common Black-Hawk	19 Mar	Jeff Davis	TX 118, Limpia Cree
83	Harris's Hawk	6 Jan	Starr	25 miles east of Falcon SP
84	Red-shouldered Hawk	7 Jan	Hidalgo	Santa Ana NWR
85	Broad-winged Hawk	29 Apr	Kenedy	Kenedy Ranch
86	Swainson's Hawk	3 Apr	Potter	I-40 frontage rd
87	White-tailed Hawk	8 Jan	Cameron	Laguna Atascosa
88	Zone-tailed Hawk	9 Apr	Jeff Davis	Davis Mountains Preserve
89.1	Red-tailed Hawk	6 Jan	Maverick	Normandy resaca
89.2	Red-tailed (Harlan's) Hawk	2 Jan	Reeves	CR 329
89.3	Red-tailed (Krider's) Hawk	15 Apr	Jefferson	TX 87, near Sea Rim

Species Name	First Sighting Date	First Sighting County	First Sighting Location
Ferruginous Hawk	6 Feb	Nueces	TX 77, south of Driscoll
Rough-legged Hawk	8 Dec	Randall	FM 1714, near Canyon
Golden Eagle	30 Jan	Reeves	CR 315
Crested Caracara	6 Jan	Dimmit	US 277
American Kestrel	2 Jan	Reeves	Lake Balmorhea
Merlin	28 Apr	Kenedy	Kenedy Ranch
Aplomado Falcon §	8 Jan	Cameron	Laguna Atascosa
Peregrine Falcon	6 Feb	Kleberg	FM 772
Prairie Falcon	23 Jan	Gaines	TX 385, south of Seminole
Plain Chachalaca	7 Jan	Hidalgo	Santa Ana NWR
Ring-necked Pheasant	3 Apr	Potter	Sand Hill Rd
Lesser Prairie-Chicken †	4 Apr	Lipscomb	north of Glazier
Wild Turkey	22 Jan	Jeff Davis	TX 118, Musquiz Canyon
Scaled Quail	2 Jan	Reeves	CR 329
Gambel's Quail	4 Jun	Hudspeth	Indian Hot Springs Rd
Northern Bobwhite	17 Apr	Chambers	FM 1985
Montezuma Quail	19 Mar	Jeff Davis	Limpia Crossing
Yellow Rail †	17 Dec	Brazoria	Brazoria NWR
Black Rail †	3 Jul	Calhoun	Magic Ridge
Clapper Rail	17 Apr	Galveston	Rollover Pass
King Rail	8 Jan	Cameron	South Padre Island bridge
Virginia Rail	30 Jan	Reeves	Balmorhea SP, San Solomon cienega
Sora	7 Feb	Victoria	DuPont wetland, Victoria
Purple Gallinule	16 Apr	Chambers	Anahuac NWR
Common Moorhen	6 Jan	Starr	Salineño
American Coot	2 Jan	Reeves	Balmorhea SP
Sandhill Crane	2 Jan	Reeves	Lake Balmorhea
Whooping Crane	24 Nov	Aransas	Aransas NWR
Black-bellied Plover	2 Jan	Reeves	Lake Balmorhea
American Golden-Plover †	3 Nov	Galveston	Bolivar Flats
Snowy Plover	18 Mar	Pecos	Imperial Reservoir
Wilson's Plover	17 Apr	Galveston	Bolivar Flats
Semipalmated Plover	15 Apr	Jefferson	Sea Rim SP, Beach Unit

#	Species Name	*First Sighting Date*	*First Sighting County*	*First Sighting Location*
122	Piping Plover	17 Apr	Galveston	Bolivar Flats
123	Killdeer	2 Jan	Reeves	Lake Balmorhea
124	Mountain Plover	20 Oct	Williamson	field bounded by C. 352, 353, Alligator
125	American Oystercatcher	8 Jan	Cameron	Port Isabel
126	Black-necked Stilt	7 Jan	Hidalgo	Santa Ana NWR
127	American Avocet	7 Jan	Hidalgo	Santa Ana NWR
128	Greater Yellowlegs	2 Jan	Reeves	Lake Balmorhea
129	Lesser Yellowlegs	6 Feb	Kenedy	Sarita
130	Solitary Sandpiper	28 Apr	Kenedy	Kenedy Ranch
131	Willet	8 Jan	Cameron	Laguna Atascosa
132	Spotted Sandpiper	6 Jan	Starr	Salineño
133	Upland Sandpiper	18 Apr	Chambers	FM 1985
134	Whimbrel	16 Apr	Jefferson	Texas Point NWR
135	Long-billed Curlew	8 Jan	Cameron	Laguna Atascosa
136	Hudsonian Godwit †	2 May	Chambers	Anahuac NWR
137	Marbled Godwit	8 Jan	Cameron	Laguna Atascosa
138	Ruddy Turnstone	8 Jan	Cameron	Laguna Atascosa
139	Red Knot	5 May	Brazoria	Quintana Beach
140	Sanderling	6 Feb	Kleberg	Kaufer-Hubert Memorial Park
141	Semipalmated Sandpiper	8 Jan	Cameron	Laguna Atascosa
142	Western Sandpiper	18 Mar	Pecos	Imperial Reservoir
143	Least Sandpiper	2 Jan	Reeves	Lake Balmorhea
144	White-rumped Sandpiper	29 Apr	Kenedy	Kenedy Ranch
145	Baird's Sandpiper	1 May	Chambers	Anahuac East Bayo
146	Pectoral Sandpiper	8 Apr	Reeves	Lake Balmorhea
147	Dunlin	8 Jan	Cameron	Laguna Atascosa
148	Stilt Sandpiper	28 Apr	Kenedy	Kenedy Ranch
149	Buff-breasted Sandpiper	17 Apr	Chambers	FM 1985
150	Short-billed Dowitcher	17 Apr	Galveston	Bolivar Flats
151	Long-billed Dowitcher	7 Jan	Hidalgo	Santa Ana NWR
152	Common Snipe (Wilson's Snipe)	5 Feb	Comal	Canyon Lake Park
153	American Woodcock †	3 Dec	Rusk	CR 286D
154	Wilson's Phalarope	22 Apr	Reeves	Lake Balmorhea
155	Red-necked Phalarope †	1 Sep	El Paso	Fort Bliss sewage ponds
156	Pomarine Jaeger †	14 Jul	Cameron	Port Isabel pelagic

Species Name	First Sighting Date	First Sighting County	First Sighting Location
LONG-TAILED JAEGER †	1 SEP	EL PASO	FORT BLISS SEWAGE PONDS
Laughing Gull	8 Jan	Cameron	Laguna Atascosa
Franklin's Gull	19 Feb	Dallas	White Rock Lake Park
LITTLE GULL	19 FEB	DALLAS	WHITE ROCK LAKE PARK
BLACK-HEADED GULL §	19 FEB	DELTA	BIG CREEK RESERVOIR
Bonaparte's Gull	30 Jan	Reeves	Lake Balmorhea
MEW GULL §	19 NOV	PECOS	IMPERIAL RESERVOIR
Ring-billed Gull	2 Jan	Reeves	Lake Balmorhea
California Gull	3 May	Galveston	Rollover Pass
Herring Gull	8 Jan	Cameron	Laguna Atascosa
THAYER'S GULL §	17 APR	GALVESTON	ROLLOVER PASS
Lesser Black-backed Gull	7 Feb	Nueces	Corpus Christi, Elliot landfill
Sabine's Gull	29 Sep	Delta	Cooper Lake
Gull-billed Tern	8 Jan	Cameron	Laguna Atascosa
Caspian Tern	8 Jan	Cameron	Laguna Atascosa
Royal Tern	8 Jan	Cameron	Laguna Atascosa
Sandwich Tern	17 Apr	Galveston	Rollover Pass
Common Tern	15 Apr	Jefferson	Sea Rim SP, Beach Unit
Forster's Tern	8 Jan	Cameron	Laguna Atascosa
Least Tern	8 Apr	Pecos	Imperial Reservoir
Bridled/Sooty Tern §	14 Jul	Cameron	Port Isabel pelagic
Black Tern	17 Apr	Galveston	Rollover Pass
Black Skimmer	17 Apr	Galveston	Rollover Pass
Rock Dove	2 Jan	Reeves	Balmorhea
Red-billed Pigeon	9 Jan	Starr	Salineño
Band-tailed Pigeon	23 Apr	Jeff Davis	Davis Mountains Preserve
Eurasian Collared-Dove	4 Feb	Travis	Austin
White-winged Dove	2 Jan	Reeves	Balmorhea, FM 2903
Mourning Dove	2 Jan	Reeves	Lake Balmorhea
Inca Dove	2 Jan	Reeves	Lake Balmorhea
Common Ground-Dove	2 Jan	Reeves	Lake Balmorhea
White-tipped Dove	6 Jan	Starr	Salineño

#	Species Name	First Sighting Date	First Sighting County	First Sighting Location
189	Monk Parakeet †	3 Feb	Travis	Austin, Krieg Field
190	Green Parakeet †	8 Jan	Hidalgo	McAllen, 10th and Violet
191	Red-crowned Parrot	7 Jan	Hidalgo	Weslaco
NC	Lilac-crowned Parrot §	15 Jul	Cameron	Brownsville, Jade St
192	Yellow-billed Cuckoo	15 Apr	Jefferson	Sabine Woods
193	Greater Roadrunner	2 Jan	Reeves	CR 329
194	Groove-billed Ani	27 May	Hidalgo	Santa Ana NWR
195	Barn Owl	6 Feb	Kenedy	Sarita
196	Flammulated Owl	9 Oct	Jeff Davis	Sierra Vieja
197	Western Screech-Owl	7 May	Brewster	Big Bend NP, Dugout Wells
198	Eastern Screech-Owl	7 Jan	Hidalgo	Anzalduas County P
199	Great Horned Owl	29 Apr	Kenedy	Kenedy Ranch
200	Ferruginous Pygmy-Owl †	28 Apr	Kenedy	Kenedy Ranch
201	Elf Owl	7 May	Brewster	Big Bend NP, Dugout Wells
202	Burrowing Owl	3 Apr	Potter	Amarillo landfill
203	Spotted Owl †	22 Jun	Jeff Davis	Davis Mountains Preserve
204	Barred Owl	4 Jul	Calhoun	Guadalupe Delta WMA
205	Short-eared Owl †	4 Dec	Hunt	Clymer Meadow
206	Lesser Nighthawk	4 Jun	Hudspeth	Indian Hot Springs
207	Common Nighthawk	28 Apr	Kenedy	Kenedy Ranch
208	Common Pauraque	7 Jan	Hidalgo	Santa Ana NWR
209	Common Poorwill	20 May	Jeff Davis	Davis Mountains Preserve
210	Chuck-will's-widow	27 Apr	Real	Lost Canyon, Barksdale
211	Whip-poor-will †	20 May	Jeff Davis	Davis Mountains Preserve
212	Chimney Swift	14 Apr	Jefferson	Sabine Pass
213	White-throated Swift	9 Apr	Jeff Davis	Davis Mountains Preserve
214	BROAD-BILLED HUMMINGBIRD §	25 APR	JEFF DAVIS	FORT DAVIS
215	BERYLLINE HUMMINGBIRD §	25 MAY	JEFF DAVIS	DAVIS MOUNTAINS
216	Buff-bellied Hummingbird	7 Jan	Hidalgo	Weslaco

	Species Name	First Sighting Date	First Sighting County	First Sighting Location
	Blue-throated Hummingbird	19 May	Brewster	Big Bend NP, Chisos Basin
	Magnificent Hummingbird	25 May	Jeff Davis	Davis Mountains
	Lucifer Hummingbird	18 May	Jeff Davis	McDonald Observatory
	Ruby-throated Hummingbird	14 Apr	Jefferson	Sabine Woods
	Black-chinned Hummingbird	19 Mar	Jeff Davis	Limpia Crossing
	Anna's Hummingbird	9 Sep	Jeff Davis	Davis Mountains
	Calliope Hummingbird	23 Jul	Jeff Davis	Davis Mountains
	Broad-tailed Hummingbird	12 Mar	Jeff Davis	McDonald Observatory
	Rufous Hummingbird	21 Jul	Jeff Davis	McDonald Observatory
	Ringed Kingfisher	6 Jan	Starr	Salineño
	Belted Kingfisher	2 Jan	Reeves	Balmorhea SP
	Green Kingfisher	9 Jan	Starr	Salineño
	LEWIS'S WOODPECKER §	17 Oct	CULBERSON	GUADALUPE MOUNTAINS NP
	Red-headed Woodpecker †	4 May	Chambers	Pinchback Rd
	Acorn Woodpecker	16 Jan	Jeff Davis	TX 118
	Golden-fronted Woodpecker	6 Jan	Maverick	Normandy resaca
	Red-bellied Woodpecker	19 Feb	Hopkins	FM 71, Hopkins-Delta Co. border
	Williamson's Sapsucker	29 Jan	Jeff Davis	TX 118, Lawrence E. Wood picnic area
	Yellow-bellied Sapsucker	19 Feb	Delta	near Cooper
	Red-naped Sapsucker	16 Jan	Jeff Davis	TX 118, Lawrence E. Wood picnic area
	Ladder-backed Woodpecker	6 Jan	Starr	Salineño
	Downy Woodpecker	19 Feb	Delta	near Cooper
	Hairy Woodpecker	27 Feb	San Augustine	Jackson Hill Park
	Red-cockaded Woodpecker †	26 Feb	Angelina	Angelina National Forest, Bannister NWR
1	Northern Flicker (red-shafted)	16 Jan	Jeff Davis	TX 118, north of observatory
2	Northern Flicker (yellow-shafted)	19 Feb	Delta	several locations along Delta Co. backroads

#	Species Name	First Sighting Date	First Sighting County	First Sighting Location
242	Pileated Woodpecker	26 Feb	Nacogdoches	Nacogdoches, Saint's Rest Rd
243	Northern Beardless-Tyrannulet	7 Jan	Hidalgo	Anzalduas County I
244	Olive-sided Flycatcher	3 May	Galveston	High Island, Smith Oaks
245	GREATER PEWEE §	21 MAY	JEFF DAVIS	DAVIS MOUNTAINS PRESERVE
246	Western Wood-Pewee	6 May	Jeff Davis	Davis Mountains Preserve
247	Eastern Wood-Pewee	15 Apr	Jefferson	Sabine Woods
248	Yellow-bellied Flycatcher	27 May	Hidalgo	Anzalduas County I
249	Acadian Flycatcher	29 Apr	Kenedy	Kenedy Ranch
250	Alder Flycatcher †	3 May	Galveston	High Island, Smith Oaks
251	Willow Flycatcher	7 May	Jeff Davis	TX 118, Musquiz Canyon
252	Least Flycatcher	14 Apr	Jefferson	Sabine Woods
253	Hammond's Flycatcher	21 May	Jeff Davis	Davis Mountains Preserve
254	Gray Flycatcher	17 Jan	Presidio	Big Bend Ranch SP, Ojito Adentro
255	Dusky Flycatcher	6 May	Jeff Davis	Davis Mountains Preserve
256	Cordilleran Flycatcher	19 May	Brewster	Big Bend NP, Pine Canyon
257	BUFF-BREASTED FLYCATCHER	23 APR	JEFF DAVIS	DAVIS MOUNTAINS PRESERVE
258	Black Phoebe	2 Jan	Reeves	Lake Balmorhea
259	Eastern Phoebe	7 Jan	Hidalgo	Santa Ana NWR
260	Say's Phoebe	2 Jan	Reeves	Lake Balmorhea
261	Vermilion Flycatcher	22 Jan	Brewster	Big Bend NP, Harte Ranch Rd
262	DUSKY-CAPPED FLYCATCHER †	3 JUN	BREWSTER	BIG BEND NP, LAGUNA MEADOW TRAIL
263	Ash-throated Flycatcher	12 Apr	Brewster	Brushy Canyon Preserve
264	Great Crested Flycatcher	17 Apr	Galveston	High Island, Boy Scout Woods

Species Name	First Sighting Date	First Sighting County	First Sighting Location
Brown-crested Flycatcher	28 Apr	Kenedy	Kenedy Ranch
Great Kiskadee	6 Jan	Zapata	San Ygnacio
Tropical Kingbird †	7 May	Brewster	Big Bend NP, Cotton-wood Campground
Couch's Kingbird	6 Feb	Kenedy	Sarita
Cassin's Kingbird	22 Apr	Reeves	Balmorhea SP
Western Kingbird	5 Apr	El Paso	El Paso Airport
Eastern Kingbird	14 Apr	Jefferson	TX 87, south of Sabine Pass
Scissor-tailed Flycatcher	4 Apr	Hemphill	FM 2266, near Canadian
Loggerhead Shrike	2 Jan	Reeves	Lake Balmorhea
White-eyed Vireo	7 Jan	Hidalgo	Santa Ana NWR
Bell's Vireo	12 Apr	Brewster	Brushy Canyon Preserve
Black-capped Vireo †	26 Apr	Crockett	canyon above Fort Lancaster, TX 290
Gray Vireo	5 Mar	Brewster	Big Bend NP, Robber's Roost
Blue-headed Vireo	7 Jan	Hidalgo	Santa Ana NWR
Yellow-throated Vireo	14 Apr	Jefferson	Sabine Woods
Plumbeous Vireo	23 Apr	Jeff Davis	Davis Mountains Preserve, Tobe Canyon
Cassin's Vireo	23 Apr	Jeff Davis	Davis Mountains Preserve, Tobe Canyon
Hutton's Vireo	9 Apr	Jeff Davis	Davis Mountains Preserve
₁ Warbling Vireo (eastern)	2 May	Galveston	High Island, Smith Oaks
₂ Warbling Vireo (western)	6 May	Jeff Davis	Davis Mountains Preserve
Philadelphia Vireo	2 May	Galveston	High Island, Smith Oaks
Red-eyed Vireo	14 Apr	Jefferson	Sabine Woods
YELLOW-GREEN VIREO †	15 JUL	CAMERON	SABAL PALM AUDUBON SANCTUARY
BLACK-WHISKERED VIREO §	5 MAY	BRAZORIA	QUINTANA NEOTROPI-CAL BIRD SANCTUARY

#	Species Name	First Sighting Date	First Sighting County	First Sighting Location
288	Steller's Jay	9 Apr	Jeff Davis	Davis Mountains Preserve
289	Blue Jay	19 Feb	Dallas	White Rock Lake Pa, Old Fish Hatchery
290	Green Jay	6 Jan	Starr	Salineño
291	Brown Jay †	29 May	Starr	Chapeño, El Rio RV Park
292	Western Scrub-Jay	4 Jan	Jeff Davis	McDonald Observatory
293	Mexican Jay	5 Mar	Brewster	Big Bend NP, Oak Creek Canyon
294	Pinyon Jay	30 Sep	Jeff Davis	Davis Mountains
295	CLARK'S NUTCRACKER §	1 OCT	JEFF DAVIS	DAVIS MOUNTAINS PRESERVE
296	BLACK-BILLED MAGPIE †	4 APR	HANSFORD	TX 136, COLDWATER CREEK
297	American Crow	6 Jan	Maverick	Normandy resaca
298	Fish Crow †	16 Apr	Jefferson	Beaumont, College
299	Chihuahuan Raven	6 Jan	Zapata	San Ygnacio
300	Common Raven	2 Jan	Reeves	Balmorhea SP
301	Horned Lark	2 Jan	Reeves	CR 315
302	Purple Martin	6 Feb	Kenedy	Sarita
303	Tree Swallow	4 Apr	Hemphill	FM 2266, near Canadian
304	Violet-green Swallow	5 Mar	Brewster	Big Bend NP, East River Rd
305	Northern Rough-winged Swallow	7 Jan	Hidalgo	Santa Ana NWR
306	Bank Swallow	28 Apr	Kenedy	Kenedy Ranch
307	Cliff Swallow	8 Apr	Pecos	Fort Stockton
308	Cave Swallow	7 Jan	Hidalgo	Santa Ana NWR
309	Barn Swallow	13 Mar	Jeff Davis	McDonald Observatory
310	Carolina Chickadee	5 Feb	Comal	Canyon Lake Park
311	Mountain Chickadee	4 Mar	Jeff Davis	Davis Mountains Preserve, Bridge G
312	Juniper Titmouse †	14 Oct	Culberson	Guadalupe Mountai NP, Frijole Ranch
313.1	Tufted Titmouse (black-crested)	1 Jan	Jeff Davis	McDonald Observatory

Species Name	First Sighting Date	First Sighting County	First Sighting Location
2 Tufted Titmouse	26 Feb	Nacogdoches	Nacogdoches, Saint's Rest Rd
Verdin	2 Jan	Reeves	CR 315
Bushtit	31 Jan	Jeff Davis	Limpia Crossing
Red-breasted Nuthatch	27 Feb	San Augustine	Jackson Hill Park
White-breasted Nuthatch	4 Jan	Jeff Davis	McDonald Observatory
Pygmy Nuthatch	9 Apr	Jeff Davis	Davis Mountains Preserve, Bridge Gap
Brown-headed Nuthatch	26 Feb	Nacogdoches	Nacogdoches, Saint's Rest Rd
Brown Creeper	19 Feb	Dallas	White Rock Lake Park, Old Fish Hatchery
Cactus Wren	16 Jan	Jeff Davis	TX 118, 10 miles south of Kent
Rock Wren	2 Jan	Reeves	Lake Balmorhea
Canyon Wren	12 Mar	Jeff Davis	Davis Mountains SP
Carolina Wren	4 May	Hardin	Village Creek SP, Silsbee
1 Bewick's Wren (eastern)	6 Jan	Maverick	Normandy resaca
2 Bewick's Wren (western)	17 Jan	Presidio	Plata
House Wren	7 Jan	Hidalgo	Santa Ana NWR
Winter Wren	19 Feb	Hopkins	FM 71, Hopkins-Delta Co. border
Sedge Wren	27 Feb	Nacogdoches	Nacogdoches, Alazan Bayou
Marsh Wren	30 Jan	Reeves	Balmorhea SP, San Solomon cienega
Golden-crowned Kinglet	19 Feb	Delta	near Cooper
Ruby-crowned Kinglet	2 Jan	Reeves	CR 315
Blue-gray Gnatcatcher	6 Jan	Zapata	San Ygnacio
Black-tailed Gnatcatcher	17 Jan	Presidio	FM 169
Eastern Bluebird	1 Feb	Jeff Davis	Limpia Crossing
Western Bluebird	16 Jan	Jeff Davis	TX 118, north of McDonald Observatory
Mountain Bluebird	29 Jan	Jeff Davis	TX 118, north of McDonald Observatory

#	Species Name	First Sighting Date	First Sighting County	First Sighting Location
337	Townsend's Solitaire	1 Oct	Jeff Davis	Davis Mountains Preserve, Madera Canyon
338	Veery	27 Apr	Nueces	Corpus Christi, Packery Channel
339	Gray-cheeked Thrush	14 Apr	Jefferson	Sabine Woods
340	Swainson's Thrush	14 Apr	Jefferson	Sabine Woods
341	Hermit Thrush	17 Jan	Presidio	Big Bend Ranch SP, Agua Adentro
342	Wood Thrush	14 Apr	Jefferson	Sabine Woods
343	Clay-colored Robin §	7 Jan	Hidalgo	Bentsen–Rio Grande
344	RUFOUS-BACKED ROBIN §	6 FEB	KENEDY	SARITA
345	American Robin	23 Jan	Lubbock	Lubbock, Clapp Park
346	VARIED THRUSH †	23 JAN	LUBBOCK	LUBBOCK, CLAPP PARK
347	Gray Catbird	14 Apr	Jefferson	Sabine Woods
348	Northern Mockingbird	6 Jan	Maverick	Normandy resaca
349	Sage Thrasher	29 Feb	Reeves	CR 315
350	Brown Thrasher	19 Feb	Delta	Delta Co. backroads
351	Long-billed Thrasher	6 Jan	Starr	Salineño
352	Curve-billed Thrasher	8 Jan	Cameron	Laguna Atascosa
353	Crissal Thrasher	17 Jan	Presidio	Big Bend Ranch SP, Black Hills Creek
354	European Starling	2 Jan	Reeves	Balmorhea
355	American Pipit	2 Jan	Reeves	Lake Balmorhea
356	Sprague's Pipit †	22 Oct	Williamson	CR 124
357	Cedar Waxwing	3 Feb	Travis	Austin, Mary Moore Seawright Park
358	Phainopepla	16 Jan	Jeff Davis	TX 118, intersection with TX 166
359	OLIVE WARBLER §	12 NOV	EL PASO	HUECO TANKS SP, MESCALERO CANY..
360	Blue-winged Warbler	14 Apr	Jefferson	Sabine Woods
361	Golden-winged Warbler	16 Apr	Galveston	High Island, Boy Scout Woods
362	Tennessee Warbler	14 Apr	Jefferson	Sabine Woods
363	Orange-crowned Warbler	6 Jan	Zapata	San Ygnacio, Washington St

Species Name	First Sighting Date	First Sighting County	First Sighting Location
Nashville Warbler	17 Apr	Galveston	High Island, Boy Scout Woods
Virginia's Warbler	23 Apr	Jeff Davis	Davis Mountains Preserve, Tobe Canyon
Colima Warbler	19 May	Brewster	Big Bend NP, Pine Canyon
Lucy's Warbler	7 May	Brewster	Big Bend NP, Cotton-wood Campground
Northern Parula	27 Feb	San Augustine	Jackson Hill Park
Tropical Parula †	27 May	Hidalgo	Anzalduas County Park
Yellow Warbler	16 Apr	Galveston	High Island, Boy Scout Woods
Chestnut-sided Warbler	14 Apr	Jefferson	Sabine Woods
Magnolia Warbler	27 Apr	Nueces	Corpus Christi, Packery Channel
Cape May Warbler §	6 Feb	Kenedy	Sarita
Black-throated Blue Warbler	14 Oct	Midland	Midland
Yellow-rumped (Audubon's) Warbler	2 Jan	Reeves	Lake Balmorhea
Yellow-rumped (Myrtle) Warbler	6 Jan	Zapata	San Ygnacio
Black-throated Gray Warbler	7 Jan	Hidalgo	Anzalduas County Park
Golden-cheeked Warbler †	27 Apr	Uvalde	Garner SP
Black-throated Green Warbler	7 Jan	Hidalgo	Santa Ana NWR
Townsend's Warbler	23 Apr	Jeff Davis	Davis Mountains Preserve, Tobe Canyon
Hermit Warbler	23 Apr	Jeff Davis	Davis Mountains Preserve, Tobe Canyon
Blackburnian Warbler	15 Apr	Jefferson	Sabine Woods
Yellow-throated Warbler	14 Apr	Jefferson	Sabine Woods
Grace's Warbler	9 Apr	Jeff Davis	Davis Mountains Preserve
Pine Warbler	26 Feb	Nacogdoches	Nacogdoches, FM 1275
Prairie Warbler §	4 May	Hardin	Silsbee, Fire Tower Rd
Palm Warbler §	18 Apr	Chambers	Anahuac NWR, Willows
Bay-breasted Warbler	27 Apr	Nueces	Corpus Christi, Packery Channel
Blackpoll Warbler	27 Apr	Nueces	Corpus Christi, Packery Channel

#	Species Name	First Sighting Date	First Sighting County	First Sighting Location
389	Cerulean Warbler	14 Apr	Jefferson	Sabine Woods
390	Black-and-white Warbler	7 Jan	Hidalgo	Santa Ana NWR
391	American Redstart	14 Apr	Jefferson	Sabine Woods
392	Prothonotary Warbler	14 Apr	Jefferson	Sabine Woods
393	Worm-eating Warbler	14 Apr	Jefferson	Sabine Woods
394	Swainson's Warbler	15 Apr	Jefferson	Sabine Woods
395	Ovenbird	8 Jan	Cameron	Laguna Atascosa
396	Northern Waterthrush	16 Apr	Chambers	Anahuac NWR, Willows
397	Louisiana Waterthrush †	11 Jul	Hays	Dripping Springs, Dead Man's Creek
398	Kentucky Warbler	14 Apr	Jefferson	Sabine Woods
399	Mourning Warbler	20 Sep	Nueces	Corpus Christi, Pollywog Ponds
400	MacGillivray's Warbler	7 May	Brewster	Big Bend NP, Sam Nail Ranch
401	Common Yellowthroat	7 Jan	Hidalgo	Santa Ana NWR
402	GRAY-CROWNED YELLOWTHROAT §	27 MAY	HIDALGO	SANTA ANA NWR, PINTAIL POND
403	Hooded Warbler	14 Apr	Jefferson	Sabine Woods
404	Wilson's Warbler	9 Apr	Jeff Davis	Davis Mountains Preserve, Jones Tan
405	Canada Warbler	29 Apr	Kenedy	Kenedy Ranch
406	RED-FACED WARBLER §	6 AUG	JEFF DAVIS	DAVIS MOUNTAINS PRESERVE, BRIDGE GAP
407	SLATE-THROATED REDSTART §	21 JUN	JEFF DAVIS	DAVIS MOUNTAINS PRESERVE, PEWEE CANYON
408	Yellow-breasted Chat	15 Apr	Jefferson	Sabine Woods
409	Hepatic Tanager	23 Apr	Jeff Davis	Davis Mountains Preserve, Tobe Cany
410	Summer Tanager	14 Apr	Jefferson	TX 87, south of Sabine Pass
411	Scarlet Tanager	15 Apr	Jefferson	Sabine Woods
412	Western Tanager	23 Apr	Jeff Davis	Davis Mountains Preserve, Tobe Cany
413	White-collared Seedeater †	28 May	Zapata	San Ygnacio, Washington St

Species Name	First Sighting Date	First Sighting County	First Sighting Location
Olive Sparrow	7 Jan	Hidalgo	Santa Ana NWR
Green-tailed Towhee	17 Jan	Presidio	FM 169, Plata
Spotted Towhee	16 Jan	Jeff Davis	TX 118, 10 miles south of Kent
Eastern Towhee §	27 Feb	Nacogdoches	CR 628
Canyon Towhee	16 Jan	Jeff Davis	TX 118, intersection with TX 166
Cassin's Sparrow	16 Jan	Jeff Davis	TX 118, 10 miles south of Kent
Bachman's Sparrow †	27 Feb	Tyler	Angelina National Forest, Boykins Springs
Botteri's Sparrow	28 Apr	Kenedy	Kenedy Ranch
Rufous-crowned Sparrow	27 Jan	Jeff Davis	McDonald Observatory
American Tree Sparrow	9 Dec	Dallam	FM 1879
Chipping Sparrow	6 Jan	Starr	Salineño
Clay-colored Sparrow	3 Apr	El Paso	Fort Bliss sewage ponds
Brewer's Sparrow	16 Jan	Jeff Davis	TX 118, 10 miles south of Kent
Field Sparrow	3 Feb	Travis	Austin, Mary Moore Seawright Park
Black-chinned Sparrow	5 Mar	Brewster	Big Bend NP, Oak Creek Canyon
Vesper Sparrow	6 Jan	Maverick	Normandy resaca
Lark Sparrow	6 Feb	Kenedy	Sarita
Black-throated Sparrow	2 Jan	Reeves	Lake Balmorhea
Sage Sparrow †	12 Feb	Reeves	CR 315
Lark Bunting	23 Jan	Hockley	TX 114, intersection with CR 197
Savannah Sparrow	2 Jan	Reeves	Lake Balmorhea
Grasshopper Sparrow	20 Oct	Williamson	Alligator Rd
Henslow's Sparrow †	26 Feb	Nacogdoches	Nacogdoches, FM 1275, private land
Le Conte's Sparrow	2 Jan	Reeves	Lake Balmorhea
Nelson's Sharp-tailed Sparrow †	17 Apr	Galveston	Bolivar Peninsula, Frenchtown Rd

#	Species Name	First Sighting Date	First Sighting County	First Sighting Location
439	Seaside Sparrow	16 Apr	Jefferson	Texas Point NWR
440	Fox Sparrow	3 Feb	Travis	Austin, Mary Moore Seawright Park
441	Song Sparrow	2 Jan	Reeves	Lake Balmorhea
442	Lincoln's Sparrow	6 Jan	Maverick	Normandy resaca
443	Swamp Sparrow	2 Jan	Reeves	Lake Balmorhea
444	White-throated Sparrow	3 Feb	Travis	Austin, Mary Moore Seawright Park
445	Harris's Sparrow	3 Feb	Travis	Austin, Mary Moore Seawright Park
446	White-crowned Sparrow	2 Jan	Reeves	CR 321
447.1	Dark-eyed Junco (pink-sided)	1 Jan	Jeff Davis	McDonald Observatory
447.2	Dark-eyed Junco (gray-headed)	1 Jan	Jeff Davis	McDonald Observatory
447.3	Dark-eyed Junco (Oregon)	1 Jan	Jeff Davis	McDonald Observatory
447.4	Dark-eyed Junco (Slate)	20 Feb	Grayson	Hagerman NWR
448	McCown's Longspur	25 Feb	Williamson	CR 353, intersection with CR 352
449	Lapland Longspur	19 Feb	Delta	various county roads
450	Smith's Longspur †	3 Dec	Rains	Lake Tawakoni
451	Chestnut-collared Longspur	16 Jan	Jeff Davis	TX 118 pond, Adobe Canyon
452	Northern Cardinal	6 Jan	Starr	Salineño
453	Pyrrhuloxia	2 Jan	Reeves	CR 315
454	Rose-breasted Grosbeak	14 Apr	Jefferson	Sabine Woods
455	Black-headed Grosbeak	6 May	Jeff Davis	Davis Mountains Preserve, near Pine Peak
456	Blue Grosbeak	14 Apr	Jefferson	Sabine Woods
457	BLUE BUNTING §	30 DEC	HIDALGO	BENTSEN–RIO GRANDE SP
458	Lazuli Bunting †	7 May	Brewster	Big Bend NP, Cottonwood Campground
459	Indigo Bunting	14 Apr	Jefferson	TX 87, south of Sabine Pass
460	Varied Bunting	22 Apr	Reeves	Lake Balmorhea

Species Name	First Sighting Date	First Sighting County	First Sighting Location
Painted Bunting	15 Apr	Jefferson	Sabine Woods
Dicksissel	16 Apr	Chambers	FM 1985
Red-winged Blackbird	6 Jan	Starr	Salineño
Eastern Meadowlark (lilianae)	17 Jan	Presidio	FM 169, Plata
Eastern Meadowlark (magna)	19 Feb	Delta	various county roads
Western Meadowlark	23 Jan	Bailey	Muleshoe NWR
Yellow-headed Blackbird	7 May	Brewster	Big Bend NP, Cottonwood Campground
Rusty Blackbird †	19 Feb	Hunt	Greenville
Brewer's Blackbird	2 Jan	Reeves	Balmorhea
Common Grackle	4 Apr	Ochiltree	FM 381
Boat-tailed Grackle	15 Apr	Jefferson	Sabine Woods
Great-tailed Grackle	2 Jan	Reeves	Balmorhea
Bronzed Cowbird	27 Apr	Uvalde	RR 387
Brown-headed Cowbird	23 Jan	Cochran	TX 214, south of Morton
Orchard Oriole	14 Apr	Jefferson	TX 87, south of Sabine Pass
Hooded Oriole	28 Apr	Kenedy	TX 77, rest stop near Sarita
Altamira Oriole	7 Jan	Hidalgo	Bentsen–Rio Grande SP
Audubon's Oriole	9 Jan	Starr	Salineño
Baltimore Oriole	15 Apr	Jefferson	Sabine Woods
Bullock's Oriole	6 Feb	Kenedy	Sarita
Scott's Oriole	7 Apr	Jeff Davis	McDonald Observatory
Purple Finch †	23 Dec	Rusk	Kilgore
Cassin's Finch	26 Sep	Jeff Davis	Davis Mountains
House Finch	2 Jan	Reeves	CR 329
Red Crossbill	23 Aug	Reeves	Balmorhea SP
Pine Siskin	1 Jan	Jeff Davis	McDonald Observatory
Lesser Goldfinch	17 Jan	Presidio	FM 169, Plata
American Goldfinch	7 Jan	Hidalgo	Anzalduas County Park
Evening Grosbeak	11 Oct	Brewster	Alpine
House Sparrow	2 Jan	Reeves	CR 329

Other Species Seen in
Texas in 2000

n addition to the 489 species I recorded in Texas in 2000, approximately another forty-two species were reported by others. As noted in chapter 27, eight of these were regularly occurring Texas species that I missed in 2000—Tundra Swan, Glaucous Gull, Black-legged Kittiwake, Black-billed Cuckoo, Long-eared Owl, Northern Shrike, Painted Redstart, and Bobolink; those are not listed here. The other additional records are briefly described in what follows. Texas Review Species are denoted by an asterisk after the species name. All other listed species are pelagic; Brown Booby is a pelagic Review Species.

Note that the listing of a Review Species record in this appendix does not imply acceptance by the Texas Bird Records Committee. If the record has been reviewed by the TBRC, the record number is given in parentheses.

In any given year, there are few pelagic data. The Louisiana State University observers stationed on offshore oil platforms during spring and fall migration and observations from birding-oriented fishermen such as Steve Welborn provided the only data other than the single Port Isabel pelagic trip (see chapter 17) in which I participated.

CORY'S SHEARWATER: Up to thirty-five birds (October 27) were seen per day from Alan Wormington's offshore platform, thirty miles east of North Padre Island. Steve Welborn described this species as "common" based on ten June trips offshore from Port Aransas.

AUDUBON'S SHEARWATER: Welborn recorded three sightings of single birds in June, twelve to twenty nautical miles offshore from Port Aransas.

BROWN BOOBY*: Alan Wormington saw a juvenile bird from an offshore platform on October 18. In early November, Billy Sanderford found a juvenile at mile marker 53, south of the Park Road 22 pavement end at Malaquite Beach on the Padre Island National Seashore.

GREATER FLAMINGO*: Two individuals of the Caribbean subspecies were present at least April 5–July 6, usually in shallow water near San Jose Island, in Aransas Bay (TBRC 2000-49). Another was reported from Calhoun County, April 15–16 (TBRC 2000-50).

BRANT*: Mike Austin reported a single bird at Lake Rita Blanca, near Dalhart, on November 28 (TBRC 2000-135). At least two other Brant were reported by Panhandle hunters in late fall (*fide* Barrett Pierce).

EURASIAN WIGEON*: A drake was found among a raft of Lesser Scaup at Imperial Reservoir (Pecos County) on April 6 by Petra Hockey and Brush Freeman (TBRC 2000-35; chapter 10).

MASKED DUCK*: Up to two individuals, one male and one female, were reported from Cattail Lakes in the Santa Ana NWR, mid-April through early May.

NORTHERN GOSHAWK*: A juvenile was discovered in Hockley County on November 26 by Rich Kostecke.

ROADSIDE HAWK*: This Mexican species appeared at Bentsen–Rio Grande Valley State Park, December 11–15 (TBRC 2001-06).

RUFF*: A single bird was discovered on private land on the lower Texas coast, December 30–31 (chapter 26).

RED PHALAROPE*: Carl Haller located a nonbreeding-plumaged individual on October 12 at the Hagerman NWR (Grayson County). The bird was seen again on the afternoon of October 13.

PARASITIC JAEGER: Kevin Guse of Sacramento, California, reported two at Boca Chica Beach on February 20, including a light phase adult harassing Bonaparte's Gulls and Forster's Terns. Mike Nelson, stationed on an offshore oil platform south of High Island, recorded a Parasitic Jaeger in mid-April. In June, Steve Welborn saw a single light morph breeding adult twenty nautical miles offshore.

BLACK-TAILED GULL*: A probable Black-tailed Gull was found on December 12 on Galveston's East Beach by Dwight and Richard Peake.

BROWN NODDY*: A single bird was discovered in Calhoun County, April 27–May 1 (TBRC 2000-32).

RUDDY GROUND-DOVE*: A single bird was photographed in an El Paso yard, March 25–28 (TBRC 2000-21).

MANGROVE CUCKOO*: On May 3, Robert Benson discovered an individual of this cuckoo species in his Corpus Christi front yard! The bird was briefly seen the following day. On August 20, a Mangrove Cuckoo was again found in Benson's yard, perhaps the same bird that was seen in May.

GREEN VIOLET-EAR*: Two individuals were seen sporadically at Joel and Vickie Simon's Corpus Christi feeders, May 6–15.

WHITE-EARED HUMMINGBIRD*: A lone bird was documented at a Fredericksburg residence, July 31–August 4 (TBRC 2000-73).

COSTA'S HUMMINGBIRD*: An immature visited a Brewster County private feeder during the month of September (TBRC 2000-116).

ALLEN'S HUMMINGBIRD*: Owing to possible confusion with rare green-backed Rufous Hummingbirds, this species cannot be identified with 100 percent confidence in Texas by sight alone. Texas hummingbird banders, however, annually catch Allen's Hummingbirds in their nets during fall migration (TBRC 2000-110 and 111).

RED-BREASTED SAPSUCKER*: A group led by Kelly Bryan observed one on December 3 at the Big Bend Ranch SP (TBRC 2001-30).

SULPHUR-BELLIED FLYCATCHER*: Mike Rogers photographed one below Falcon Dam on April 29 (TBRC 2000-31).

PIRATIC FLYCATCHER*: Only the second Texas record for the species, excellent photos were obtained of a weary bird at Alan Wormington's offshore platform, thirty miles east of North Padre Island, on October 21–22 (TBRC 2000-126).

FORK-TAILED FLYCATCHER*: Alan Wormington studied and photographed an immature that did not tarry long at his offshore platform on November 1. Mike Sims and his father observed an immature in Bexar County on September 9 (TBRC 2000-108).

ROSE-THROATED BECARD*: An immature male was at Los Fresnos (Cameron County), January 27–29. A male was seen sporadically at Anzalduas County Park from February 8 through early May. After an interval of no reports, a male and a female were reported June 17 from Anzalduas.

BLUE MOCKINGBIRD*: The single bird that arrived in Weslaco in early May, 1999, was occasionally glimpsed by observers in 2000. The TBRC's acceptance of this record was one of the committee's more controversial decisions.

BOHEMIAN WAXWING*: A single bird was found in a Cedar Waxwing flock near Peerless, in rural Hopkins County, by Matt White on January 26 (TBRC 2000-37). Another was observed in Tarrant County on April 1 (TBRC 2000-36).

CONNECTICUT WARBLER*: Jason Leifester discovered a male at the Quintana Neotropical Bird Sanctuary on May 6. The bird was seen well for half a minute, then it disappeared. Another one-day wonder, a male, was observed on October 18 in Alan Blankenship's Central Texas yard.

RUFOUS-CAPPED WARBLER*: Ro Wauer discovered a single bird in Big Bend National Park's Green Gulch on May 1 (TBRC 2000-41). A male was studied at the Dolan Falls Nature Conservancy property from spring through August.

BAIRD'S SPARROW*: Ro Wauer reported one at Daniels Ranch near Rio Grande Village in Big Bend NP on May 7 (TBRC 2000-42). Another was located in Brewster County on May 10 (TBRC 2000-60). Kelly Bryan observed one at the Fort Davis High School football field on May 4. Others were documented in Lubbock on September 23 (TBRC 2000-114) and in Bailey County on October 15 (TBRC 2000-117).

GOLDEN-CROWNED SPARROW*: A bird observed on May 2 in Hockley County was well documented (TBRC 2000-28). Phil Rostrum also observed an immature at the Guadalupe Mountains NP Pine Springs campground on November 4 (TBRC 2000-98).

SNOW BUNTING*: First discovered on December 26, 1999, at the Lake Tawakoni dam by Matt White, this bird was seen by several observers in 1999. Birders chasing the bunting in the rocks along the dam worried local authorities, resulting in unfortunate access restrictions. Matt White saw the Snow Bunting for the last time on January 15.

SHINY COWBIRD*: Jim Stevenson reported a single bird at the Quintana Neotropical Bird Sanctuary on April 9 (TBRC 2000-66). Alvin Cearley reported another at a Kingsville feeder in early December.

PINE GROSBEAK*: On November 24, Eric Carpenter photographed a female Pine Grosbeak along the Tejas Trail in Guadalupe Mountains NP (TBRC 2000-104).

Index

All abbreviations used are defined in
Appendix A.
Italics indicate pages with illustrations.